Genesis of the Financial Crisis

Genesis of the Financial Crisis

Roderick Macdonald
Associate Professor of Management and Technology
École des sciences de la gestion
Université du Québec à Montréal

© Roderick Macdonald 2012

All rights reserved. No reproduction, copy or transmission of this publication may be made without written permission.

No portion of this publication may be reproduced, copied or transmitted save with written permission or in accordance with the provisions of the Copyright, Designs and Patents Act 1988, or under the terms of any licence permitting limited copying issued by the Copyright Licensing Agency, Saffron House, 6–10 Kirby Street, London EC1N 8TS.

Any person who does any unauthorized act in relation to this publication may be liable to criminal prosecution and civil claims for damages.

The author has asserted his right to be identified as the author of this work in accordance with the Copyright, Designs and Patents Act 1988.

First published 2012 by
PALGRAVE MACMILLAN

Palgrave Macmillan in the UK is an imprint of Macmillan Publishers Limited, registered in England, company number 785998, of Houndmills, Basingstoke, Hampshire RG21 6XS.

Palgrave Macmillan in the US is a division of St Martin's Press LLC, 175 Fifth Avenue, New York, NY 10010.

Palgrave Macmillan is the global academic imprint of the above companies and has companies and representatives throughout the world.

Palgrave® and Macmillan® are registered trademarks in the United States, the United Kingdom, Europe and other countries

ISBN: 978–0–230–29853–8

This book is printed on paper suitable for recycling and made from fully managed and sustained forest sources. Logging, pulping and manufacturing processes are expected to conform to the environmental regulations of the country of origin.

A catalogue record for this book is available from the British Library.

A catalog record for this book is available from the Library of Congress.

10 9 8 7 6 5 4 3 2 1
21 20 19 18 17 16 15 14 13 12

Printed and bound in Great Britain by
CPI Antony Rowe, Chippenham and Eastbourne

Contents

List of Tables	vii
List of Figures	viii
Preface and Acknowledgements	ix

Part I The Crisis of 2007–2010   1

1 The Nature and Effects of the 2007–2010 Crisis and
    Ways to Resolve It   2
    The nature of the 2007 financial crisis   3
      An overview of the 'financial sector'   4
      Was this a crisis for everyone?   11
    Some effects of the toxic assets   13
      First effect: difficulties in routine economic transactions   13
      Second effect: shrinkage of habitual sources of financing   14
      Third effect: deflation   16
    Why we should care: what happens if there is no
      bailout – the mainstream view   21
    An alternative view on the crisis: Austrian economics   30

Part II The Genesis of the Crisis   35

2 The Roots of the Crisis   37
    Some basics about shelter and homeownership   37
    The historical context   41
    The mechanics of the crisis   47
      Investment banking and various fund managers   47
      Mortgages and the hierarchy of markets: from
        construction to mortgage-backed securities   52
    Securitization   55
    Imperfections in the markets linking home buyers and
      investors in securities   59

3 Three Chronologies and the Genesis of the 2007–2010 Crisis   69
    Overview   69
    Chronology of US government interventions in housing   70

Spasms in US housing	74
The ABCP (securitization) bubble that preceded the 2007 financial crisis	84
Securities	84
The ball of yarn unravels	87
Conclusion	93

Part III Remedies and Repartee — 95

4 Saltwater Economists	98
Saltwater economist number one: Paul Krugman	98
Saltwater economist number two: Joseph Stiglitz	109
5 Freshwater Economists, Austrian Economists and Popular Opinion	119
Introduction	119
Freshwater economist number one: Luigi Zingales	119
Freshwater economist number two: John Cochrane	122
Austrian economists	124
Austrian economists on the bailout	127
Peter Schiff on stimulus	128
Popular opinion	132
6 Conclusion	137
Notes	158
Bibliography	162
Index	173

Tables

1.1	Citigroup liabilities as of June 2008	27
2.1	Goldman Sachs liabilities	50
3.1	Sales of new single-family homes in the United States	75
3.2	Number of existing homes resold in the United States	75
3.3	Employment in real estate services in the United States	77
3.4	Prices for new single-family homes in the United States	78
3.5	Number of houses sold in the United States, grouped by selling price	83
3.6	Volume of the subprime mortgage originators	89
3.7	Top issuers of subprime mortgage-backed securities	89
4.1	A list of financial and banking crises in the last 50 years	108
4.2	Outside-the-box suggestions by Joseph Stiglitz on the use of bailout funds	115
5.1	Booms, busts and schools of economic theory	126

Figures

1.1	Debt for different sectors of the US economy	19
1.2	Map of one day's transactions between banks in the Fedwire interbank payment network	23
1.3	Impact of the Lehman Brothers bankruptcy on its creditors	29
2.1	Financial services as a fraction of US GDP	45
2.2	American financial sector wages compared to all wages in non-agricultural industries and to oil and gas wages	46
2.3	Profits in the financial sector compared to total business profits in all non-financial industries in the United States	47
2.4	Flow of payments from homeowner to the investor holding a mortgage-backed security	56
2.5	Schema of the securitization process	62
3.1	Number of mortgage brokers in the United States	78
3.2	Evolution of the importance of prime mortgages	78
3.3	Evolution of the importance of subprime mortgages	79
3.4	Number of foreclosures initiated in Pennsylvania, 2006	79
3.5	Categories of mortgages originated, 2001–2009	79
3.6	US house price index	84
3.7	Volume of securities issued in the United States, 1996–2009	85
3.8	Issuance in the US bond markets	86
3.9	Agency and private-label mortgage-backed security issuance	86

Preface and Acknowledgements

This book began as a chapter of another book. The other book was an explanation of business for people with a humanities or science background. I had hoped to explain the impact of macroeconomics on businesses with a chapter on the case of the financial crisis. That chapter grew into something too extensive for the original project, and I decided to turn it into the volume you hold. It retains the ambitions of the original work: to make complicated issues accessible to the uninitiated and to offer the initiated a coherent and synthetic purview of the basics. The reader must judge the degree of my success.

This book attempts to gather *all* of the factors contributing to the crisis brought to the public eye on 15 September 2008. It is not meant to provide a simplified explanation that the capitalist system is broken or that our system is one in which the rich, powerful and initiated appropriate the dwindling wealth of the poor and the middle class, or that what we need is better regulation of the financial sector. It has been written without any ideological agenda. However, the best way to defuse any bias in this exposition is to declare my opinion at the outset. This opinion is that the financial sector shares a management problem with much of business in the Anglo-American world: incentives. The problem usually manifests itself at the level of CEOs and top management, where the unscrupulous may pillage a firm's resources or weaken its mid-term strategic position in the pursuit of short-term performance goals which either directly trigger bonuses or else increase the value of shares and thus that of the options that form part of their compensation. The case of the financial sector is far more dramatic in its consequences and displaced to other echelons of the firm, because in the financial sector it is the traders – the blue-collar workers of the financial world – who pocketed huge bonuses based on falsely valued performance, although top management also benefited from this misperception of performance.

However, many, many factors and influences had to be in place for this defective management tool spawned by agency theory to have the devastating effect it had. To explain the 2007–2010 financial crisis by poor employee evaluation techniques alone would be to misunderstand the crisis.

The first draft of this book was completed as the National Commission on the Causes of the Financial and Economic Crisis in the United States published its final report. The ten-person commission had a staff of 80, powers to obtain documents and testimony under oath and seven months to acquire data. I was eager both to fill in any lacunae in my own work and to see how badly I had been scooped.

The final report was in fact a 'majority report'. Four of the ten commissioners dissented from the final report, and two brief dissenting statements (one by three commissioners) are included in the published book. The majority report provides a reasonably complete catalogue of the various factors contributing in some way to the crisis, but fails to give much insight into the relationship between the different factors. There is no evident discernment between context, causes, catalysts and motives, nor does the report give a sense of the weight of the various causes. Further, the vast powers of the commission to obtain and analyse data seemed to have remained untapped. For example, both majority and dissenting commissioners take for granted conventional wisdom that subprime mortgages are what made so many securities perform poorly. Given the considerable manpower and coercive powers of the commission, many real estate and other researchers must have hoped that the staff would have been directed to do the dog work of breaking down a statistically useful sample of mortgage-backed securities to find out whether the prime loans indeed contributed little or nothing to the non-performance. The report refers to a website (http://fcic.law.stanford.edu/) where the commission had archived extensive resources, but unfortunately only a single 'story' of a mortgage-backed security is related, with information about aggregate performance of the bundle of mortgages. The data for the security is provided, including the FICO rating and delinquency status for each loan, so it is technically possible to drill down for the information. (The meaning of the technical terms used in this paragraph will become clear later in this book.)

The critiques of the dissenting reports are partly valid, but underestimate the moral and financial influence of the US economy. The conclusion of this book will discuss the first and more substantial of the two dissenting statements, although the body of this book does not benefit from the report of the commission.

Tiurlan Sihaloho and Jonathan Deraiche helped finalize the typescript for submission to the publisher. Lisa von Fircks, my editor, provided patient moral support and humour as well as technical guidance. Marc Stern, Raymond Théoret and Yong Lee answered my technical questions in finance; Jean Canonne and Unsal Ozdilek provided expertise in real estate. John Singleton read a couple of chapters and offered critiques from the economist's and economic historian's viewpoints. Marc Stern read the entire book and corrected my English as well as my Finance. Terry Ryan, former economic secretary of the Kenyan Ministry of Finance, initiated me into the mysteries of economic policy long before I undertook this project. The Waikato School of Management provided New Zealand hospitality and encouragement that transformed a chapter into a book. The School of Economics and Finance – Victoria University of Wellington, across the street from the parliament of New Zealand, also provided one week of intensive consultation with several researchers as well as new friendships. Numerous students and professors in Canada, Indonesia, New Zealand and Vietnam have been subjected to the ideas contained in these pages.

In the final vetting of the manuscript, Vidhya Jayaprakash, Will De Rooy and the entire team at Newgen Publishing & Data Services saved me from many mistakes and helped make the final work more elegant. I wish to thank them as well as all readers who advise me of any errors I have overlooked.

Part I
The Crisis of 2007–2010

The financial crisis of 2007 led to an economic crisis that continued on into 2011, amplified by the influences of the debt crises in Europe and worries about US debt, and we may well be witnessing the first salvoes of a currency war, in part to protect internal economies and in part to protect the value of debt on the books.

Chapter 1 provides an explanation of the financial crisis: its nature, its extent, and how it came about.

1
The Nature and Effects of the 2007–2010 Crisis and Ways to Resolve It

Many ordinary people became aware of the financial crisis of 2007–2010 with the failure of investment bank Lehman Brothers in September 2008.

Serious professionals had been aware of a brewing crisis since at least the previous year, but only a very few had realized the extent of the problem, and fewer of these dared to speak out. Peter Schiff, CEO of Euro Pacific Capital, had warned of the coming bust since at least 2006. Nouriel Roubini, professor of economics at the Stern School of Business at New York University, had been predicting a crisis since even earlier. Neither was popular when he predicted doom. Schiff was laughed at during television appearances, and Rubini was cast as a gloomy doomsayer. Raghuram Rajan (2005), Professor of Finance at the Booth School of Business at the University of Chicago, was greeted by silence when he warned of the dangers of growing risk. The awareness of the crisis grew, first among professionals within their specialities (for example, among a few real estate observers) and then among a very few investment experts, such as Michael Burry of Scion Capital (Burry [2006] provides a primer to the investments he had been making in previous years), who were either gifted with deeper insight than even the serious finance professionals (as opposed to floggers of whatever their employer promoted) or simply lucked out in their own little theory of the economy.

Earlier in the 2008, the US Federal Reserve system had acted to facilitate a soft failure for Bear Stearns, a smaller US investment bank. This new failure of Lehman Brothers was more spectacular, since many had felt Lehman Brothers to be too big for the US government to allow it to fail.

The notion 'too big to fail' was first applied in the United States by Treasury Secretary William Gibbs McAdoo while coming to the rescue of the municipal government of New York City in 1914. The notion refers to the fact that, while the success or failure of an individual or of a single small organization usually has little impact on a society, the failure of a large organization will have a large impact. The dividing line is not simply one of size, of course, because the role played by a large organization also affects the impact of its failure.

Was Lehman Brothers too big to fail? What about Citigroup or Goldman Sachs or American International Group (AIG)? Citigroup was a commercial bank bailed out with government monies. Goldman Sachs, an investment bank, was also bailed out. AIG, an insurer, was also bailed out. Each was arguably the largest American player in its industry. In 2009, the predominant estimate for the total bailout of the American financial industry was US$8 trillion. That works out to US$30,000 for each US citizen. Had Washington written a cheque to every household for an amount equal to US$30,000 for each household member, would this have not avoided many foreclosures, supposedly the root cause of the crisis? In other words, if a household of four received US$120,000, would they not easily meet their mortgage payments, assuming responsible use of the funds on their part? Wouldn't this be fairer than rewarding precisely those institutions that seemed to have provoked this crisis? Wouldn't this have the advantage of treating every citizen equally, rather than rewarding those who had squandered their money?

In the following pages we will try to arrive at answers to these questions by examining, in order, the nature of the crisis (what was the problem), why it was a crisis (what effects have been felt or could have been felt by all members of society), and finally the genesis of the crisis (how it came about) and how it played out.

The nature of the 2007 financial crisis

The essence of the crisis was that a large number of institutions owned assets of dubious value: the so-called toxic assets. These institutions included private financial firms, such as investment banks and commercial banks; public bodies, such as municipal governments; foundations, such as university investment funds and retirement funds. To understand the nature of the crisis, we need to have some understanding of these different kinds of financial institutions. This involves going over some basic definitions and descriptions, as misunderstandings in economics, particularly about business, often involve disagreements or misinformation about basic facts. Further, specialists from many different fields may read this book, and what is obvious for someone whose expertise is in capital markets may not be obvious for someone in real estate. Finally, many people are in such a hurry to learn and to publish about advanced topics that clichés rather than facts become established as the basics.

An overview of the 'financial sector'

A bank is an institution that holds assets for someone else and then invests these assets in other projects. In other words, a bank is a business which provides the service of holding cash and also expediting payments with that cash. It makes a profit by charging for some transactions made with that cash and also by investing that cash in different projects during the period it is held. A commercial bank holds deposits for consumers and businesses and then invests these assets in loans of various sorts (mortgages, business loans, student loans, other consumer loans). It makes its money by charging higher interest on the loans it makes than it pays on its customers' deposits. It may also make money in other ways (credit card payments, what appear to be outrageous charges for money transfers and the like), but the interest spread between deposits and loans is the heart of the matter. The amount of money a commercial bank can make is thus limited by two factors: the interest spread and the total volume of loans it makes.

The total quantity of loans a bank can make is regulated. This is done in different ways in different countries. US regulations are the most relevant because the crisis began mainly in the United States.

At the time of the crisis, commercial banks in the United States were being brought under the rules of the Basel II agreement, which foresaw a complex combination of ratios to be respected. For simplicity's sake, however, we will make a first approximation using the earlier 10:1 capital requirement in order to understand the nature of regulation of commercial banking activity in the United States.

Individuals deposit their money in banks for three reasons: (1) a bank account is a convenient device for paying bills, (2) banks pay interest on deposits to certain kinds of accounts and (3) banks are safer than mattresses and socks.

The last reason holds true only if the bank does not fail. From 1929 to 1933, many banks did fail. These failed banks were merged into surviving banks, and depositors were partially compensated. The Glass-Steagall Deposit Insurance Act of 1933 created the Federal Deposit Insurance Corporation (FDIC), which insured the deposits in commercial banks. The insurance was limited (at the time there was a $2500 limit; today accounts are guaranteed up to $250,000) and was paid for by participating banks. Because this insurance inspires confidence in the vast majority of the US population, it would be difficult for a bank not to participate in this insurance programme and still get depositors.

The FDIC offers the insurance in exchange for regular payments by the participating banks; in addition, these banks must meet certain requirements. Among these requirements was a minimum ratio of capital to assets. A well-capitalized bank, in the FDIC's view, had $1 of capital for every $10 of assets.

With $1 million in capital stock, and $1 million in profits accumulated over the years and not paid out in dividends, a bank would have $2 million in equity capital and could thus make up to $18 million in loans and accept as many million dollars in deposits (for banks, loans are assets and deposits are liabilities). If this ratio fell to 1:11, the FDIC would issue a warning to the bank.

The reason for this ratio is that every loan involves a bet that the borrower will be able to pay back the loan as agreed. Although banks are notoriously conservative in granting loans to consumers and small businesses, defaults still occur. If 10 per cent of borrowers were to default, the bank's capital would be completely wiped out. Since the deposits are still insured, there would not be a run on the bank, but it makes sense for the FDIC, the insurer, to limit the risks. This is particularly true because there is a motivation for banks to loan more money. Banks can increase their profits by lending more on the same capital base. Even without the FDIC regulations, there is a commonsense reason to limit this profit seeking: a given bank does not want to fail by taking too great a chance on borrowers' not defaulting. Nonetheless, the FDIC would not want to leave the judgement as to the appropriate ratio to bank managers, who might be more or less competent or scrupulous.

Why is the United States adopting the more complicated regulations of the Basel agreements? The reason is that the 10:1 capital-to-assets ratio is too simplistic. It assumes that one loan is as risky as another. This is obviously false, because Microsoft founder Bill Gates could easily repay a $10 million loan, whereas a university professor with a large family may have difficulty repaying a $10,000 home improvement loan. Further, loans are not the only kind of assets that a bank holds. At the end of June 2008, Citigroup had US$2.1 trillion in assets against US$136 billion in equity (thus roughly a 15:1 ratio). Loans accounted for only one-third of the bank's assets. Trading account assets (securities bought by the bank for resale) and 'Federal funds sold and securities borrowed or purchased under agreement to resell' (in other words, very short-term investments, held for one or a few days) together accounted for another third of assets, while longer-term investments accounted for about a tenth of the assets. The levels of riskiness of these different categories vary, and each individual category will vary in riskiness as economic conditions change. This is the motivation behind the more complicated Basel I and Basel II accords. They attempt to impose more realistic risk requirements on banks.

The situation is even more complicated when we consider the different kinds of banks. Investment banks are different from commercial banks. They do not take deposits. Instead, they are financed by sources of capital looking for higher returns than a simple cash deposit account. Sovereign wealth funds, pension funds, hedge funds and commercial banks are among the sources that confide their money to investment banks. Thus, the commercial banks that pay you 5 per cent on a long-term deposit may turn around and lend your deposit to the investment bank for a 10 per cent return. Unfair? Then go directly to the investment bank to lend them the amount that you had deposited in the commercial bank. Your loan will not be insured by the FDIC, but you will get a higher return for that risk. On the other hand, you will be lost among giants, because many of the institutions providing funds to the investment bank will be lending (not 'depositing') hundreds of millions of dollars.

In December 2007, Goldman Sachs, the most prestigious investment bank in the United States, had US$43 billion in shareholders' equity against $1.1 trillion in assets, a 30:1 ratio. In December 2008, after some bailout and more conservative management by Goldman Sachs, this ratio was down to a little over 15:1. Investment banks are not covered by the FDIC, which thus cannot stipulate any requirements such as a maximum assets-to-equity ratio. However, Goldman Sachs (along with Morgan Stanley) transformed into a bank holding company at the end of September 2008 in order to qualify for bailout and thus became subject to the FDIC and its capital requirements.

Pension funds are also in the list of institutions holding assets of dubious value. Why would pension funds have such assets? Answering this question requires a summary of how the financial system works.

To finance means to provide funds and thus capital; we can use it in the passive sense of obtaining funds and capital. Almost any wealth-producing activity requires capital. A sewer system requires some real estate, machinery to dig holes and trenches, piping, and funds to pay salaries. Baking a cake for a bazaar requires flour, eggs and sugar, but also an oven, electricity and so on. Anyone who wants to start or enlarge a business needs capital, and thus the availability of capital is a major factor limiting the capacity of an economy to produce wealth. Anyone providing capital chooses between financing a bake sale or financing a sewer system construction project and other endeavours. That choice is made according to a variety of criteria: moral and social considerations, superior return on investment (conventionally quantified and incorporated into the estimated return), riskiness of the venture, one's expertise in evaluating the project, and so on.

Now, any one investment project is going to be risky, whereas investing in a pool of projects can be seen as reducing risk. This is in part an illusion of arithmetic, but it has practical consequences, as we shall see. Suppose all projects are equally risky (which of course they are not). Suppose the risk is a one in ten chance that a given project will fail. If I invest in one project, there is a 10 per cent chance of failure. Suppose I invest in ten projects and expect one failure in ten. Thus I will succeed almost all the time and simply receive a lower total return than if I succeeded all the time. This is the principle of diversification and/or spreading the risk.

By making a large number of investments and building a certain level of failure into my expectations, I have conjured risk away. This is no mere illusion. It is true because human work does tend to produce far more than it consumes, so that the occasional failure can be absorbed by the more frequent successes.

As a consequence, we can reduce risk by making many investments instead of one single investment. The larger the number of investments we make, the more the risk is diluted.

On the other hand, not all investments are equal. Some are riskier than others; some promise greater returns than others. So work is required to select projects for investments. Expertise is also required. Not only are some projects in themselves more risky, but my personal ability to evaluate that risk may be inferior for some projects. That is why there are individuals and institutions that invest on behalf of others: investment managers (for example, money managers). This means that the people confiding their money to investment managers are exposed to less risk than they would be if they invested on their own, because the investment manager spends all his professional time investing and thus has developed a greater expertise. Further, he usually invests in a large number of projects, particularly since he is using the money of several clients and so has more funds to invest in a larger number of projects. Again, he may form part of a larger team or organization of investors who share experience and insight.

There is a downside to confiding your money to an investment manager. First, he has to make money, so he will not pass on all the investment returns to you. He will take a cut on those returns – usually a percentage as well as a fixed fee. Second, a new risk is introduced by hiring an investment manager: the risk that he will do a poor job. Part of the risk is that he will be dishonest, as the Earl Joneses, the Vincent Lacroix and the Bernie Madoffs of this world have reminded us. Part of the risk is that the investment manager will be less competent than others. Both of these risks can be controlled by some due diligence examining past results and reputation.

Investing funds that belong to someone else involves a moral obligation that is usually enshrined in legal obligations. These obligations are called 'fiduciary duties'. Fiduciary duties are juridically formulated according to the mandate of the fund manager. They may be imposed by regulations or else issue from the contractual agreement between the funds provider and the investor. These agreements are usually standardized by the investment manager, who doesn't want to deal with varying obligations across his various investors.

Investment managers are usually classified according to the nature of the fiduciary obligations they undertake. For example, pension funds manage the savings of employees and contributions of employers with the goal of providing an income to these same employees when they retire. It is more critical that some income be provided once they retire than it is to maximize that income, so the pension funds do not invest in riskier projects even if they promise a high return. It is for this reason that pension funds may decide to provide funds to another investment firm such as a money manager: precisely because their fiduciary duty precludes or limits riskier investments, such as an investment in a single business venture (with a few exceptions). This second investment firm then combines these funds with other money and invests in a plurality of projects.

A pension fund is basically a corporation whose job is to save the money of workers and use that money to support them when they retire. The pension fund could stuff that money into socks – so could the workers, for that matter – but that is a guaranteed way of losing the value of the pension. Twenty-five cents bought you a milkshake in the 1960s; the price is over $3 now. Other things we purchase with money have also increased in price, so the purchasing power of money stuffed into socks decreases over time (except in times of deflation). The solution is to use your cash to participate in the growth of the economy, so that the value of your assets purchased with your cash grows as quickly as prices inflate – or even more quickly. This will be the case when the economy has the opportunity to grow and there is no hyperinflation; in other words, this is the case most of the time. How does one use his cash to participate in the growth of the economy? He cannot buy everything, so he has to buy some specific things. While the entire economy will almost always grow in value more than the inflation rate, individual purchases are more risky. Certainly many things decrease in value: clothing, most cars and consumer goods in general, even if we don't use them. Houses usually rise in value, so real estate should ordinarily be a wise investment. However, a neighbourhood may decline, a house must be maintained, and local economics and demographics may also affect the price of a building, so that investing in real estate requires considerable work to manage the investment and pull out if trouble occurs.

The low-maintenance solution is to get someone else to administer your money.

Pension funds administer other people's savings so that they may have a comfortable retirement, and for that reason they must make very safe investments. While investing in a single home is usually a good investment, it is still too risky for a pension fund, particularly if someone else is living in the home and managing its upkeep and taxes. If these people do a good job, the investment is safer. If they are negligent, the investment is in danger. One way to reduce the risk is to invest in a large number of homes. In a way, this is what a mortgage company does (actually, it lends funds to people who invest in their own homes). But the level of risk is still too high for pension funds. They need to invest in several pools of mortgages made by diverse lenders for homes in different parts of the country.

At the opposite extreme from pension funds (in terms of fiduciary duties) are hedge funds. Hedge funds have investment managers who promise high returns on investment by taking on greater risk. They attempt to manage this risk by betting against their investment – hence the term 'hedge funds' (we will see elsewhere how it is that they can 'hedge'). Another class of provider of funds and investor is constituted by the so-called sovereign funds: pools of capital managed by governments that have accumulated years of budget surplus, typically from revenues accruing when petroleum is among the nation's natural resources.

Now we can repeat the essence of the 2007–2010 financial crisis: a large number of institutions owned 'toxic' assets. These institutions included private financial firms, such as investment banks and commercial banks; governments, such as municipal governments; foundations, such as university investment funds; and other savings and investment vehicles, such as sovereign funds and retirement funds.

Besides each of these large pools of capital caught holding toxic assets, another kind of institution also had serious problems: financial guarantors. Even the largest of these firms are comparatively modest in size at US$5 billion in assets, but they are crucial for the financial industry because they insure debt, such as bonds and other securities. Should these insurers disappear, many financial instruments would lose their appeal to investors. People with money would opt for the least risky investments: deposit accounts in banks and (ironically) real estate. It would become very difficult for small businesses or governments to get loans, and most households would be forced to rent their homes from wealthier people.

How were these financial guarantors at risk? Like everyone else, in the final analysis they were caught holding assets that had been overvalued – 'toxic' assets. This is a direct result of the manner in which financial guarantees were provided.

The core field for these financial guarantors was municipal bonds.

Municipalities, like other forms of government, don't seem to require insurance because governments don't default – if we forget the earlier reference to New York City in 1914 and the cases of several countries in the 1980s and 1990s. Recently a banking analyst, Meredith Whitney (2010) has raised awareness of the possibility of municipality defaults, but this was unimaginable at the turn of the twenty-first century, although municipalities were short of money even then. So there *was* a small possibility of default under such financial conditions that even bond holders would receive only a fraction of every dollar lent. Investors expect a premium interest rate if they are going to face any risk, so municipal bonds would have to carry a higher interest rate to attract investors. An alternative would be to insure the bonds against the bankruptcy of the issuer. Should a municipality go bankrupt, the insurer would take over the payments. As a consequence, municipalities may consider issuing insured bonds if the additional cost (the premium they pay to the insurer) is lower than the interest premium they would have to offer on uninsured bonds.

This makes sense, and the consequence was that financial guarantors had clients coming to them and asking for insurance on a rather sure thing. Municipalities were in no danger of defaulting: even if municipalities across North America experienced a financial squeeze, other levels of government usually have been there to back them up – if somewhat grudgingly.

Financial guarantors moved beyond this safe and profitable but small haven out onto the ocean of insuring pools of bonds.

These collections of bonds are called 'collateralized debt obligations' (CDOs). In some ways they were very safe. First, because a CDO is a collection of bonds, risk is spread across several bonds. Suppose that on the average one bond in a hundred goes bust, and you have a collection of a hundred such bonds. It is quite probable that you will have one go bust, maybe perhaps two; three is practically impossible. So you can calculate your total rate of return by supposing such a failure rate as almost a sure thing, and anything better (unlikely) is gravy. Second, the obligations are collateralized. In other words, if an obligation fails, you get to seize the assets that have been assigned as guarantees, so there is a fallback in the case of such a default. Apparently very safe, although not in retrospect, as we shall see.

The insurance on these collections of bonds is done through 'credit default swaps' (CDSs). Basically, the client promises to pay the guarantor a fixed fee in exchange for the guarantee that if a bond defaults, the guarantor will redeem it.

This seems to be the same business as insuring municipal bonds. There are two differences: (1) the client is no longer the issuer of the bonds, but the acquirer who would be paid if there is a default, and (2) the issuer of the bonds is no longer a municipality, but anybody who issues CDOs. It is this latter that is the rub. From the accountant's viewpoint, financial guarantors, like everyone else, got stuck holding some toxic assets; in their case, CDSs. From the viewpoint of the average person, they got caught *insuring* toxic assets and thus had to pay up to redeem all the defaults.

To summarize this section once again, the essence of the financial crisis lay in the devaluation of the assets of a large number of organizations, such as investment banks and commercial banks; governments, such as municipal governments, foundations, such as university investment funds, retirement funds and hedge funds. Further, a number of institutions had insured these assets, and not only were they unable to provide the promised coverage, their capacity to provide unrelated coverage was also threatened.

Was this a crisis for everyone?

This general overview of the facts in the previous paragraphs reveals the essence of the crisis: different institutions caught holding toxic assets. These institutions played a real role in the economic life of most people. In other words, the financial crisis led to an economics crisis: the US economy shrank, it became more difficult to find a new job, many people lost their old job, most businesses made less money or even a loss.

In some cases it is obvious. Consider pension funds. The failure of a pension fund means that a portion of the ageing population may not be able to provide for itself as it loses its capacity to work. The effect is not immediate but gradually increments as new cohorts reach retirement age. This might be beneficial for society. These people can be very productive after their retirement date and can benefit society in better ways than playing golf. Nonetheless, their savings are lost because they were not put to productive use.

Insurance companies were among the firms caught holding toxic assets. Besides the specialized financial guarantors ('monoline insurers'), some general insurance companies also ventured into the field of financial insurance. The most spectacular case was that of AIG. If a large insurer, such as AIG, fails, then a large number of people and organizations are suddenly uninsured. A portion of these will fail, and their creditors or dependents, who would have been covered by the insurance, now would lose the proceeds. This is an obvious harm to the common citizen.

In other cases, the damage for all is less obvious, as in the case of hedge funds. If it is true that a large sum of money has been wasted, it is not evident that the demise of a hedge fund hurts the common citizen.

To understand the role of financial institutions in our economy, we need to remember that they are businesses: at least in theory, they reap a profit by providing a benefit. This is true on both the asset and the liability side of the balance sheet. People confide money to them because they provide a return with lower risk. They provide financing to various projects because (among the other reasons mentioned above) these projects can provide a return on that financing. When a financial institution is not profitable – not successful as a business – then those projects the institution might have financed had it been successful must look elsewhere for financing, or do without, while the people that provided it with funds may see their returns diminished and perhaps even run the danger of losing their entire initial investment. This second effect is more obvious, but the first effect is the reason invoked by Washington to intervene vigorously in an effort to stem the crisis. Without a vigorous financial sector, less capital would be made available to businesses, and thus the wealth-producing capacity of the nation would be hobbled.

The demise of these other kinds of investors does not remove money from the pocket of the common citizen. Rather, their demise means that less money can be borrowed. The common citizen would no longer be able to obtain credit whether he wanted to start or expand his business, or if he wanted to purchase a new home or a new car – or to go to university.

The availability of capital is the theoretical reason there was indeed an economic and financial crisis for everyone. Does this theory hold in practice? Was the failure of some and the imminent failure of countless other financial institutions really a threat to the lives of ordinary people?

In the next section we will consider a few of the effects of these events on daily life and then examine why the fate of the investment banks is relevant to the rest of us. This will give us an understanding of the mainstream view that there was a crisis and that the US government should have intervened by creating money to stabilize the situation. We will then examine the alternative viewpoint of the Austrian school of economics.

Some effects of the toxic assets

First effect: difficulties in routine economic transactions

Many Canadians are snowbirds: they spend most of the year in Canada, but arrange to spend part of the winter (January and February, for example) in the southern United States or somewhere else warm. Consider someone who rents a condominium in Florida from early February till the end of March every year. Every year he mails a cheque to the owner of the condominium. In the fall of 2008, the owner of the condominium writes back:

> I received your check last week. I tried to deposit it last Friday. Because it is drawn on a Canadian bank, they told me it would take 90 days to clear. It was not a problem last year, but the bank said there have been issues and this is their new policy. I will call you tonight to discuss options with you. I will mail the check back to you. The bank will accept a money order if it is issued from an American bank. The other option is wiring the money. I will pay for the wire service; you can deduct the amount from the check. (This is taken from a real transaction.)

Thus, she explained that her bank would take three months to clear the cheque written by the Canadian client on his current account with Scotiabank. Scotiabank is a Canadian bank that held $CDN34 billion dollars in ready cash and deposits at other banks at the time. Supposing his cheque was for $5000, it would seem that Scotiabank had the wherewithal to respect the cheque. Today it is a notorious fact that Canadian banks (as opposed to some American banks and a number of Canadian pension funds) were relatively unaffected by the crisis. Yet, as a consequence of the financial crisis, the American bank required three months to clear the cheque drawn on a Scotiabank account.

Another example: in 2009, one Canadian in Toronto experienced a strident response to his first late credit card payment in years: *all* of his credit cards were suspended. In normal times, the credit card company would simply charge him the exorbitant interest rate that such companies are permitted to charge.

These administrative decisions – perhaps software adjustments in automated account management – by the credit card company help us understand what happened to the cheque of the snowbird. Banks in the United States were nervous about cashing cheques drawn on other banks because there was a real possibility that some banks would disappear – and thus not be around to honour those cheques. The solution (of the top management of the condominium owner's bank) was to draw up a list of 'safe' banks. That list included 40 banks, all of them American. Information was still pending on international banks. They would 'eventually' get around to it.

One of the effects of the toxic assets, then, was to make banks skittish about cashing the cheques of other banks. If the other bank had considerable toxic assets, then perhaps its real net worth was zero or negative after discounting those bad assets. In that case the other bank already owed the cash it seemed to have, and it would be unable to honour the cheques made on accounts it held. This skittishness translated into heavy-handed administrative procedures that limited the effectuation of payments among clients of different banks.

Second effect: shrinkage of habitual sources of financing

Canadian farmers sell their produce (milk, eggs, grains, etc.) to various cooperatives and boards, which market to domestic and international markets, among which the United States is dominant. As a result, revenues of Canadian farms are sensitive to US agricultural importations, which in turn are dictated by international competition (farmers of other nations), policies (tariffs and 'buy American' campaigns), and the purchasing power of the US market. The fall of 2008 saw storm clouds with respect to these latter two factors.

Farming in Canada, as in most developed countries, is a large-scale and heavily financed business. Machinery is financed over several years, the farm is mortgaged, and seed, fertilizer and other consumables of agriculture are sold on credit knowing that the farmer will get his revenue at the time of harvest. The farmer does not wait for the harvest, however, but rather sells the crop ahead of time.

Most farmers contract their crops. This means they sell the year's harvest before seeding the ground. Contracting the crop does not mean earlier payment. It means that the amount of payment is settled today, and the risk regarding price (per bushel) is thus transferred to the purchasing party. If prices rise, he gains. If prices fall, he loses. Similarly, the farmer loses if the prices rise, but at least he is certain of the contracted income, and he can also transact against that certain income. There are times when money can be made by gambling on the open market. The general trend is to contract the crop to eliminate the insecurity of doubt.

This understood, we can imagine the yearly cycle for a Prince Edward Island (PEI) potato farmer as follows:

- April to April/May: the farmer gets a line of credit or 'operating loan' (to be repaid in full each year before a new loan can be authorized) from a chartered bank or credit union. The chartered banks and credit unions normally take the crop (and crop proceeds, i.e. accounts receivable) as their security. If they feel the crop of 2009 will be worth less because the US economy is shrinking, they may offer less credit to the PEI potato farmer.
- May to June: the farmer purchases supplies (seed and fertilizer), signs a transport contract for delivery to the chip plant, sells his crop and purchases insurance on the crop. The insurance premium is immediately payable; the receipt for the crop will come after delivery.
- September to October: the farmer harvests potatoes and other crops and puts them in storage.
- October to May: potatoes are delivered to the plant as contracted, the payment on the contracted crop becomes due 30 days later and is made to the farmer, who then can pay back the operating loan or line of credit.

Sometimes the farmer cannot repay the operating loan (due to a shortfall) and requests a lending institution, such as Farm Credit Canada, to amortize the shortfall over a long-term period secured by a mortgage on the farm. This can happen only a limited number of times before the farm equity gets used up.

Without going further into all details of the farm business, the upshot is that each farmer is dependent on the financial judgement of his creditors, and this judgement was not rosy in the fall of 2008, because the United States suffered a great reduction in purchasing power and showed signs of being about to 'buy American'. It followed logically, in the mind of the creditors, that Canadian farmers should be offered less credit. These conditions did not reduce the fixed expenses of Canadian farmers in the fall of 2008. The payments for the farmers' machinery were the same; the mortgage payments on the farms were the same. As a result, farmers across Canada found themselves in a cash crunch, as a result of the weakening of the US economy caused by toxic assets.

That is a second effect of the financial crisis: diverse businesses that seem to have no connection to mortgages in the United States or to Wall Street suddenly found themselves short on credit.

Third effect: deflation

The great spectre of the economic crisis for North Americans was deflation. Deflation means that your dollar buys more in 2010 than it did in 2008. If you hold dollars, this seems like a good thing: your purchasing power has increased. While inflation is the great bogeyman in South America and Europe, in North America – or at least in the United States – deflation is more feared. The reason is not that evil economists want prices to be higher rather than lower. Obviously, when clothing imported into North America allowed Mexican, American and Canadian families to clothe their children with a smaller portion of their after-tax wages, those families were better off, no matter what North American clothing manufacturers may say. Access to cheaper (but same quality) goods is beneficial. Are we worse off today if five MB of hard disk memory has a price of $US .001 rather than a $US 50,000 as in 1956?

The reason deflation is feared is that, historically, deflation tends to be linked to recessions and depressions and economic problems for everyone, if we look back at the twentieth century. General deflation can bring three problems. Two damage the economy: the deflationary spiral and deflation-debt mutual reinforcement. The third problem with deflation is that it makes it more difficult for central banks to stabilize the economy.

The deflationary spiral is a vicious circle. If the prices of goods are falling, we will wait until later to purchase goods because we believe they will be cheaper. Inventories of goods build up, so manufacturers slow production.

There is less overtime, perhaps there is job-sharing, and eventually manufacturers begin to lay off employees. As a consequence, purchasing power diminishes and demand decreases. Because demand decreases, prices drop. This brings us back to step #1, and the circle is complete.

This mechanism should not be understood as a series of causes. Economists do not think that a declining price *forces* you to delay purchase. Rather, we have a series of contexts for deciding about purchasing, about manufacturing and about hiring, or allocating hours of work, and so on. In those contexts, the same influences, catalysts and commonsense factors continue to operate. The point is that there is an additional effect which is self-reinforcing, so that this effect can begin to dominate other influences. This impact is not universal, however. For example, even if the price of food is decreasing, no one can afford to wait very long before buying more food.

Deflation-debt reinforcement. This tendency of declining prices feeding into a deflationary spiral is exacerbated when society is debt ridden. If prices are dropping, then the return on my assets is dropping through the floor. If these assets are heavily leveraged – in other words, if I have borrowed money to pay for them – my net return may even become negative.

Suppose a small business makes soft ice cream with a $10,000 Sweda machine, acquired at the start of summer with $1000 cash and a promise of $1000 payment every month after that until one year from the day of purchase. That is 20 per cent for interest. The owner can reduce the total interest in dollar terms by paying back $2000 a month – say in five monthly payments, to keep it simple – but if she spends her cash on that, she won't be spending it on something else. If she sells her ice creams for $2 each and sells 2500 per month, and with a profit of 50 cents per ice cream, then her return on the Sweda machine is $1250/$10,000 or 12.5 per cent each month – not a bad business before she takes into account her general expenses. Now suppose demand for ice cream drops as the seasons change and she lowers her price to $1.75 to get some more business. Her return on investment drops to 6.25 per cent! She begins to worry about perhaps having to cut the price to $1.50 an ice cream...As demand for ice cream continues to fall, she begins considering the possibility of reselling the Sweda machine. After all, she may not be making any money on it, so why not simplify her life? If she can persuade someone else to take over the monthly payments, any cash he would give her up front would be gravy! In other words, she would be happy to take a cash payment equivalent to her original $1000 down payment and a couple of monthly payments and have someone else walk away with the machine and the burden of future payments. She would have made a little money over the summer and wouldn't have to worry about the future of business amid declining prices. The new owner has to worry about these new conditions, but his machine is costing him a lot less.

In other words, deflation + debt leads to distress selling of assets. It makes sense to sell your assets at a loss now rather than retain them and pay interest for them.

According to the *Economist*, Irving Fisher is the economist who warned of the dangers of deflation when debt is rampant: '…he described debt deflation as a sequence of distress-selling, falling asset prices, rising real interest rates, more distress-selling, falling velocity, declining net worth, rising bankruptcies, bank runs, curtailment of credit, dumping of assets by banks, growing distrust and hoarding' (*Economist*, 12 February 2009, 'Out of Keynes's Shadow'). The reason has to do with the use made of ready cash by debtors in times of deflation. The interest on the debt is fixed and does not decrease with time as do other prices, so it makes sense to pay interest and to reduce the principal on debt by deferring other expenditures.

From the viewpoint of mainstream economics, as bank loans are paid off, less money is in circulation, which means there is less money chasing the goods for sale in the economy, and thus reduced prices, and back to the beginning of the spiral.

Financial distress (in the form of lower or delayed revenues, higher costs or accelerated expenditures, or problems of solvency) leads to deflation in at least three ways:

1. To reduce their burden of debt ('indebtedness'), firms sell assets to raise cash. When most firms do this, there is a contraction in the money supply which leads to deflation.
2. Distress selling reduces asset prices, causing losses to agents with maturing debts. This reinforces distress selling and reduces consumption and investment spending, thus deepening deflation.
3. Debt-deflation involves widespread bankruptcy, impairing the process of credit intermediation, occasioning credit contraction which depresses aggregate demand and thus reinforces deflation.

Figure 1.1 illustrates that the United States was indeed in a situation of surging debt.

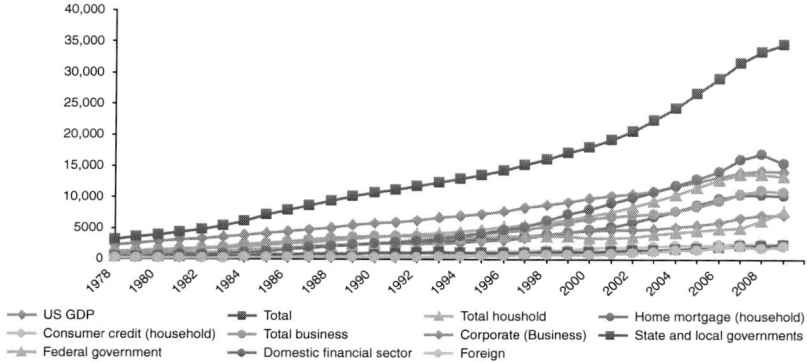

Figure 1.1 Debt in billions US$ for different sectors of the US economy

Stabilizing the economy. This deflation makes government intervention more difficult. The interest rate is the principal instrument of economic policy today. Central banks can affect the money supply through the interest rate: when interest rates are higher, it becomes more expensive to borrow; when interest rates are lower, it is cheaper to borrow. If other factors in the profitability or interest of a project do not change, then a reduced rate makes a project more profitable or attractive: there is more profit left over after paying for interest. As a result, more projects are undertaken when interest is lower, and thus more money is borrowed, so that there is more ('a greater supply of') money in circulation. Thus it becomes easier to buy a new car or expand a factory, and the members of society can participate in the economy more fully by consuming as well as through their paid labour. Similarly, the central bank can reduce the amount of economic activity by increasing interest rates. How high can rates be raised? There is no absolute limit, although it is not hard to imagine a practical absolute limit on the downside: zero per cent. If the central bank establishes a rate which is below zero per cent, then it begins to pay people to borrow money. Borrow $1000 from me, and I will pay you $50 cash each year until you pay me back. Will you ever want to pay me back?

There are two ways to look at this limit. The pessimistic way is to assume that zero per cent interest is a floor to the influence a central bank can have by manipulating the interest rate. The optimistic way of looking at this limit is to see it as asymptotic: as central banks massage the interest rate closer and closer to zero, spectacular effects are had on the economy. Unfortunately for central banks, history does not support this second vision. For example, the Bank of Japan maintained an interest rate between zero per cent and 0.5 per cent over the decade 1990–2000. This did *not* stimulate the Japanese economy, and the period is considered a 'lost decade' in the sense that the Japanese economy lost ground in the nineties after gradually catching up to the US economy for several decades. The Bank of Japan had recourse to various other measures in attempts to spur growth, with few or no results.

In a 2004 paper, Ben S. Bernanke, Vincent R. Reinhart and Brian P. Sack formulated the problem as one in which a central bank can no longer stimulate aggregate demand by further interest-rate reductions and must rely instead on three 'non-standard' policy alternatives (p. iii): 'spin' (communications policies to shape public expectations about the future course of interest rates); increase the size of the central bank's balance sheet; and 'quantitative easing' by loans to troubled institutions. Thus, when the New York Federal Reserve created a loan facility for AIG that could grow to US$182 billion, it created the possibility of increasing its assets by US$182 billion, changing the composition of the central bank's balance sheet through, for example, the targeted purchases of long-term bonds as a means of reducing the long-term interest rate.

In other words, the central bank has to do a lot more 'work' (loaning and purchasing rather than a simple declaration of the interest rate) and get a lot 'dirtier' (choosing to make specific interventions by loaning to one institution rather than another, committing to the purchase of 10-year Treasury bonds, etc.) to pursue alternative policy levers, and retiring these actions may be difficult.

This third effect of deflation has been a little technical, so we need to situate our argument once again. We have seen that the essence of the 2007–2010 financial crisis is that a number of institutions owned assets of dubious value. We then asked whether this was indeed a crisis or simply a problem for the institutions caught with those assets. The response is that there was indeed a crisis, as can be verified by three economic effects that seem distant from these 'toxic assets'. First, there was an effect on the circulation of payments (illustrated by the cheque of the snowbird). Second, there was a cash and a credit crunch, as illustrated by the plight of Prince Edward Island potato farmers. Third, there has been a danger of deflation which Washington has struggled to contain – in spite of the fact that Washington has injected over US$8 trillion dollars into the economy. (Well, it's more complicated than that, but US$8 trillion available for the balance sheets of distressed institutions must still have some inflationary influence!)

Were there signs of deflation in the 2007–2010 crisis? Deutsche Bank Securities Inc. Global Economic Perspectives (26 November 2008) observed that 'break-even inflation rates have dropped to record lows and talk of deflation is rampant'. The publication argued that these fears were overdone. On 16 December 2008, Bloomberg reported: 'The cost of living dropped 1.7 percent last month, more than economists had forecast...Worsening residential construction means the economy will likely shrink by 6 percent or more this quarter, the most since the early 1980s, some analysts said.' On 4 August 2009, Bloomberg reported: 'Wages and salaries decreased 0.4 percent in June, the ninth drop in 10 months.'

On 2 December 2009, Alex Carrick, chief economist for CanaData, was able to write: 'Earlier this year, considerable concern was expressed over the possibility of deflation. A general decline in overall prices is still a problem in some countries, such as Japan. For the US and Canada, however, it seems that deflation is one more concern that has been taken off the table.' However, Bloomberg once again argued that the 'U.S. Economy Isn't Out of the Deflation Woods Yet' on 23 February 2010.

The financial crisis has real effects on the lives of many people. Should we care? The snowbird eventually purchased a bank draft drawn on an American bank and paid that way. 'Damn queer way of doing business, eh?' Potato farmers are getting their bridge financing from the Farm Credit Canada (FCC), and those of us – the vast majority – who did not lose our jobs seem to muddle along. Should we want taxpayers' money – even if they are American taxpayers – to bail out AIG, Citibank and Goldman Sachs?

Why we should care: what happens if there is no bailout – the mainstream view

The mainstream view – which is not unanimous – is that government should intervene to keep too many financial institutions from failing and thus protect the financial system and the overall economy. The phrase 'too big to fail' suggests that some institutions are so big that their failure would have irremediably catastrophic consequences for the economy.

The general argument for government intervention goes as follows:

Stage one is in the financial world (investment banks, pension funds, hedge funds, sovereign wealth funds, etc.):

1. Financial institutions are interrelated by a huge number of short-term transactions – loans and borrowing.

2. If one institution is in distress, then it cannot pay back its loans.
3. If it cannot pay back its loans, then everyone else that lent to it is now in distress.
4. Loop back to number (2).

Figure 1.2 gives an actual map for one day of transactions among American commercial banks, which are far more numerous than investment banks. They nonetheless give a sense of the dependency between institutions in the financial world.

This looks similar to the chain reaction at the heart of a nuclear bomb. The government must intervene quickly to avoid the first distress having an opportunity to propagate.

Stage two is in the 'real' economy (the three Bs: commercial Banks, Businesses and everyBody).

Effect A, toxic assets:

1. Some of the players in the real economy may have invested in the financial world (some American commercial banks, for example, held and hold the infamous toxic assets; Chief Financial Officers (CFOs) of cash-rich firms may also have invested in such assets).
2. No one knows whether a given player in the real economy does indeed hold toxic assets – they may not have time to consult that player's balance sheet, or that balance sheet may be out of date or, in the case of banks, those assets are magically 'off balance sheet'.
3. No one knows, then, whether the other bank will still be around to settle a cheque, or whether another non-bank player will be able to pay back credit.
4. Cash on delivery is accepted, but other terms, even cheque on delivery, become suspect.
5. Because circulation of payments is impaired, the whole economy is impaired, leading to fewer goods available, jobs lost and the deterioration of public works (unless government expressly promotes public works). Something like this happened in the years leading up to World War II.

Effect B, financing:

1. The distress in the financial world slows down the activity in that world, including different ways real-world businesses raise capital, such as issuing new shares or floating new bonds.

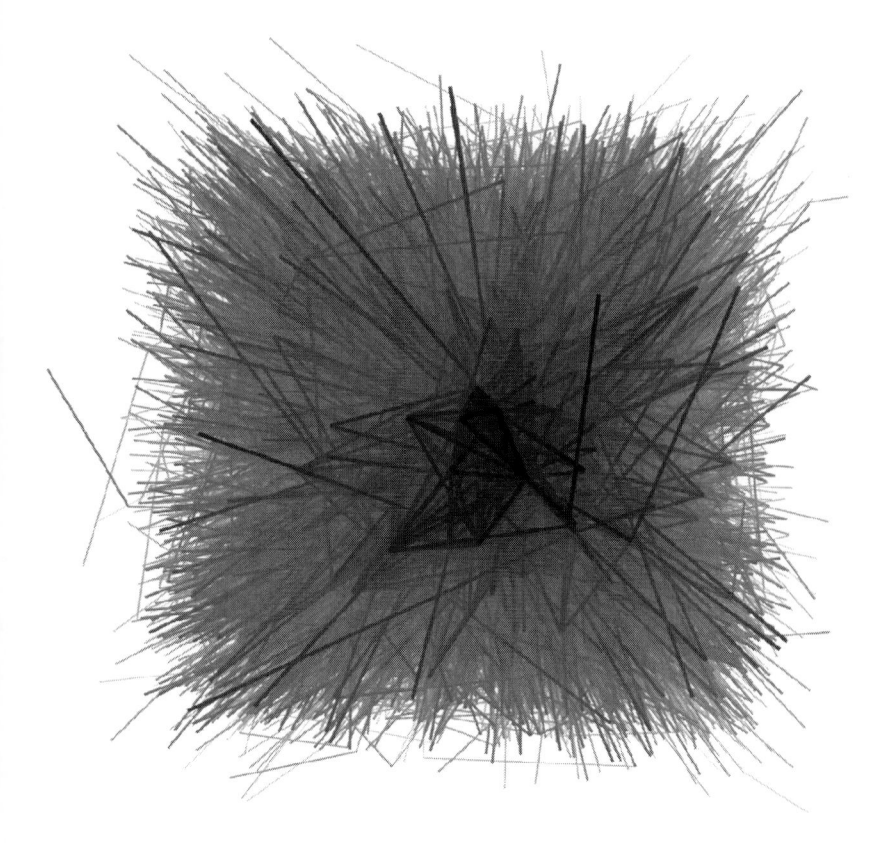

Figure 1.2 Map of one day's transactions between banks in the Fedwire interbank payment network – 6600 nodes and 70,000 links
Source: de Nooy et al., 2005.

2. Real-world businesses thus have less capital to work with, which restricts all their uses of capital – salaries, inventory levels, accounts payable, cash in the bank.
3. Banks become loath to lend to businesses.
4. As a consequence, there is a liquidity squeeze in the real world.
5. As a consequence, managers tend to cut costs rather than spend: people lose their jobs or have less overtime; some really essential activities may be compromised, for example maintenance of machinery; inventories may be cut, which may lead to some clients being served late or simply lost.

The mainstream argument, then, is that events in the world of finance have repercussions on the 'real' world in which we live because the (necessary) participation of businesses in the world of finance transmit the contagion to them both (i) via solvency (which leads to liquidity problems) because some business (foolishly) abandoned their core expertise and invested in exotic financial instruments (effect A) and (ii) via limits to the raising of capital (effect B), again leading to liquidity problems.

What would happen if Washington were not to intervene? The easy answer is that the financial system would implode because of the chain reaction mentioned above. But that is a vague answer if we don't specify what we mean by 'implode'. A guess is that some institutions would disappear, while others would muddle through under duress.

One of the programmes under which Washington intervened was the Troubled Asset Relief Program (TARP), in which the US Treasury bought and insured 'troubled' assets. If we look at one source's guess of the recipients of TARP (the figures were not made public as of the summer of 2009), three of the top five recipients represent different classes of financial institutions: Citigroup is a commercial bank, AIG is a general insurer and JPMorgan Chase was an investment bank until the fall of 2008, and presumably most of its liabilities were still characteristic of investment banks under TARP. What would happen if these institutions were not helped?

There are three possibilities. They might be acquired by other institutions, they might be reorganized under chapter 11 of US bankruptcy law, or they could simply be liquidated under chapter 5 of US bankruptcy law (bankruptcy is simply title 11 of the US code of law; see http://www.law.cornell.edu/uscode/text/11).

What happens when one financial institution is acquired by others? The demise of Bear Stearns (where, as in the case of Lehman Brothers, government agencies chose not to intervene beyond encouraging J.P. Morgan to acquire it) illustrates the answer. The carcass is divided up into interesting parts, which are kept, and uninteresting parts, which are sold or simply thrown away. The shareholders of Bear Stearns held shares that had been valued at $172 a year earlier. They had to sell them to J.P. Morgan at $10 a share (the original price was $2, but a class-action suit quintupled the price). Many employees and suppliers of Bear Stearns found themselves without an employer or a customer. These are the usual effects of a failure of any company in the United States. The most talented employees (or at least the ones with a best fit for the needs of J.P. Morgan) found themselves with a new employer, while the clients simply found themselves served by the acquiring bank.

What happens when a financial institution goes bankrupt? The assets of the bankrupt institution are used to pay off creditors to the extent possible. Chapters 5 and 11 of US bankruptcy law provide two procedures for doing this. Under chapter 5, the court appoints a trustee to liquidate the assets of the firm and pay off the creditors. Under chapter 11, the debtor continues to run the company but under rules that protect it, so that assets may continue to grow, benefitting everyone and perhaps allowing the company to emerge from bankruptcy as a going concern. The 'debtor' means the stockholders who choose top management via the board of directors and most likely will *not* have a special meeting to choose either a new board or new top management. In the case of chapter 5, there is a pre-established pecking order in which various creditors (the people who are owed money) are paid off. In the case of chapter 11, the debtor proposes a plan to pay off the different creditors, and the court accepts the plan as fair or rejects it. If the court accepts the plan, it is then proposed to the creditors, who vote to accept or reject it. If the debtor is unable to come up with a plan that is accepted by creditors within a given time period – usually four months – then other parties can propose a plan for adoption. 'Fair' usually means respecting the same pecking order as required by chapter 5, but more leeway is given to judgement, allowing management to continue using assets to improve the chances of paying more back to creditors. Employee salaries owed have great priority, but the current labour union contract, which governs future earnings among other things, may be annulled if in the interests of all parties. Employees would rather have a job with a lower salary than a higher salary for a non-existent job with a defunct company.

So what is the point of bankruptcy law? While it aims to govern an orderly repayment of creditors to the extent possible with remaining assets, bankruptcy law brings with it an 'automatic stay': in other words, no more debt collection can be imposed on the company, since the bankruptcy procedure now governs reimbursement. As a result, creditors are paid back as much as possible, in as fair a way as possible. Of course, this law and its implementation are as imperfect as all other things human.

Part of the bankruptcy procedure may be to pay creditors in kind, since cash will be limited and a sale of assets may not bring much more cash if too many are sold when the economy is weak. Once again we see that the 'toxic' assets are transferred to an existing firm, with their 'realizable value' (i.e. that recorded by the accountants) reduced to a more credible level. This, in lieu of a larger cash payment that would never be forthcoming. If the toxic asset originally had been valued as equivalent to the amount owed, and that value was maintained after transfer to the creditor, then someone else now has toxic assets which they may be able to hide if their other assets are extensive enough. If, on the other hand, the new account value is the true value of the asset, then the creditor would have gotten some money back, but the full impact of the debtor's misjudgement would be visited on the creditor. The third extreme case is that the toxic assets be revalued to credible terms, and then sufficient assets transferred to creditors to reimburse the full amount owed. That would be fair, if there were enough such assets to go around. There would be enough such assets to go around if the debtor firm were richly capitalized, since the difference could be made up for with the equity of the debtor firm. In this case, the only losers would be the shareholders of the debtor firm, who took the risk of trusting the managers of the firm and lost. However, the firms in question were *not* richly capitalized. On the contrary, the nature of these firms is to have low capital ratios, and in practice the debts of these firms were 30 or even 100 times the equity of the firm. Consider what would have happened if Citigroup had gone bankrupt. All deposits under US$250,000 would be returned by the Federal Deposit Insurance Corporation, so that most consumers would not lose their shirts. The FDIC, on the other hand, would lose these dollars paid out to 'small' depositors. The FDIC acts as receiver in the closure of the bank and can recoup some of the funds paid to depositors through the liquidation of the bank's assets. As these assets are liquidated (sold for cash), the proceeds are allocated to the remaining creditors following priorities: uninsured deposits, then general creditors, and then stockholders.

In September 2008, Citigroup had US$780 billion in deposits and averaged US$287 billion in consumer deposits. Suppose we very conservatively guess that a little more than a third of those deposits were in accounts under US$250,000. The FDIC would thus have to pay out US$100 billion. How much cash did the FDIC have on hand? As of 30 June 2008, the FDIC fund balance was US$45.2 billion. It had been higher. On 30 June 2007, it was US$52.4 billion. It was never anywhere near US$100 billion. The FDIC would have been hard pressed to meet the payments it had 'guaranteed' with its insurance. The spirit of insurance is that by spreading risk over a large number of players, no one single person has to face catastrophe. Yet here we have one single player bringing catastrophe on the whole banking industry, for if the FDIC falls, bank runs will surely follow. (Of course, one could imagine Washington stepping in to provide the FDIC with sufficient funds.)

The role of the FDIC does not end with payments to insured depositors. The FDIC also acts as receiver to resolve the failed bank by liquidating all assets and using the proceeds to (usually partially) reimburse itself, uninsured depositors, general creditors and (almost never) shareholders, or alternatively arranging for a healthy institution to take over a portion or all of the assets and perhaps some deposits and using the proceeds of that sale as well as the proceeds of the liquidation of further assets to partially reimburse the remaining creditors and the shareholders.

In summary then, the failure of a bank (especially such a large one) like Citigroup is most unpleasant for the uninsured depositors and for general creditors, and it may be catastrophic for the FDIC and thus the current US commercial banking system if the bank is large enough. Who are the general creditors? The beginning of an answer comes from an examination of the liabilities on Citigroup's balance sheet (as of 30 June 2008; see Table 1.1).

The uninsured depositors would be on the hook for some US$700 billion according to our earlier guesstimate. They would be some extremely wealthy individuals, and then a large number of corporations, some of

Table 1.1 Citigroup liabilities as of June 2008

Deposits	Non-interest-bearing deposits in US offices	49,636
	Interest-bearing deposits in US offices	210,916
	Non-interest-bearing deposits in offices outside the US	46,765
	Interest-bearing deposits in offices outside the US	496,325
	Total	803,642
Fed funds purchased and securities loaned or sold under agreement to repurchase		246,107
Brokerage payables		96,432
Trading account liabilities		189,468
Short-term borrowings		114,445
Long-term debt		417,928
Other liabilities		95,502
Liabilities of discontinued operations held for sale		456
Total liabilities		**1,963,980**

Source: Citigroup consolidated balance sheet for December 2008.

them from the world of finance (such as investment managers, hedge funds, insurance companies and brokers) and some from the 'real' economy (the Exxons, General Electrics and US Steels of the world). Suddenly Exxon would have difficulty paying suppliers and employees because the current account would be non-existent. After a few years (because these things take time), a portion of the deposit would be returned to Exxon by the FDIC upon resolution of the failed bank. Meanwhile, however, Exxon would suddenly be cashless. The participants of the financial world would also suddenly be cashless – at first sight this is not a problem, since their other assets are so liquid... but once again we must recall the degree of contagion in the financial world. Financial institutions are closely linked by short-term exchanges, and any potential partner that appears to be strapped for liquidity is quickly shunned.

After deposits, the next largest figure is 'long-term debt'. What is this – a loan from another bank? The long-term debt of Citigroup is composed of bonds issued by Citigroup and its subsidiaries. (I omit the complication of consolidated balance sheet accounting. Suffice it to say that rules of consolidating balance sheets of related firms is a (best) effort to represent the state of the holding firm by adding the assets and the liabilities of all related firms to the degree that these assets and liabilities are part of the 'empire' of the holding company.)

Besides using shares to finance its operations, Citigroup also issues bonds, which are part of the long-term debt. As of 30 July 2008, the bonds accounted for $171 billion of the long-term debt. For example, someone could purchase a 10-year bond of Citigroup with 6 per cent interest. During ten years, he or she receives payments of 6 per cent annually. After ten years, the bond is redeemed for the full purchase price (if Citigroup still exists). With the US government around to bail out Citigroup, this may appear a better deal than buying US Treasury bonds, which are also (more closely) guaranteed by the US government, but at a lower interest rate. Whether one purchases Treasury bonds or Citigroup bonds, one is really lending money. Who does this? Many, many individuals, but the vast majority of these bonds are held by pension funds and other pools of capital that either are restrained to low-risk investments or need a portion of low-risk investments to anchor their portfolio. The failure of these bonds (in the case of the failure of Citigroup) would constitute not a failure in the liquidity of these pools of capital, however, simply a reduction of the performance of their investments. It is the clients of these pools of capital who lose. By and large these are the same people who are funding the government bailouts: ordinary citizens participating in a retirement fund, middle- and also of course upper-class citizens who have a nest egg with investment fund managers, and so on.

Lehman Brothers provides a (once) live example. Lehman Brothers, an investment bank, filed for bankruptcy on 15 September 2008. Figure 1.3 summarizes the impact of the Lehman Brothers bankruptcy on creditors. Detailed analysis can be found in Valukas (2010) and an overview in the Wikipedia article on the Lehman Brothers bankruptcy.[1] As in the imaginary scenario of a failure of Citibank, we see a large number of middle-class and upper-class investors losing part of their nest egg; in this case the international impact is more evident.

How should we perceive this loss of investment by large numbers of people? The reality is that investment involves risk. Investment is made in the expectation of increased wealth, but under the risk of losing all or part of one's investment. This is tough, but it is what happened with the failure of Lehman Brothers and is what would happen with a failure of Citibank.

There is, however, a less tangible effect of a failed financial institution – whether by distress acquisition or by bankruptcy. The less tangible effect is the diminished confidence of financial agents when the failed firm enjoyed great standing. Put into clear terms, if I yesterday considered firm X to be solid and it turns out that it wasn't solid, then perhaps I am wrong today in considering firms A, B and C to be solid. Is it wise to lend to firms A, B and C? Is it wise to confide my capital to firms A, B and C?

This leads to two related issues that require examination. First, how many similar hits can investors take before we have a catastrophe for all of society? Second, do such banks as Lehman Brothers and Citibank have any role other than providing investment opportunities, and how many hits can that role take before there is a catastrophe for all of society?

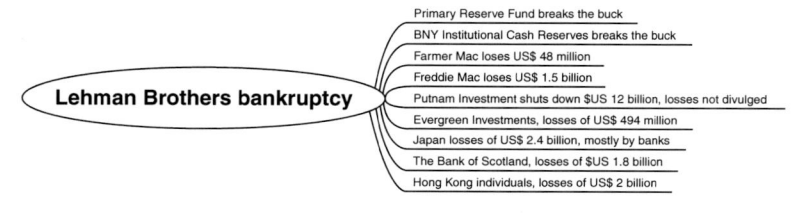

Lehman Brothers bankruptcy
- Primary Reserve Fund breaks the buck
- BNY Institutional Cash Reserves breaks the buck
- Farmer Mac loses US$ 48 million
- Freddie Mac loses US$ 1.5 billion
- Putnam Investment shuts down $US 12 billion, losses not divulged
- Evergreen Investments, losses of US$ 494 million
- Japan losses of US$ 2.4 billion, mostly by banks
- The Bank of Scotland, losses of $US 1.8 billion
- Hong Kong individuals, losses of US$ 2 billion

Figure 1.3 Impact of the Lehman Brothers bankruptcy on its creditors
Note: 'Breaking the buck' means that the value of shares in a fund falls below one dollar.

The financial world is an intermediary between the capital and debt markets. In other words, it takes the wealth accumulated by some individuals and moral persons (companies, pension funds, etc.) and invests it in various projects in the real world.

The theory is that this service is done in such a way as to provide the highest possible return for the clients who provide wealth, by investing in the best-performing projects. This is beneficial not only for those clients, but for society as a whole because these 'best-performing projects' are precisely the ones which maximize the new wealth of society.

That theory may be disputed, but now the question is what happens if current financial institutions are impaired in fulfilling that role. The fear that a catastrophe would occur is what motivated massive government intervention beginning in 2008.

An alternative view on the crisis: Austrian economics

> What should have happened in 1929 is precisely what should happen now. Let the price system prevail! The government should completely remove itself from the course of action and let the market reevaluate resource values. That means bankruptcies, yes. That means bank closures, yes. But these are part of the capitalistic system. They are part of the free-market economy. What is regrettable is not the readjustment process, but that the process was ever made necessary by the preceding interventions. (Rockwell, 2009)

Austrian economics is a school of thought about economics (and has the United States and to a lesser extent the United Kingdom as its venue). The moniker derives from derogatory comments made (in the late nineteenth century) by students of the German Historical school regarding the arguments of Carl Menger, who was from Austria. The German Historical school argued that the key considerations of economics change from society to society, from historical context to historical context, whereas Menger argued that nonetheless we can observe universal economic laws.

This observation that there are universal economic laws is neither original nor the principal characteristic of Austrian economics, however. Wikipedia says that Austrian economics 'is a school of economic thought that emphasizes the spontaneous organizing power of the price mechanism'.[2]

This is not simply neoclassical economics with an assertion of efficient markets. The point of Austrian economics has as much to do with economic policy as it has to do with the theory of what the economy is and how it operates. Government should intervene little, and only with the goal of permitting the market to operate properly – in other words, effectively and efficiently. The market is not some anonymous force, but simply the cumulative effect of millions of decisions by individuals, both physical and moral. Government intervention, in contrast, replaces these cumulative decisions with a single wilful decision based on 'expert' analysis. It should facilitate the market process rather than substitute it.

One specific case in point is the operation of the banking system. Without government intervention, banks are in competition and their managers must keep pace with market developments if they wish to pursue profits with a reasonable level of risk. If they do not do so, then they will lose the support of the other banks, who will retire all cash in anticipation of a bank failure:

> For if banks were truly competitive, any expansion of credit by one bank would quickly pile up the debts of that bank in its competitors, and its competitors would quickly call upon the expanding bank for redemption in cash. (Rothbard, 1969)

In the United States, for example, banks are not in a truly competitive market because they are forced to keep their reserves in the Federal Reserve System. Thus the disposition of these reserves obeys no longer the influence of the market (again, the accumulated decisions by many) but rather the dictates of the central bank. Because the central bank has the power to expand these reserves by fiat, all banks can enter into an expansionary strategy with reduced risk of any demand to render all cash.

> So now we see, at last, that the business cycle is brought about, not by any mysterious failings of the free market economy, but quite the opposite: By systematic intervention by government in the market process. Government intervention brings about bank expansion and inflation, and, when the inflation comes to an end, the subsequent depression-adjustment comes into play.

How would this apply to the financial crisis of 2007–2010? Austrian economists were almost alone in predicting the crash and in bearing witness to the antecedent bubbles. This is no surprise, since one of the more prestigious Austrian economists, Friedrich Hayek, received a Nobel Prize for his theory of business cycles and their cause. However, the advice of Austrian economists as to the resolution of the crisis has been ignored, perhaps because this advice is unpalatable both to politicians and to the financial industry.

So what is their advice?

Do nothing.

This is unpalatable to politicians because it means they have no power, and also because they do not want to appear indifferent or lazy to their constituents. It is unpalatable to the financial industry because it means the financial sector must suffer the consequences of decisions made by the finance gurus of the turn of the millennium.

This advice to do nothing is born neither of callousness nor of an ideological bias against government intervention. Rather, it follows logically from the analysis made by Austrian economists. What we call an economic crisis is a crash in asset prices after a prolonged inflation of those prices: a bubble has burst. The distortion thus is not the bursting of the bubble, but the inflation of the bubble. The inflation is pleasant for most, while the bursting is painful for just about all. Unfortunately, the pleasant situation was entirely artificial and unsustainable. The unpleasant situation is merely the correction of the error.

There are two causes to every bubble: the accumulated decisions by large numbers of people (more or less talented and diligent) seeking to improve their personal prosperity (what some stereotype as selfishness or greed) and the context within which those decisions were made. The pursuit of improved prosperity for oneself and one's household is a reasonable endeavour and sustainable in spite of all the obstacles fate may throw in one's way. What may be artificial is the context within which individual decisions are made. Any arbitrary human influence on the economy is artificial for the Austrian economist. In practice, the only human influence with sufficient power to influence the economy is government (with the possible exception of a large and centralized hedge fund – one person having the power to decide – in extreme conditions). Government replaces the 'natural' governance of the economy by the massive accumulation of individual decisions, with economic policy exercised through the interest rate by which the central bank lends to private banks (monetary policy), through the budgetary issues of taxation and spending (fiscal policy) and through other creative ways of influencing specific parts of the economy. Austrian economics accuses government (specifically the US government, although there were parallels in Britain and other countries) of bringing two artificial influences to bear on the economy: (1) making too much money available by lowering interest rates (here Federal Reserve Chairman Alan

Greenspan is seen as the bogeyman) and (2) policies which skewed the housing market. We will examine the dynamics behind the housing boom in the next chapter; at present we simply want to understand the reasoning of Austrian economics.

The reasoning is thus that the harm is already done and that the cause was government intervention. The two artificial influences (low interest rates and housing policies) contributed to a squandering of society's wealth, and the pain of the crash is simply a recognition of this fact. Spending taxpayers' money to hide this fact does not change it. In more specific terms:

1. Maintaining a low interest rate to 'stimulate' the economy only prolongs one of the artificial influences which produced the bubble and so cannot be a remedy.
2. 'Rescuing' those institutions which gambled (or, more kindly, misjudged the best investment of assets), be it by paying money to them ever so temporarily, also skews the market and encourages more risk-taking in the future.
3. Stimulating the economy by increased spending on public works also skews the market if the projects are not part of normal infrastructure improvement.

In summary, the criticism of Austrian economics is that the remedies are unlikely to be effective because they attempt to replace a resolution of the crisis via the accumulative decisions of the mass of participants in the economy with a decision or a series of decisions by some very smart people with a limited understanding of the crisis –even supposing their objectivity and the absence of any ulterior motives.

'The government package is not going to rescue the economy, but it will rescue activities that the economy cannot afford and that consumers do not want. It will sustain waste and promote inefficiency, draining resources from growth and efficiency' (Shostak, 2008).

In the Austrian view, then, government intervention caused the crisis, exacerbated the crisis, and prolonged the crisis.

Part II
The Genesis of the Crisis

The genesis of the 2007–2010 financial crisis may be distilled into two complementary processes. The first is a boom in housing (see Chapter 3). This was provoked by a series of government interventions earmarked to improve the lot of the disadvantaged, but which led to increased demand for houses, and thus to an increase in housing construction and in house prices, the granting of a large number of injudicious mortgage contracts and ultimately the failure of a large number of the parties to fulfil those contracts. The second process was the growth of securitization[1] in general, and the securitization of mortgages in particular (see Chapter 3). This growth multiplied the impact of government interventions to increase ownership and supported the explosive growth of mortgages, even among people unable to support mortgage payments.

The two processes had two effects. On the ground, a large number of people saw their homes foreclosed as they failed to make mortgage payments. In the financial world, a large number of investors discovered that the 'nearly risk-free' securities were in fact of very uncertain value. It is this latter issue that is at the heart of the financial crisis, rather than

---

1. Securitization is explained in Chapter 2. If you own something that can make money on a reliable basis, in finance-speak you have an asset that generates cash flow. If you want, you can sell the opportunity to share in that cash flow. You could even sell the rights to all of the cash flow and make a little profit by selling those rights at a higher price than you paid for the asset. This is securitization, and that little profit when earned a multitude of times made the securitization of mortgage loans a sustainable business. Unfortunately, the purchase of those securities was predicated on the faulty assumption that real estate values were going to continue to increase in value uninterruptedly.

the former issue. The nearly total seizing up of the credit markets was due in large measure to these 'nearly risk-free' securities.

In order to understand the genesis of the crisis, we must first examine the roots before studying the sequence of events leading up to the bust of 2007: the historical context of the crisis and the mechanics behind the sequence of events. That examination is the topic of Chapter 2.

2
The Roots of the Crisis

Some basics about shelter and homeownership

The average house costs the equivalent of two to five years of the average person's revenue, and few people ever save that much cash. Those who do have already been working for more than five to ten years, since they have to spend money to eat, get to and from work, and pay for their shelter during that time. If a couple in their twenties wants to marry and start a family, it may be difficult for them to own their own home, since their expenses will be rising as the family grows, and as parents they will probably not both work outside the home continuously. Yet these are precisely the people who would most benefit from owning a home.

How can young families acquire their own home? One solution is intergenerational solidarity. Parents can help children buy their own home. This can become difficult, however, if parents have several children in their twenties. The irony of the situation is that these same young people in their twenties will be earning more money in their fifties, when they no longer need such a large house to live in.

Mortgages are the solution to this problem.

A mortgage is a special kind of loan. By promising to cede ownership of their house to the lender should they cease to make regular payments over a long period of time, a couple can receive a loan of the cash necessary to buy a house. This is an elegant solution if both sides come out winning. This will be the case if the couple has access to better living conditions and eventually ownership of the home with a paid-off mortgage and if the person or company doing the lending also makes some money on the transaction.

Several factors need to be in place to assure this.

One is the terms of the mortgage itself: is it a fair deal? We will come back to this question later. For the time being, we will let the market be the judge: can the couple get a better deal elsewhere? Could the lender make more money doing something else with its money? For example, if the lender charges exorbitant rates, it's not a fair deal. If the couple gets the mortgage almost interest free, it's not a fair deal either.

Another factor is the mortgage's appropriateness for the borrowers. Perhaps the terms of the mortgage are fair according to the market, but the borrowers will be unable to meet the terms. This could be because the borrowers are trying to buy a house that remains beyond their means even with the aid that a mortgage gives. If a cashier in Montreal tries to buy a mansion in Beverly Hills, California, or a condominium in Naples, Florida, or near Les Invalides in Paris, he or she would be unable to keep up the mortgage payments. Of course, this is not a problem of the mortgage, but of the underlying purchase. The terms of the mortgage may be inappropriate even if the house being purchased is unpretentious. If the payments are not uniform over time, or if the mortgage period is too short, it may become difficult to continue paying.

How should the mortgage be structured? There is room for judgement here. A young couple may have to pay off student debt for a few years, and anticipate an increase in salaries, and so prefer to pay less the first few years, increasing payments thereafter. This will work well if everything goes as planned. If the primary earner falls ill or is injured, this may affect the couple's capacity to meet payments. To prevent this problem, they may have an insurance plan ... or they may not. The terms of the mortgage may require this. Or not.

In various countries, governments intervene by establishing guidelines as to what is a standard structure for a mortgage, particularly with respect to:

the absolute amount mortgaged (more expensive houses have their own risks);
the portion of the price of the house which is lent to the borrower; and
the borrower's capacity to meet the loan payments.

In the United States, where the 2007–2010 financial crisis primarily originated, mortgages which do not conform to the first criterion above are called 'jumbo asset' mortgages. Mortgages which do not conform to the second criterion or for which there is incomplete documentation of the borrower's income are called 'Alt-A' mortgages. 'Subprime' mortgages are those in which the borrowers do not meet credit criteria (the third criterion), namely:

1. The ratio of monthly payments to monthly income
2. Past credit performance – missing payments by 30 days or 60 days
3. A judgment about the stability of income flow, usually based on the nature of the employment contract and past employment history (see Office of the Comptroller of the Currency et al., 2001).

In appraising the riskiness of a mortgage, the key factors are the borrower's capacity and willingness to persevere in making monthly payments. Of the three kinds of non-standard mortgages, the riskiest is obviously the subprime mortgage. When a company invests in a series of riskier investments, a greater portion of those investments will fail compared to investments in a series of less risky investments. In other words, the investor will not make money on some of those risky investments. He will have to make up the difference on the remaining investments. That is the reason the interest rate on that class of mortgage will be higher. Otherwise no one would volunteer to make funds available.

This creates an ironic situation. Precisely those borrowers least able to pay a higher rate are those who are condemned to do so. How large and what is the shape of the window within which people with poorer credit can afford a mortgage? The availability of mortgages allows people to own homes before they can accumulate the cash necessary to purchase them, but only people with a certain financial capacity. That capacity is defined by the potential to save that amount of cash over a given period of time, say 30 years, plus a further amount of cash to allow the lender to make money off of the loan, and another sum of cash to cover the risk taken by the lender. To understand the latter factor, consider that the risk translates into a certain percentage of defaults on loans. Those who don't default contribute an extra amount to pay for those defaults. Nobody wants to pay for others' defaulting, and lenders would just as soon not take the risk if there is no extra money to be made. For these two reasons, and also for the historical reason in various countries that mortgages were originally limited to 'prime' borrowers, there is a going rate for low-risk borrowers and higher rates for higher-risk borrowers, rather than one slightly higher rate for everyone. As a consequence, poor credit risk borrowers have a smaller window of access to mortgages.

Since the same range of mortgage structures is possible when lending to both prime borrowers and subprime borrowers, it follows that the price of the house is the key factor for subprime borrowers to make it through the window. This appeals to common sense.

Even the ironic situation that those least able to pay high interest on a mortgage are precisely those who must pay it also loses its irony if we consider the role of mortgages in the overall economy. Most people cannot buy a house with 100 per cent cash down. Mortgages allow some of these people to buy a house by anticipating the cash they will be able to accumulate over the years. This divides the population into three groups: those able to pay cash, those able to purchase a house with a mortgage, and those who do not qualify for a mortgage. You can qualify for a mortgage if you can eventually accumulate enough cash to purchase a house and some more to pay the profit of the lender. In other words, you can qualify for a mortgage if your income is high enough. The frontiers between the three parts of the population are defined in terms of your capacity to accumulate cash. That is why the frontier between populations seems so strange if we expect a physical wall or a clean dividing line. The difference between the top (in terms of creditworthiness) two parts of the population is that one qualifies for mortgages and the other qualifies so well that it could purchase a house without mortgaging it. The difference between the lower two parts of the population is that the top part qualifies for mortgages, whereas the bottom part does not. The frontier could be very gradual, since so many factors – such as the structure of the mortgage and the willingness of the borrowers to defer other expenses – feather the frontier. However, the rise in interest rates for riskier borrowers helps make the frontier more brusque, selecting out potential borrowers who would be borderline.

This may raise questions of social justice: Is it fair that some can afford their own home and others cannot? The practical question: Is it better if more people can own a home? The current system allows more people to own a home, and this is as fair as possible until someone can find another system to let even more people own a home. That being said, it is not always wise to own a home. The conventional wisdom is that homeownership is the best expenditure: since the asset is retained, you are investing your money, not spending it. A fancy car, on the other hand, loses its value over the years and the parts wear out. Food, clothing and other expenditures are consumed, with nothing to show once consumed. In contrast, you may use a house, but you do not 'use it up' because it retains its value.

That is conventional wisdom.

Things are a bit more complicated in reality. Further expenditures are necessary to maintain the house: repairs and landscape maintenance (even if only to mow the lawn) and taxes are also inevitable expenditures. Further, the mortgage payments do not all go to ownership – part of them go to paying a profit to the lender, as we have seen. If we compare ownership with rental, we must sum all of these expenditures and compare these as well as the final value of the house. In point of fact, in some (exceptional) circumstances, ownership is not as good as rental from the financial viewpoint.

Another factor which influences whether the mortgage will work out well or not is the relationship of the mortgage to the rest of the economy as it evolves, not only to current mortgage rates. Mortgages are typically long-lasting contracts – commitments of 30 or 40 years. What is reasonable in 1981 – when the rate was 19 per cent – may not be reasonable in 2003 – when the rate was 5.5 per cent. That's why there are fixed-rate mortgages and variable-rate mortgages. No one knows the future, least of all the average consumer – or for that matter, the average bank employee – so having a variable rate means that the payments may vary wildly in the future. Still, they may be lower in the short term, if currently interest rates are low. Some mortgages split the difference, with a portion of the payment being fixed and another portion of the payment varying as a function of current interest rates.

Further, the borrowers are usually able to renegotiate their mortgage at specified later dates. Sometimes they can do so outside of these dates, subject to certain penalties.

The upshot of this is that mortgages are extremely varied in their terms and, if less sophisticated than other financial instruments, are a great deal more complicated than buying a new dress or a case of beer. A 2006 survey conducted on behalf of the Mortgage Bankers Association revealed that half the 'borrowers who had bought a house within the previous 12 months...couldn't recall the terms of their mortgage' (Brooks and Simon, 2007). There is room for confusion here. If we add to this any incidence of dishonesty on either side – some borrowers trying to get better terms by misrepresenting their credit situation, or brokers trying to get either more numerous mortgages or else mortgages with higher rates – it is not surprising that this mechanism for buying homes has unfortunate side effects.

The historical context

There are five factors in the historical context which are relevant: the rise of new sources of mortgages, new circumvention of banking regulations (especially by off-balance-sheet holdings), the deregulation of the banking industry, spectacular incentives for workers in the finance industry, and the dot-com boom and bust at the turn of the millennium.

The first part of the historical context to emphasize is a modification in the operation of the mortgage banking system. Traditionally, banks would accept deposits and then re-lend that money at a higher interest rate than that paid on the deposits. They made their profit on that spread and also by making a reasonable guess about when they would actually have to produce the cash corresponding to the deposits made. This guess allowed them to loan out several times as much as the amount in deposit, which is how the banking system 'creates' money or has a 'multiplier' effect.

This changed. As Brunnermeier has observed (2008), the 'originate and distribute' model replaced the 're-lend deposits' model. In this model, loans are originated by firms with limited working capital, and then securitized in order to multiply the reach of that working capital.

Fifty years ago, most mortgages in the United States were a contract between the homeowner and the bank that originated and held the mortgage with its own funds. The mortgage was simply one of the various types of loans on the bank's books. Beginning in the 1990s, however, a new kind of institution began to occupy more space on the mortgage market: specialized mortgage originators who worked with a few million dollars in capital and thus had the cash to fund the purchase of a couple dozen houses.

If you sign a mortgage deal every few hours, it won't take long to use up that kind of capital. The solution is to resell this block of mortgages to someone else with deeper pockets. That someone else accumulates a few such blocks of mortgages and resells them, typically by creating a corporation to hold the pool of mortgages and issue securities backed by that pool. We will examine this mechanism more closely further on. The point here is that the appearance of specialized mortgage originators meant that more mortgages became available in the economy and that the person who ended up owning the mortgage was no longer the person who originated it.

A second part of the historical context consists of clever legal ways in which banks in the United States circumvented regulations. It should be noted that there are two justifications for US regulation of banks: (1) banks have an important fiduciary role, since common citizens are entrusting their hard-earned funds to the care of their bank; (2) the Federal Deposit Insurance Corporation provides a service to the banks (inasmuch as it inspires greater consumer confidence in participating banks) and thus can stipulate conditions for that service.

The relevant regulations have to do with the level of risk taken by banks. Once government intervenes, market discipline is severely diminished and must be replaced by regulation. The fundamental risk taken by a bank resides in the proportion between money deposited and money lent out (in the case of commercial banks; the regulator was different and more distant for investment banks, but similar rules applied). Still, the riskiness of loans and the timing of deposits vary, so that the rules about capital reserves – the ratio of capital to the various loans – were evolving. The rules were based in large part on an analysis of the balance sheet of each bank, where one could read in black and white the bank's total equity (in all its complexity of retained earnings, ordinary shares, preferred shares, trust preferred shares, etc.), liabilities (deposits) and assets (different loans). The problem was that if a bank created a subsidiary that held a pool of loans and that subsidiary then issued securities to all and sundry, the risk involved in that subsidiary was 'counted' in the reserve ratio according to the methodology then in place. Put simplistically, banks which were required to limit their loans to 15 or 20 times their equity could comply according to the methodology in place, even though the effective ratio was closer to 50 times the equity. It was circumvention of the law, but everyone did it, and the extent of this practice grew bit by bit, like the slow heating up of the proverbial pot of water containing the oblivious frog.

The consequence of this was that commercial banks and investment banks were far more at risk than regulators and shareholders realized.

This off-balance-sheet activity implied not only the existence of other institutions involved in the banking function (multiplying money), such as the originators, but also those involved in the securitization and re-securitization of the pools of mortgages and other kinds of loans. These constitute what is known as the 'shadow' banking system, and it grew to be larger than conventional banking.

Related to this is a third part of the historical context of the crisis: the deregulation of the banking sector. The Glass-Steagall Act of 1933 had forced banks to choose between commercial banking (holding deposits and lending to individuals and to businesses) and investment banking (raising capital and investing it in various ways). Bit by bit, the dividing line between the two became diffuse, and the act ended up being repealed in 1999 under President Clinton. At the same time, little was done to regulate investment banking, which was outside the purview of the bodies regulating commercial banks. Further, the entire regulatory apparatus for the financial industries was very fragmented, and large institutions incorporated special subsidiaries to operate under different regulatory regimes to ensure that the applicable regulations were as simple and as liberal as possible. Capital requirements for investment banks were monitored by the Securities Exchange Commission, which modified its rules in April 2004 in order to allow the firms to regulate themselves.[1]

On top of this, the labour pool among regulators of investment banks had a peculiar relationship with the firms they regulated. The pool of expertise is and was limited, so people would migrate from regulated companies to regulator and back. Knowledge of how the business worked was important to regulate proficiently; knowledge of the regulatory apparatus was similarly valuable in industry. There was a major difference, though: the big money was and is in industry (the banks). Several commentators – some more and some less radical – have witnessed and decried the intimacy of Wall Street and Pennsylvania Avenue in magazines varying from the staid *Atlantic Monthly* to the (once) trendy *Rolling Stone*.

A related development, although not involving regulation by any government agency, was a change in the policies of the New York Stock Exchange. Prior to 1970, the NYSE required approval for each owner of its member firms, who were in fact the most important investment banks. After 1970 these firms voted to permit public ownership (cf. von Nordenflycht, 2008), and the major investment banks were thus able to expand their equity base in subsequent years. This allowed them to expand their volume of activity considerably.

A fourth part of the historical context of the crisis is the evolution of the US economy. The accepted wisdom in economics is and was that the portions of the economy represented by agriculture and by manufacturing were destined to shrink. Indeed, although agriculture's productivity and absolute output grew by leaps and bounds throughout the twentieth century, it shrank to about one per cent of the whole economy (as a percentage of GDP). Manufacturing also shrank in the last years of the twentieth century and in the first decade of the twenty-first century. There were two causes. Unlike agriculture, manufacture experienced a real decline as low-end and not-so-low-end manufacturing emigrated to other countries. The automobile industry is a case in point. Another cause of the relative decrease in importance was the rise of another sector of the economy: services, and financial services in particular. 'Size' in economics is measured by the price paid by the last purchaser. Thus, the size of the financial sector with respect to the entire US economy is roughly indicated by the total revenues of that sector compared to US GDP for the year. Figure 2.1 shows that the relative importance of the sector nearly quadrupled from the 1940s to the 2000s.

This increased size was accompanied by a growth of salaries in the sector: after some 50 years of a steady decline that began with the Great Depression, wages in the financial sector rose from a rough equality to other non-agricultural wages (1980) all the way to 170 per cent of other wages (2007).

That superior salaries lie within the grasp of workers in the financial industry is clear. It is also interesting to see how those earnings are structured. Although a handsome salary is at the base, in most case the bigger portion of take-home earnings is merit-based bonus, where 'merit' is the money brought in to the employer. That money is not all that easy to measure, however, as many investment funds discovered to their dismay in 2008. A lot of it took the form of toxic assets or was tied to sources that then discovered some of their assets to be toxic. The incentive mechanisms that governed the bonuses earned by workers in the financial sector rewarded aggressive revenue expansion at the expense of realistic risk control. This is now seen to be obviously

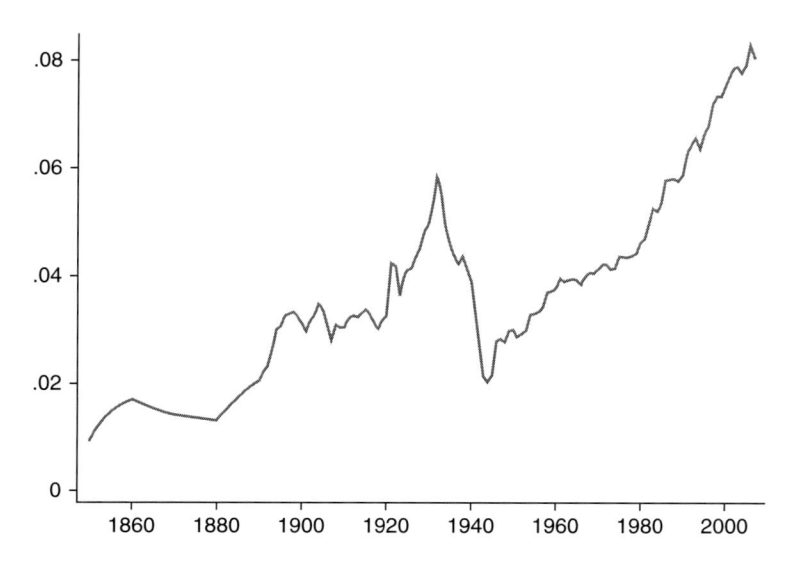

Figure 2.1 Financial services as a fraction of US GDP
Source: Philippon, 2007.

counterproductive, for shareholders if not for employees, including the topmost layers of management, who get to walk away with their bonuses – but at the time it seemed to be the only way to exploit the market instead of leaving it for the competition to exploit. This is illustrated in Figures 2.2 and 2.3, which graph the importance of wages and profits in the financial sector relative to those in other industries. Profits peaked in 2005 and then dropped in the following years; wages, on the other hand, grew until the end of 2007 and diminished only microscopically in 2008.

The final piece of the historical context is a bubble that preceded the bubble in housing prices that input directly into the current crisis. That previous bubble was the telecommunications/dot-com bubble. The dot-com aspect of the bubble was visible to everyone who wasn't actively throwing away their money on all sorts of silly ventures, but the telecommunications-hardware aspect caught most people by surprise. Cisco in the United States and Nortel in Canada were some of the most spectacular cases of firms caught overproducing and overinvesting in production capacity. In 2000, freshly graduated electrical engineers found themselves competing for jobs with seasoned veterans of ten, 15 or even 20 years of leading-edge experience. The shareholders of telecommunications stock also found themselves in an unpleasant situation.

Investors had placed their money in the real economy and had been burnt. They were looking for somewhere more secure than the real

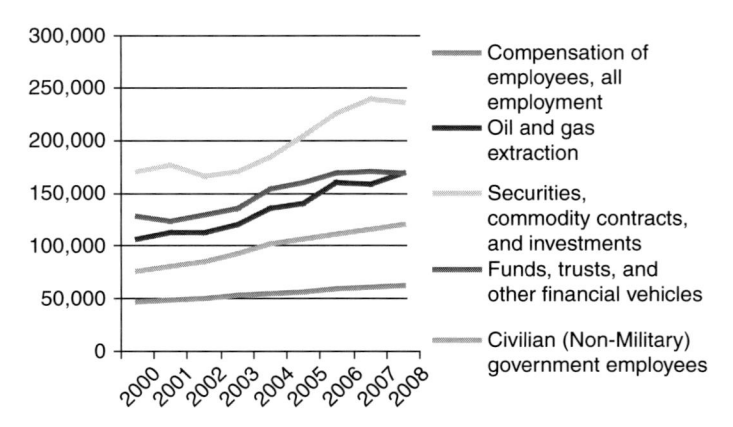

Figure 2.2 American financial sector wages compared to all wages in non-agricultural industries and to oil and gas wages

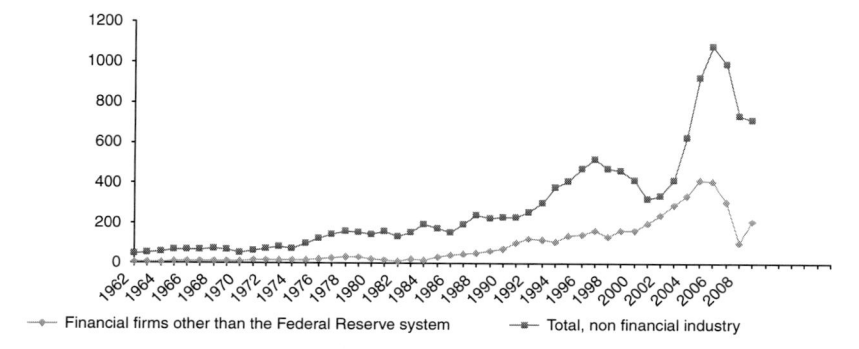

Figure 2.3 Profits in the financial sector compared to total business profits in all non-financial industries in the United States

economy for investment, and they found that security in the world of finance.

They made a lot of money. At first.

The mechanics of the crisis

Before we walk through the chain of events that led to the crisis, we need to have an understanding of the actual mechanics of the crisis, in addition to the understanding we now have of the historical context. There are only two simple things to understand: the locus from which the crisis emanated and the linkage between home mortgages and that locus. The locus is the extreme sensitivity of investment banking to real and perceived liquidity fluctuations. The linkage is what is called the 'securitization process'.

Investment banking and various fund managers

Investment banks do not hold deposits the way commercial banks do. Whereas commercial banks lend out several times their equity based on a conservative projection of the flow of funds into (from deposits) and out of (via loans) the bank over time, investment banks are constantly making huge short-term investments in stocks and various securities. These investments are short term because the goal is not to invest in the different securities, but to hold them long enough to sell them at a profit on the market. Most of the top-tier investment banks (previous to September 2008) were also dealers, brokers and underwriters. In some cases different aspects of the business were assumed by a distinct corporation that belonged to the bank; in others they were merely different divisions of the same corporation. The exact legal status of the different aspects of a given investment bank's business could be complex – byzantine, even. This was not because these banks wanted to hide their activity, since on the contrary they wanted to exploit the reputation attached to their name and as well let potential clients know that they were a full-service operation. The causes were current opportunity and the specific legal requirements and advantages of different juridical entities.

In any case, most of the top-tier investment banks helped companies issue new shares and new bonds. If the city of Milwaukee wanted to issue bonds to finance the construction of new schools at $50 million, it could go to one of these dealers, which would provide the legal services and then issue the bonds and buy up all those that were not immediately purchased on the market. If the city issued two million bonds at $25 each, perhaps only the first million would be purchased on the market at $25. Thereafter the price would drop until a new buyer became interested. Perhaps the second million would sell at prices varying from $23 down to $10. If the bank purchased the second million shares at $25 each and sold them over the next month, then the city would raise the $50 million it needed to construct the new schools. This process of buying and holding the excess bonds and/or shares is called 'underwriting'. Of course, it is in the bank's interest to correctly guess how much the market is willing to pay and how many units it is willing to buy in the short term. Put into cynical terms, it is in the bank's interest to underestimate the price and number of shares so that it can quickly sell at a profit. On the other hand, this could hurt the bank's reputation for fair treatment of its clients.

The bank engages in analogous activities of easing capital from seller to buyer, and the ensemble of these activities is called 'making markets'.

The bank's revenues come from fees for providing various services and also from the profits made while making markets. It can of course suffer a loss rather than make a profit in making a market. Much of the expertise of investment banking lies in managing this risk. The other part of the expertise lies in the technicalities of executing tasks for its clients.

Investment banks make markets far beyond the capacity of their equity base, even more so than commercial banks extend loans beyond their equity base. How does the investment bank finance (fund) this market making? If we look at the liability side of the balance sheet of

Goldman Sachs (Table 2.1), we can see a 'mere' $28 billion in equity out of a total of $800 billion on the liability side that finances the assets. Long-term loans to Goldman Sachs totalled $168 billion. The rest of the liabilities varied from accounts payable (30 days) to 'securities sold under agreements to repurchase' (usually overnight). The biggest item is 'payables to customers and counterparties', which is mostly cash either generated on client accounts and thus owed to them, or else a portion of the cash deposited by the investing client and still not used.

Whereas commercial banks lend out the funds that arrive in the form of deposits, investment banks use funds that arrive in the form of loans. In a sense, that is not a great difference because, of course, depositing money in a bank is pretty much like lending money to the bank. Commercial banks may pay interest on deposits, but the depositors are clients of the commercial bank and accept a lower rate of interest for the ready access and manoeuvrability of funds provided by the commercial banks. They also pay for a myriad of services, from cheques to overdrafts to conversion of currency. Like commercial banks, investment banks have clients on both sides of the balance sheet. Besides the legal and procedural niceties, however, there are a couple of major differences in these loans. First is their size. We are talking about blocks of $100 million, $1 billion. The second difference is the duration of these loans: many of them are loans for 24 hours. Thus the liability side of investment banks' balance sheets is made up of large blocks of rapidly turning over loans. You lend a couple hundred million to your neighbourhood investment bank knowing that tomorrow it will pay you back the full amount, plus one day's interest or about $20,000 (a guesstimate of three per cent for a 300-day year, or 0.01 per cent of $200 million). The investment bank needs to make more than $20,000 with the loan over that 24-hour period: that is how it makes a profit. And investment banks do make better than $20,000 with that money in 24 hours, sometimes much better – that is their expertise.

However, to do this, they need someone to lend them $200 million. Pension funds, insurance companies and hedge funds are among the large sources of overnight loans. From the 1980s onwards, the funds came increasingly from Asian and other foreign sources. However, no one will lend money if they think the investment bank won't be able to pay them back the next day. That is where the locus of the crisis lay.

Investment banking is a very profitable business with an important Achilles heel: liquidity. This Achilles heel becomes very exposed when

Table 2.1 Goldman Sachs liabilities

Liabilities and shareholders' equity, Goldman Sachs, in millions of dollars	2008	2007
Deposits (includes $4,224 and $463 at fair value as of November 2008 and November 2007, respectively)	$27,643	$15,370
Collateralized financings:		
Securities sold under agreements to repurchase, at fair value	62,883	159,178
Securities loaned (includes $7,872 and $5,449 at fair value as of November 2008 and November 2007, respectively)	17,060	28,624
Other secured financings (includes $20,249 and $33,581 at fair value as of November 2008 and November 2007, respectively)	38,683	65,710
Payables to brokers, dealers and clearing organizations	8585	8335
Payables to customers and counterparties	245,258	310,118
Trading liabilities, at fair value	175,972	215,023
Unsecured short-term borrowings, including the current portion of unsecured long-term borrowings (includes $23,075 and $48,331 at fair value as of November 2008 and November 2007, respectively)	52,658	71,557
Unsecured long-term borrowings (includes $17,446 and $15,928 at fair value as of November 2008 and November 2007, respectively)	168,220	164,174
Other liabilities and accrued expenses (includes $978 at fair value as of November 2008)	23,216	38,907
Total liabilities	820,178	1,076,996

Source: Goldman Sachs annual report, 2008.

investment banks have their fingers in the derivatives pie. A derivative is a security whose value is derived from the performance of another security. Warren Buffet (Chairman of Berkshire Hathaway Inc. and considered the most successful investment manager ever) explained the risk that derivatives pose for liquidity with clear and simple terms in a letter to shareholders accompanying the Berkshire Hathaway annual report for 2002:

> Another problem about derivatives is that they can exacerbate trouble that a corporation has run into for completely unrelated

reasons. This pile-on effect occurs because many derivatives contracts require that a company suffering a credit downgrade immediately supply collateral to counterparties. Imagine, then, that a company is downgraded because of general adversity and that its derivatives instantly kick in with *their* requirement, imposing an unexpected and enormous demand for cash collateral on the company. The need to meet this demand can then throw the company into a liquidity crisis that may, in some cases, trigger still more downgrades. It all becomes a spiral that can lead to a corporate meltdown.

Derivatives also create a daisy-chain risk that is akin to the risk run by insurers or reinsurers that lay off much of their business with others. In both cases, huge receivables from many counterparties tend to build up over time. (At Gen Re Securities, we still have $6.5 billion of receivables, though we've been in a liquidation mode for nearly a year.) A participant may see himself as prudent, believing his large credit exposures to be diversified and therefore not dangerous. Under certain circumstances, though, an exogenous event that causes the receivable from Company A to go bad will also affect those from Companies B through Z. History teaches us that a crisis often causes problems to correlate in a manner undreamed of in more tranquil times.

* * *

Many people argue that derivatives reduce systemic problems, in that participants who can't bear certain risks are able to transfer them to stronger hands. These people believe that derivatives act to stabilize the economy, facilitate trade, and eliminate bumps for individual participants. And, on a micro level, what they say is often true. Indeed, at Berkshire, I sometimes engage in large-scale derivatives transactions in order to facilitate certain investment strategies.

Charlie and I believe, however, that the macro picture is dangerous and getting more so. Large amounts of risk, particularly credit risk, have become concentrated in the hands of relatively few derivatives dealers, who in addition trade extensively with one other. The troubles of one could quickly infect the others.

On top of that, these dealers are owed huge amounts by non-dealer counterparties. Some of these counterparties, as I've mentioned, are linked in ways that could cause them to contemporaneously run into a problem because of a single event (such as the implosion of the telecom industry or the precipitous decline in the value of merchant power projects). Linkage, when it suddenly surfaces, can trigger serious systemic problems. (Buffet, 2003)

These considerations about the need of investment banks for liquidity allow us to understand why the best known twentieth century economist, John Maynard Keynes, likened a liquidity crisis to a game of musical chairs. When confidence drops around investment banks, the bank most in need of a cash loan suddenly finds that no one is willing to lend to it. In this way, one institution and then another is caught in the snares of the crisis. The analogue of the stoppage of music is the suddenly growing conviction that this institution or another would be unable to meet new obligations, as we have seen. The passage between music playing to music stopped – from confidence to doubt – is sudden, because of the mechanisms described by Brunnermeier (2008) and others. The vulnerability of investment banks to liquidity variations and the sensitivity of their partners to the onset of weakness were both enhanced by the systemic risks deriving from hedge funds.

Buffet's words also point to the concentration of risk – accumulation of assets characterized by similar risk within individual institutions – and easily lead us to observe that a large number of institutions faced identical risks.

We now understand how weakness would lead to sudden death for one investment bank after another, but we have yet to understand the initial source of weakness. The initial source was poor-quality mortgages, but in order to understand the relationship between any given mortgage and investment banks, we need to understand the mortgage industry and, in particular, the securitization process as it applies to mortgages. It is this securitization that links mortgages to the locus from which the financial crisis emanated.

Mortgages and the hierarchy of markets: from construction to mortgage-backed securities

Shelter is a fundamental human need. Not only do we need protection from the elements, but a home allows for the storage of property that is not currently being used, allows the individual to retire from the throng, and provides a physical support for gathering family members.

It can be made more functional and beautiful to provide repose to the human spirit.

Homes can be procured either through purchase or by rent. A purchased home, once it is paid for, provides security in old age and eliminates an important expense from the family budget. Rental leaves no residual rights beyond the time period paid for. On the other hand, homes are not eternal, and they require maintenance, so that even a home that has no payments outstanding requires continued expense. Further, the financial analysis of home purchasing reveals that in some (probably exceptional) circumstances, rental is actually cheaper than ownership. Given the uncertainties of life and the certainty of old age, however, homeownership does seem the better road to economic freedom.

The cost of urban land and interest in larger profits are among the factors which explain why most housing construction is usually priced for middle class or richer. In this way, lower classes have more difficulty in accessing the advantage of homeownership and must always dedicate a major part of their reduced budget to the acquisition of shelter by renting.

Because the price of a home is some two to five times annual salary before taxes, few homebuyers dispose of all the cash necessary to buy their home outright. We have seen how mortgages are the usual solution in the contemporary Occident and most of the Orient. A household pays a certain amount of cash down, and the balance is provided by a financial institution which loans that sum against the collateral of the building. The household must then make monthly payments to pay back the loan. The payments cover both the principal amount loaned and the interest owed. The terms of repayment are decided in the mortgage contract, which must obey certain rules established by the government. The rules were quite limited in the United States at the start of the twenty-first century, in the laudable hope of making homeownership accessible to more households.

A financial institution provides mortgages as a way of doing business. In other words, that institution loans money in order to make a profit. By doing so, it provides a service to homebuyers (allowing them to purchase a home today rather than when their children have grown up).

How does this business work? In simple terms, the interest rate paid by the homeowners should be higher than the cost of the principal for the financial institution.

Suppose the owners of the financial institution have invested $1 million, and they issue ten mortgages of $100,000 each. If they charge ten per cent interest, then the institution makes $100,000 a year. Not too bad. In September 2009, the fixed rate for a 30-year mortgage was around 4.5 per cent per annum. Not quite as good.

While the price of a home is a lot of money for one family, one needs many times that amount of cash to make a business of lending that sort of money. This is the reason that banks and credit unions have traditionally been the sources of this funding. A little company with 'just' $10 million wouldn't be able to fund the purchase of more than 50 homes. Since mortgages last 20 or 30 years, that wouldn't be much of a business. There is a way of getting a higher return on that capital. The trick is to loan the same amount of capital several times. In order to do that, the institution that issues the mortgage must sell the mortgage to get that cash back, lend it again, sell the new mortgages, and so on. A mortgage is a contract between lender and borrower in which the borrower promises to make a series of cash payments, so the lender can transfer the rights to these payments to another party in exchange for cash. The lender has lent out $10 million in exchange for promises to make payments over 20 years. It sells the rights to these payments for a profit. The company that buys this set of mortgages then bundles them with other sets and resells them to an investor with really deep pockets, such as a pension fund. The lender charges an origination fee to the home purchaser, keeps that and passes the monthly payments on to the company that buys the block of mortgages. He must make his money on the origination fee, not the interest.

The origination fee (between 0.5 per cent and two per cent of the loan) provides some return on the equity of the mortgage originator, which the lender is able to turn around ten times a year by reselling the blocks of mortgages. But the lender has to pay brokers and their loan officers, as well as their own employees and administrative expenses. Mortgage lenders need to get origination fees on mortgage originations corresponding to many more times their equity in order to get a higher return.

And so it is that, like most businesses in the later half of the twentieth century and so far in the twenty-first, mortgage originators fund their activity with debt rather than with capital. For example, with $1 million in capital, the issuer borrows another $10 million and pays prime rate plus one per cent, which in September 2009 would come out to a little less than 4.5 per cent. It borrows the money for a month, and then reimburses it once it has sold a block of mortgages. Then it again takes out another $10 million loan for another month. The difference between the fees it charges and the interest paid to the 'warehouse lender' is the net revenue. To increase the return on its equity, the originator has only to borrow more money. For example, a lender may have $1 million in equity and $19 million in warehouse debt, a ratio of 19:1. Ratios as high as 40:1 occurred in 2005 and 2006. The mortgage lender then could originate five mortgages a day for a month and then sell the block of mortgages to an arranger who took care of issuing securities based on this pool of mortgages combined with others, as we have seen.

The larger financial institution which purchases the block of mortgages wants to make money with the mortgages, and not on repossessing homes and administering real estate, so it makes an effort to ensure that the mortgages are solid. This effort is reduced to a couple of bureaucratic procedures which require the originator to take out 'mortgage insurance' and also a certain documentation of the mortgages.

Finally, homebuyers rarely deal directly with the originator, but go through an intermediary called a 'mortgage broker', who will shop around for mortgage deals.

As a result, the simplest universe of the homebuyer involves seven different visible players – the homebuyer, the constructor/seller, the real estate appraiser, the mortgage broker, the originator, the mortgage insurer, the mortgage servicer (who collects payments) – and two other players not visible to the purchaser: the warehouse lender and the larger financial institution that acquires blocks of mortgages from the originator.

Securitization

The larger financial institution that purchases a block of mortgages is also in business and must turn a profit. How does it do so? Once again, the interest payments on the mortgages represent a return on the capital of the larger financial institution, but it can fund the purchase of those mortgages with someone else's money in order to increase the return on its own capital.

The way it does so is a little more complicated than simply borrowing the money. What it does is collect several blocks of mortgages from several originators, until it has a pool of some thousands of mortgages. Then it creates a company: a legal entity called a 'mortgage trust' or a 'special purpose vehicle', depending on the context and depending on local laws. This trust then purchases the pool of mortgages from the financial institution that created it. In order to pay for the purchase, the trust issues a sort of bond – in other words, the *trust* borrows funds from fixed-income investors. It is not truly borrowing, however, because the bonds have a limited lifetime (30 years, or however long it takes the homeowners to pay off their mortgages) and the trust will not have to give any money back at the extinction of the securities.

The 'sort of bond' – the security, the infamous mortgage-backed security – is not really a fixed-income investment. Rather, such a security gives the holder the right to participate in the mortgage payments by the various purchasers of houses. The security gives the right to not the payments on any one mortgage, but rather a percentage of the total payments (less administrative fees for the trust). Suppose for example there were two thousand mortgages with payments varying from $700 to $1500 a month, for a total $2 million in payments each month, and that a total of one thousand participations were issued; then each security would have the right to $2000 a month. Such a security would be worth $350,000, at a guesstimate. Figure 2.4 relates home owner to security investor.

But things are slightly more complicated than that.

As we saw above, some mortgages are riskier than others. In other words, there is a greater chance that certain mortgagors will default on payment. As a consequence, these securities were not that easy to sell. A solution for this problem was to reorganize that risk.

What risk was there in mortgage-backed securities?

A specific risk for the special interest vehicle resides in the fact that it has purchased the pool of mortgages from the arranger using a line of credit or a loan with a variable interest rate. Many mortgages also had variable rates, but these kicked in a few years after the origination of the mortgages. Thus the early years of each mortgage (and ultimately of the securities issued) carried an interest-rate risk. The special purpose vehicle can buy insurance for these payments in the form of an

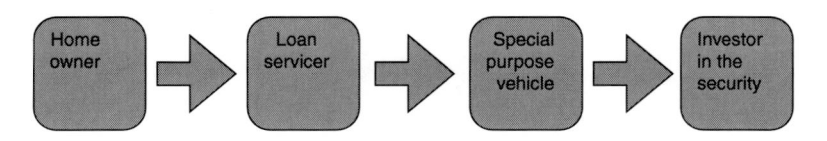

Figure 2.4 Flow of payments from homeowner to the investor holding a mortgage-backed security

interest-rate swap. The following paragraphs focus on risk for the investors. However, one of the risks for the investor is that other parties to the securities fail. This is reduced in part by the creation of a distinct legal entity (the special purpose vehicle) which would be unaffected by the failure of the originators of the mortgages or of the arranger of the issue. This separation of the securities from the arranger is called 'de-linking' and is an important element in the management of risk. There remains the possibility of failure of the special purpose vehicle, and this is managed to a great extent by the interest-rate swap.

Risk is a variation in the cash flow of an asset. In other words, variations in the payments associated with these securities pose a risk. These payments came from the monthly mortgage payments made by homeowners. The homeowners make the payments to the loan servicer, who then forwards them on to the special purpose vehicle that issues the securities, and it allocates payments to the various holders of the securities.

The mortgage payments could vary for several reasons besides inability or unwillingness to make the payments. For example, a household could decide to sell their home and buy another. This would lead to a block payment to close the mortgage (and probably negotiating another mortgage for the new house). Again, the household may take advantage of a windfall or other increase in available cash to accelerate payments. It may also renegotiate a new mortgage. All of these occasions upset the smooth flow of payments; the last two usually occur when there is a drop in mortgage rates, which means new mortgages will not be as interesting (for investors – they *will* be interesting for homebuyers!). Closing mortgages to purchase a new house is a frequent enough occurrence that it can be dealt with by the law of large numbers: one can assume that a given fraction of the mortgage pool will have accelerated payment. This can be built into the valuation of the securities. The effect of the drop in mortgage rates, however, is a risk that can only be reckoned with as a possibility.

Should the homebuyer become unable or unwilling to meet his payments, the loan servicer will have to manage this issue. The way it does so is dictated by the terms of the mortgage. In principle, the terms can be changed only by the two parties to the mortgage: the mortgagor and the owner of the mortgage, now the special purpose vehicle that has constrained itself by the terms of the issue. The terms of the issue have been formulated in order to enhance the attractiveness of the securities to investors and thus not introduce any further complications into the flow of funds. There is no room for consideration of exceptional mitigating factors. As a consequence, after a certain number of missed payments, the mortgage is foreclosed and the home is repossessed. Administrating this real estate is a burden and an unsatisfactory replacement for the monthly payments. The property must now be maintained without payments and probably sold at a loss. This has a severe impact on that mortgage's contribution to the payments accruing to the securities. It is for this reason that the Federal National Mortgage Association (FNMA, 'Fannie Mae'), the Federal Home Loan Mortgage Corporation (FHLMC, 'Freddie Mac') and the Government National Mortgage Association (GNMA, 'Ginnie Mae') guarantee the mortgage payments, the former two for the securities they issue, and the latter for securities, issued by private-label firms, based on Ginnie Mae mortgages. (It was Ginnie Mae that invented mortgage-backed securities in 1970 (see Dodd, 2007), making the risk palatable by the just-mentioned guarantee of payments.)

The spectre of these vagaries of mortgage payments decreases the attractiveness of the securities. How can the arranger diminish this effect? Simply by being overly generous in the pool of mortgages underlying the securities. This pool of mortgages can be overly generous in two ways. 'Overcollateralization' is when the total value of (the principal balance of) all the real estate (or other assets) which is collateral to the mortgages (or other loans) exceeds the balance of the principal assigned to the securities. This is used especially for prime and 'jumbo' mortgages. Securities based on subprime and Alt-A mortgages that carry a higher interest rate usually apply 'excess spread': monthly payments exceed the payments due to the security holders.

It becomes clear that even in the case of a simple 'pass through' mortgage-backed security issue, only a portion of the payments pass through. A small fraction is retained as profit, and a small fraction is reserved as insurance for regular payments.

What else can be done to reduce risk? Further steps to reduce risk bring us into the domain of structured finance. In simple terms, structured financing provides funds with a structured instrument. In other words, the different participants to the financing participate in diverse ways. Securitization is the first and foremost way this is done. The instrument is sliced (hence *tranche*, the French word for 'slice') into various classes, of which some are subordinate to others: there is a pecking order for receiving payment. When the underlying mortgage payments are insufficient, senior tranches are paid first, and the remaining funds are then applied to the next class, and so on, down to the most junior class. This last, most junior class has the greatest risk of not receiving payment.

Why would anyone buy a junior tranche? They buy them because of a higher yield accompanying the higher risk: higher monthly payments and perhaps a good chunk of the excess spread once the shortfalls in payments to the senior tranches are covered (this could result in an increase in the payment that month).

These structured mortgage-backed securities are called 'collateralized mortgage obligations' (CMOs), a category within collateralized debt obligations (CDOs).[2]

Thus, tranched securities are not completely identical, but organized into categories of risk. Suppose that, in general, one per cent of homes are foreclosed. Everyone could participate in that problem, so that everyone would have one per cent lower return once those loans are defaulted on and no one would face a catastrophe. Alternatively, one could offer a class of securities that would give rights to the worst-performing ten per cent of the mortgages. This experience would suggest that one mortgage in nine will fail – possibly more, possibly less. To entice investors to purchase this class of security, it would be necessary to give them a better price (which works out to giving them a terrifically higher return on the purchase price if the mortgages work out). Similarly, the best-performing 20 per cent of mortgages could be sold to another class of investors who would accept a lower rate of return in exchange for the greater security – in other words, pay a higher price to purchase the security. Experience quickly showed that it was easier to market these securities by breaking them down into several layers of risk in this way. The reason is that this allowed investors to choose a rate of return and a degree of risk that best corresponded to their investment strategy and fiduciary responsibilities.

The effect of all this investment activity was that more money was available for mortgages. One result was that mortgage originators had to decrease their interest rates to compete for potential homebuyers, and thus offer mortgages at rates accessible to new households that normally wouldn't qualify.

Imperfections in the markets linking home buyers and investors in securities

Ashcraft and Schuermann (2008) provide an interesting insight into the linkages from mortgages to the locus of the 2007–2010 financial crisis by listing the 'frictions' and market imperfections in the securitization process. The following paragraphs follow their analysis to a great extent and attempt to render the relevant factors accessible to a non-specialist audience. Figure 2.5 helps situate each imperfection.

A market friction or imperfection is simply any factor that renders the market a poor way to allocate money. For example, if you know which store has the best price on toothpaste, you can go to that store to purchase toothpaste if it is not too inconvenient. That is an efficient allocation of money. However, if you don't know any better, or if you are in a rush, you may purchase your toothpaste at the pharmacy downstairs and pay a higher price. Information about prices and the distribution channels of products are thus important factors in making an economy more efficient.

If market imperfections seem unimportant, consider an economy in which decisions about purchasing and selling are routinely made for personal benefit. To start, imagine that you are a purchasing agent for a carpet retailer, and you purchase from wholesalers or other suppliers who offer you a yearly vacation on Hainan Island, instead of purchasing from the supplier with the best designs, quality and prices. Imagine an entire economy that works like that. Consider that in South America, for example, without getting any more specific, purchasing agents in mid-sized firms are usually family members, since they can be controlled and are loyal to the family cause. When mediocrity can be made to succeed with 'encouragements', the whole economy becomes less efficient and society as a whole is impoverished – although a rich minority may continue to thrive off the 'encouragements'.

Imperfections can cause havoc in an industry if systematic, and this can propagate to the whole economy if the industry is key. Although securitization increased the amount of money available for mortgages and thus should have benefitted homeowners and the economy, there were 'frictions and imperfections' in the securitization process which contributed greatly to the financial crisis of 2007–2010.

A young couple seeking to buy a house may set their heart on a bungalow that is just a bit too expensive for them, deciding that they can make the payments if they scrimp and save. This decision to cut on other less essential items on the budget (like cappuccinos and nights out) is a realistic way to marginally increase the ready cash of a household, but it is not an argument which will convince an accountant. So perhaps when they visit the mortgage broker, they 'enhance' their income or 'forget' some debts. Salary can be checked with payslips or the equivalent, but other forms of income may be difficult to verify;

similarly with debt to family members. The point is that it may be possible to deprive the broker of some information relevant to his decision as to whether to accord the mortgage or not.

The incentive to cheat is increased by the way loans work. As loans get riskier, lenders demand higher interest to compensate the risk they are taking. From the perspective of the lender and viewed through the prism of statistics and overall return on investment, this makes sense. If a loan is riskier, then there is a greater chance of default; more loans out of a hundred will fail. In order to make as much money on the remaining loans that don't fail, the lender charges more interest per loan. This is what happens in reality, although typically the higher-risk lenders and the lower-risk lenders are different people. From the perspective of anyone who wants to enhance the probability that a loan will succeed (be paid back), of course it would make more sense to charge a *lower* interest rate to the less privileged borrower. However, the lender is in the business of lending. He survives and thrives only if he makes some profit while providing the public with this service of lending money. Thus, the philosophy of the lender is simply that you should not borrow if you can't afford it. If you think you can afford it but the lender doesn't agree, well, you will have to show you can pay higher interest.

Sneaky behaviour on the part of people soliciting a mortgage is just the start of imperfections.

If you obtain a mortgage from a regular bank, that mortgage usually is held by the bank, which thus has a motivation to make sure that the borrower is capable of meeting the payments in order to avoid the burden of having to repossess and administer real estate (which is not what a bank is good at and represents a distraction rather than a way to make money). On the contrary, the bank does not want to have its capital sunk into something that is not returning a steady cash flow.

If you get a mortgage from a broker, his motivation is different. He makes his money on volume – the more mortgages, the better. This is also true for the originator. Neither holds on to the mortgage. Even the larger financial institution that purchases blocks of mortgages and accumulates these blocks into pools might not really worry about foreclosures, because the pool of mortgages will be sold to investors via the trust's securities. Of course, the large financial institution does have the motivation of keeping its reputation (of supplying quality securities, among other things) intact. The mortgage insurer would also seem to be motivated to avoid foreclosures, but we will examine this case separately.

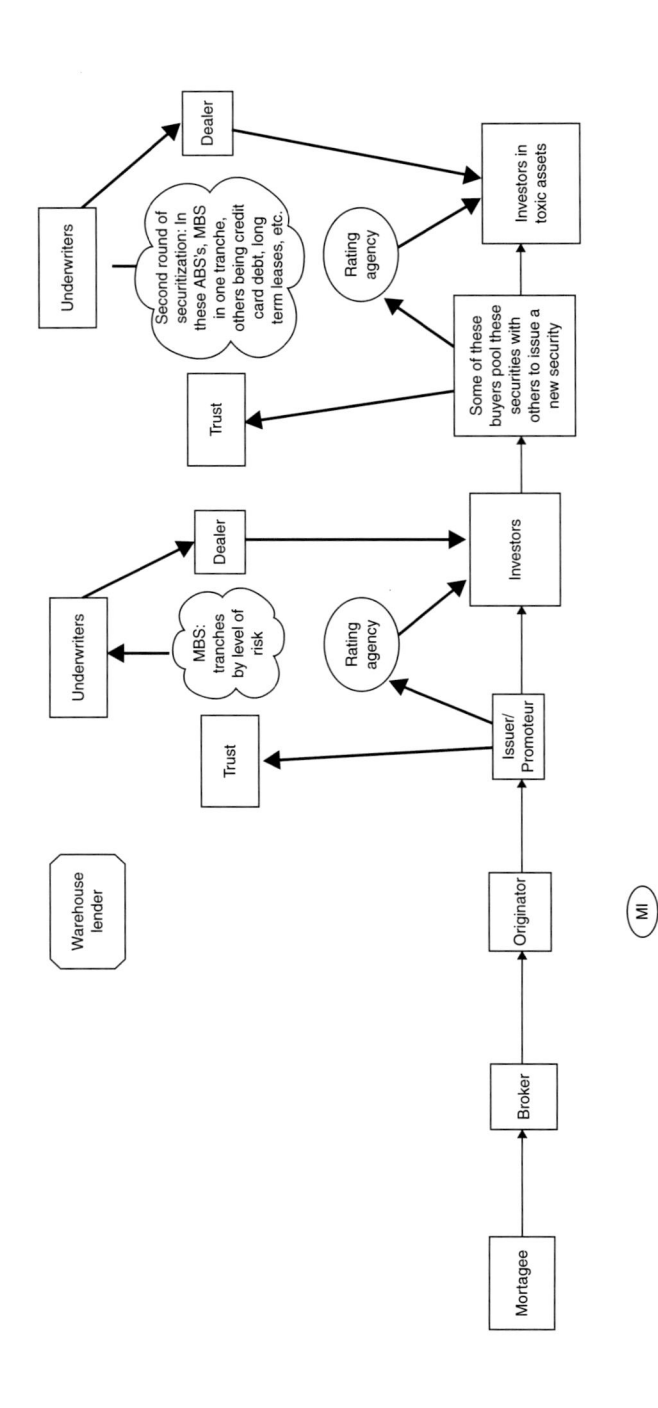

Figure 2.5 Schema of the securitization process

The broker, the originator and the large financial institution that does the securitization make more money when the package of mortgages is large, with big payments. So the incentives they send down the pipe will be to turn over more mortgages with higher payments. The upshot of this is that loan officers may more easily allow themselves to be duped by homebuyers. They may well also dupe the homebuyer in turn: offering them a more costly mortgage as if it were the best deal available. The incentives encourage more and bigger loans, and at higher interest rates.

This predatory lending seems indeed to have been widespread. But it is a little hard to tell. The reason is that mortgages became more complicated.

In order to understand this complication, we should consider the life cycle of a growing family: the couple works, and at a certain point perhaps the mother decides she wants to be a full-time mum. Luckily, the career of the husband takes off and his salary begins to increase. It is quite reasonable to expect a family's purchasing power to increase, even as the number of children increases. Why buy a modest house now if it is going to be too small in two years? Why not buy a bigger house immediately? Well, the answer could be that the mortgage payments are too high.

A simple financial solution is to establish varied mortgage payments – lower payments at the start of the repayment period, and then more ambitious payments later on. These are called 'ARMs': adjustable-rate mortgages.

Perhaps this was not the original rationale of variable-rate mortgages, but we would like to think so.

In some – many – cases, what happened in practice is that couples that had to take a bus to the mortgage broker because they could not afford a car, with a demonstrable income in the low five figures, were offered mortgages that were accessible for two years and then inflated beyond reach thereafter.

Even this seeming predatory lending has a certain justification, though. Recall the context in the housing market. Prices were rising. People were purchasing houses to live in for a short period of time, then resell them at a profit. They did not consider the later payments, although those payments could eventually complicate the sale if the new owner wanted simply to take over the mortgage payments. But the mortgage could be closed and a new mortgage negotiated for the new owner. A variable-rate mortgage could be a way for families flipping houses (buying and then reselling a year or two later) to enhance their profits. As brokers became used to such mortgages, less experienced brokers may have begun to offer them to all and sundry, whether or not they intended to flip the house – in practice, the homebuyer would not reveal that information anyway.

There were plenty of inexperienced brokers at the time because the mortgage business was booming, and more and more mortgage brokers were opening offices across the country. The number of people employed by mortgage brokers in the United States increased from 26,760 in 1999 to 66,210 by 2007. Used-car salesmen with high school educations were hired and found themselves making hundreds of thousands of dollars a year – if they were willing to be aggressive in closing numerous mortgages.

This was perhaps the greatest source of predatory lending in the mortgage market: a vast cohort of mavericks out to make fast money according to the simple rule of big numbers: many mortgages; the bigger the payments, the better (even if the really big payments only started in two years, there were 28 more years of payments to come).

On the borrowers' side, there could be some soliciting of such loans, for the reasons given.

The large financial institution – in this context called the 'arranger' or the 'issuer' because it arranges the issue of securities – that would ultimately securitize the pools of mortgages is not totally disinterested in the quality of the mortgages. It would not want to be criminally negligent or guilty of securities fraud. Also, its reputation as a financial institution is in play: without a reputation for reliability, it would quickly find itself without customers. Further, there really are people in these institutions who are honest and do not want to sell valueless securities.

Even if the arranger did not have intrinsic motivation to avoid bad mortgages, the procedure of issuing securities protects against such an eventuality, precisely because such intrinsic motivations may not be sufficient to countermand the drive to increase volume. The arranger must carry out due diligence – in other words, verify the terms of the mortgage as well as the identity and other data regarding the originator, the broker and the mortgagor. The originator, on his part, had to follow a formal underwriting procedure – which means that he had to arrive at an appreciation of the probability that the mortgagor will meet the payments (typically showing his capacity to pay, his willingness to pay, and the existence of sufficient collateral should he not pay). The originator must make 'representations and warranties' about the mortgagor and the underwriting process, which reinforces the due diligence by the arranger. The originator must buy back the loan if the representations and warranties prove false.

Of course, the originator could buy back only a few such loans – that is precisely the reason he is reselling them – or at least that was the reason in the original business plan. So the proviso of buying back the loan is of limited value if there are numerous problems.

The originator, the mortgagor and the broker all have incentive to make a little mortgage fraud here, at least in the sense of not being careful to verify the household income and the stability of the mortgagor's job, of encouraging the appraiser to be aggressive in his evaluation, and so on. And so we have a second point where the market may be deformed.

A third imperfection is somewhat more subtle. The arranger may not securitize all the mortgages, or it may have several issues of securities. Thus, it may choose the best (most likely to be paid) to retain for itself and securitize the weaker mortgages, assuming it has sufficient information from the originator. This becomes a question of confidence for all parties dealing with the originator and is called the problem of 'adverse selection' in economics. One would suppose that an arranger that was 'in it for the long term' would wish to maintain its reputation by the quality of the issue. However, it is also true that the careers of the employees of the arranger are short, with huge bonuses, and that the culture inside these firms is to make a lot of money quickly. This does not require dishonesty, but may tempt people to be a little superficial in order to produce volume.

One of the ways to control for the quality of the issue is to have a third party evaluate the securities.

This was done, but in a clumsy way. The US rating agencies industry is an oligopoly composed of three firms: Standard and Poor, Moody's and Fitch. Theoretically, of course, an oligopoly can be hotly contested – an example is the retail grocery industry in Canada from 1970 to 2000. In order to make the evaluations available to all potential customers (thus avoiding that only the rich have access to evaluations), they are paid for by…the issuing firm. The rating agencies' revenue depends on the very firms whose work they are evaluating! As a consequence, the rating agency may fear losing future business if it is too severe with a big customer. This alone might lead to hesitation to downgrade an evaluation, although principle will win out in the end – out of the employees' principles and also out of fear of lawsuits and loss of the value of the agency's ratings.

The real problem that occurred was not out-and-out corruption but over-expediency in the execution of the ratings.

How did agencies rate these mortgage-backed securities? A mortgage was a very safe kind of debt historically (i.e., in the twentieth century) because no one wants to lose their home or their life's savings, so that banks granting mortgages had only to second-guess homebuyers' realism about their economic capacity. Further, the odd foreclosure was a lot of administrative work, but the value would be there in the repossessed home. Suppose one per cent of mortgages were foreclosed. All the rating agencies had to do was verify that a one per cent failure rate was incorporated into the pricing of the securities, and then give the security a good rating. The actual mechanism was somewhat more complicated, but this is the gist of how a rating agency could evaluate a mortgage-backed security, once it had assured that the whole business set-up was legitimate (real mortgages, the originator was a documented firm, insurance and servicing of the mortgage, and so on). The complications would take into account the geographic areas of the buildings for which the mortgages were contracted, the firms involved, the kinds of houses and any other factors that characterized the profile of the pool of mortgages being securitized. (See Baily et al., 2008) So, even with a nice quiet mortgage market, a large amount of data was necessary to create a model capable of predicting the probable failure rate in the pool of mortgages.

The mortgage market did not remain quiet and humdrum, however, in the first years of the millennium. Many people were flipping houses, and sometimes they had a second residence, so that their attitudes towards the houses and towards the monies involved had changed. Further, mortgages were no longer held by the originator, but passed on down the line through securitization, as we have seen. Finally, both pressure from the government to extend mortgages to minorities, who were typically in poorer financial health, and the pull of investors' dollars seeking more securities to buy (translated into incentive schemes for the employees of the brokers) led to an expansion of the mortgage market to poorer-quality loans (Alt-A and subprime) for which there was a higher frequency of default. The quality of mortgages was no longer even and perhaps was degrading over time.

Rating agencies, meanwhile, were slow to update their models, which would have required time, energy and money; further, the implementation of new models would probably disrupt the workflow precisely while the demand for ratings of mortgage-backed securities was increasing.

And then there was the lingering question as to the effect of new models. Most people realized they would probably be more demanding and thus perhaps lead to a downgrade of the ratings of the securities of... their paymasters!

In any case, we have here a third imperfection in the market: inaccurate information about the quality of the securities.

The fourth imperfection has the effect of a gatekeeper that hustles anyone hesitating about a mortgage payment into the default mode. When meeting payments becomes difficult, homeowners gird their loins to meet the difficulties over a few months unless circumstances make this effort seem hopeless or make the rewards of sacrifice seem minimal. If it looks hopeless, then the homeowner/mortgagor loses all incentive to maintain the property and keep insurance and tax payments up to date. In order to protect themselves against losses caused by such delinquency previous to foreclosure, the originator and mortgage servicer require the mortgagor to establish an escrow fund from which taxes and insurance payments will be made if the mortgagor misses a payment and thus incurs a risk of an uncompensated destruction of the property (by fire for example), or tax payments to be made, so that the value of the foreclosed home is diminished. Little can be done to protect against limited maintenance, from small repairs and gardening to remedying plumbing accidents. As a consequence, not only do the escrow funds decrease the cash available for the mortgagor, but also the mortgage servicer is more likely to move quickly once foreclosure is legally possible, in order to avoid property degradation.

The fifth imperfection has an effect contrary to that of the fourth. The fourth imperfection could accelerate and increase foreclosures, whereas the fifth has the effect of avoiding foreclosure. This raises the issue of whether foreclosures are favourable or not to the value of the securities. Obviously foreclosures mean someone is losing their home – although, if early mortgage payments are low enough, the cost/benefits comparison with renting may not be that dramatic. Here, however, the question is rather the impact on the value of securities. Foreclosure is a complication of the entire process because, instead of merely cashing in the monthly payments, a property must be managed and then sold – incurring unforeseen expenses and extra work – and the sale price may be superior or inferior to the effective value of maintained payments. For the servicer, this is just part of doing business – because there will always be a percentage of defaults – unless the level of defaults increases beyond the usual level. The question is whether the management expenses and the compared values of sale price and the flow of maintained payments constitute a major loss for investors in the securities. In practice, the value of mortgage payments was greater than the proceeds from the sales of foreclosed homes, and thus the drop in real estate prices over 2007 was one cause of the financial crisis.

3
Three Chronologies and the Genesis of the 2007–2010 Crisis

Overview

The real price of housing decreased 15 per cent in the United States over the years following the end of the Second World War to the end of the sixties (see Baker, 2007). Increased access to housing was part of the tremendous spurt of prosperity experienced in the United States at that time, a spurt that made the idealism and 'rejection of materialist values' of the countercultural movement possible. Part of this prosperity was homeownership, because independence of any landlord was seen as freedom from subservience. Financially, this meant the virtual elimination of the cost of shelter once a home was paid for –homeownership is almost always preferable to renting from the financial viewpoint, although there have been occasions isolated in time and location in which renting is cheaper than ownership.

Not everyone participated fully in this increased prosperity, however. The civil rights movement in the United States would help provide blacks and 'Hispanics' with not only some access to power, but also access to greater material well-being. From the late sixties onward, the US government began to seek ways of promoting homeownership among the poor, with particular attention to blacks as well as other racial and ethnic minorities.

Ironically, perhaps even as a result of government intervention, the tendency of real house prices reversed. Prices for new houses tripled from 1969 through to 2006. There were brief periods of hesitation in the seventies, eighties and nineties. This cost of sheltering a family rose even as the size of families in the United States dwindled during this same period, with birth control becoming virtually universal among the middle class. Real prices dropped 15 per cent from 1953 to 1969, then increased slightly before dropping back again in the mid-seventies, and then began to rise and by 1990 eventually increased to 20 per cent higher than 1953 prices. Prices then dropped a little and subsequently remained flat until 1997.

Although real prices tripled over the last 40 years of the twentieth century – in other words, prices tripled even after we take inflation into account – ten years stand out as a period of tremendous appreciation in new house value: from 1997 to 2006.

What factors led to the gradual increase in real prices for three decades and the spurt at the turn of the millennium?

Two sets of factors contributed to the rise of house prices. On the one hand, government efforts to make housing accessible to poorer people increased prices slightly for the first 30 years. On the other hand were the changes we have already seen in the US financial system (in part thanks to government intervention and in part thanks to private ingenuity). These made cash available for purchasing houses, but also led to a house taking twice as big a chunk out of consumers' wealth as it had after the Second World War. This was not the intent of government (on the contrary!), nor the intent of financial innovators. It was the result of the economy adjusting to human action rather than to human intent.

Chronology of US government interventions in housing

Washington created the Federal National Mortgage Association (FNMA, 'Fannie Mae') in 1938 in order to make mortgages available to households with modest incomes. It operated by buying blocks of mortgages and securitizing them. Because Fannie Mae was a government agency, the securities were seen as risk-free and were purchased at a low interest rate. In this way, Fannie Mae provided cheap financing to anyone in the mortgage business, which at the time of the agency's creation meant banks.

Fannie Mae established criteria for deciding whether a mortgage was admissible for securitization, as is logical. The consequence of this was that Fannie Mae established the criteria used by all lenders in according mortgages, since these lenders wanted to be able to sell blocks of their mortgages to Fannie Mae. If Fannie Mae became more strict, lenders would use more stringent criteria; if Fannie Mae became more lax, lenders could be more lax and still see their mortgages securitized.

Fannie Mae was split into two entities in 1968: the newly created Government National Mortgage Association (GNMA, 'Ginnie Mae') continued operations as a government agency guaranteeing a reduced subset of mortgage loans (for veterans, American Indians, etc.), making it easier for private firms to issue securities based on them. (It later would invent the securitization of mortgages by private financial institutions.) The lion's share of operations remained with Fannie Mae, which was privatized. This removed Fannie Mae from the government's balance sheet and raised the interest rates required to sell Fannie Mae's securities. The rise was slight, however, since these securities were still seen as having a low risk because of the volume of operations and because of the arm's-length relation to government. In 2008, the US government intervened to keep Fannie Mae from failing.

In order to keep Fannie Mae honest – that is to say, making a profit but not too much in order to pass the benefits on to homeowners (in the form of lower interest rates on mortgages) – the US government followed the privatization of Fannie Mae with the 1970 creation of the Federal Home Loan Mortgage Corporation (FHMC, 'Freddie Mac') to compete with Fannie Mae. The two have the same mission and differ only in size (Fannie Mae is larger because it is older) and in the history of choices made by management that for a period saw Fannie Mae dealing with banks whereas Freddie Mac tended to deal more with thrifts.[1]

The effect of the creation of Ginnie Mae and Freddie Mac was an increased capacity for securitization within the US economy. However, until securitization itself changed at the turn of the millennium, this impact was slight.

The Equal Credit Opportunity Act of 1974 attempts to assure all consumers an equal chance to obtain credit by prohibiting discrimination on the basis of race, color, religion, national origin, sex or marital status, or age. In 1977, the Community Reinvestment Act extended this notion of discrimination from individuals to neighbourhoods and required federal banking agencies (The Federal Reserve System (FRB), the Federal Deposit Insurance Corporation (FDIC), the Office of the Comptroller of the Currency (OCC), and the Office of Thrift Supervision (OTS)) to evaluate whether banks (and 'thrifts') provided credit in modest-income neighbourhoods. Non-compliance was taken into account when judging whether to permit bank expansion. Banks were thus motivated to provide some credit in neighbourhoods which previously had been completely 'redlined' (excluded) as high risk. Mortgages are considered to be a safe form of credit and were thus affected by this legislation.

The Garn-St Germaine Depository Institutions Act of 1982 included Title VIII which may be cited as the 'Alternative Mortgage Transaction Parity Act of 1982'. Around this time, interest rates had suddenly approached 20 per cent. The volatility of the market had made it difficult for lenders to provide anything but prohibitive fixed-rate mortgages until federally chartered depository institutions[2] had been authorized to engage in alternative mortgage financing. This new act allowed other lenders to offer alternative (non-fixed-rate) mortgages. Thus, the intent of this act was to make a greater variety of mortgages available to more people; the most notorious effect was to make predatory mortgage lending possible.

Real new house prices rose 20 per cent from 1982 to 1990.

The Home Mortgage Disclosure Act (1975) was updated in 1989 to require most mortgage lending institutions to file a report on each application for a mortgage and the outcome of that application. In itself simply a tool to eliminate discrimination, a side effect was to encourage lending institutions to be more lax in evaluating the capacity of poorer lenders to meet mortgage payments. This is a result of the previous history of US society: minorities tended to be poorer, so any effort to avoid even the appearance of discrimination would of course tend to involve lower-income applicants.

The Housing and Community Development Act of 1992 established the Office of Federal Housing Enterprise Oversight within the US Department of Housing and Urban Development (HUD) to oversee Fannie Mae and Freddie Mac with respect to the promotion of loans in support of affordable housing (via the securitization of such mortgages). US president Bill Clinton sent 'a memorandum to the four federal banking regulators that requires them to implement a series of reforms around CRA – designed to increase investment in communities that need it, while simultaneously streamlining and clarifying the regulatory process...' (Clinton, 1993). This led to a 1995 regulations reform of the Community Reinvestment Act (mentioned above for the year 1977) which empowered community groups with information (by making home loan data available along race and neighbourhood blocks as well as by income) and funding (by allowing them to earn a broker's fee when marketing loans) and as well made it easier for Fannie Mae, Freddie Mac and others to claim subprime securities as being in support of affordable housing. Frequent comments suggest that the regulations change required lenders to lower their standards in approving mortgages, but this is inaccurate and probably explained by Internet gossip: the tendency of blog authors to convert innuendoes into assertions as they paraphrase the blogs of other authors. Journalists and other professional commentators were also guilty of simplifications of reality (see, for example, Liebowitz 2008).

The Taxpayer Relief Act of 1997 increased the capital-gains exclusion from $125,000 to $500,000 (per couple). Most observers argue that this increased consumer investments in a second residence. Their reasoning is that the increase in value of a house is an increase in the capital of the owner, and this 'capital gain' is a form of taxable income. Should a $500,000 house appreciate ten per cent in one year, the household enjoys a capital gain of $50,000. If the household also has a similar experience on the stock market, then it has a prosperous year of $100,000 in capital gains, well within the $125,000 exclusion of capital gains for taxes. It needn't free ready cash to pay taxes on capital gains, which could be difficult in spite of the apparent prosperity of the household – possibly because of that apparent prosperity, because the family may well be meeting mortgage payments for the house and loan payments for the stock-market holdings. There is no room to acquire a sizeable second house (as an investment) because that may bring the capital gains into taxable territory. The increase to $500,000 capital gains exclusion makes that second home purchase more attractive. It has the effect of allowing a larger portion of the US middle class to invest their way into the upper middle class, although probably maintaining or even augmenting the stress of financial pressures.

Fannie Mae made a key relevant announcement in 2000: a commitment to securitize US$2 billion of affordable housing–related mortgages as per the 1995 regulations reform of the Community Reinvestment Act with the goal of increasing this to $500 billion by 2010. The reason: the Department of Housing and Urban Development was going to require Fannie Mae to dedicate 50 per cent of its business to the 'affordable' market. The same ratio was to be required of Freddie Mac.

When the dot-com stock-market bubble burst, there was fear of a recession, and Alan Greenspan, chairman of the Federal Reserve Board at the time, began to cut the prime interest rate in an effort to keep the economy vibrant: a series of cuts decreased the interest rate from 6.5 per cent on 16 May 2000 to 1.75 per cent on 11 December 2001, and ultimately to one per cent on 25 June 2003. One effect of this was to make it possible for lenders to offer lower mortgage rates and still make a profit. As a result, homebuyers would get lower mortgage rates or would be able to acquire a more expensive home for mortgage payments equal to those on a less expensive house under a higher interest rate regime. The same household could afford to pay a higher price on a house because the mortgage payments would be lower than with a higher interest rate. This increased the demand for more expensive homes (as we shall see). Also, households that could not meet mortgage payments on cheaper homes when the interest rate was higher could now meet the smaller mortgage payments at the lower rate. This increased the demand for homes in general.

When demand increases for a given supply, two things happen:

1. Prices rise.
2. Builders increase supply.

The millennium housing bubble had begun.

Government intervention stimulating the bubble did not cease, however, nor did the changeover from Clinton's Democratic presidency to Bush's Republican administration signal a change of pace.

On 17 June 2002, the new president announced his intention to increase minority homeownership via the action of Fannie Mae combined with subsidies and tax credits. The American Dream Down Payment Act of 2003 provided down-payment assistance of up to US$10,000 or six per cent of the purchase price. In 2004, the Department of Housing and Urban Development increased the target ratio for affordable housing–related activity required of Fannie Mae from the 2000 figure target of 50 per cent up to 56 per cent. (Leonnig, 2008)

Spasms in US housing

This section examines the evolution of the housing industry at the turn of the millennium using various statistical sources. Mark Twain was not merely joking when he said that there are three kinds of lies: lies, damned lies, and statistics. Numbers can reveal, but numbers can also hide, so the reader needs to be aware of what is being measured.

Statistics about an industry can be about the number of firms selling, the number of people buying, how many items are bought, how much is paid for the items, how many people are employed, and so on. Each statistic tells us a part of the story. Understanding a statistic also leads us to understanding our preconceptions and assumptions.

Suppose we would like to know approximately how many people bought a new home. There is no such statistic. Suppose the author buys a new home. Is he buying it alone, or is he part of a more numerous household? So what do we mean when we ask, 'How many people bought new homes?' Again, some people buy a physically separate dwelling, others buy a flat/condominium. Others buy a duplex with the intention of renting out another floor. How do we count each of these transactions?

Things become even more complicated if we suppose that all the homes are brand new. When we stop to think about it, most homes purchased have already been lived in. Indeed, many middle-class families buy a new house for their first home, and then move up to a 'used' home after that – in a way, the opposite to what happens with cars and clothing. This is due in part to the nature of housing as a longer-lasting good and also in part to the maturing of neighbourhoods.

There is no magic or mystery in descriptive statistics, but there are a lot of little complications that need to be noticed. Often we will notice them only if we have prior experience which teaches us the questions to ask and the details to look for.

There was a bubble in housing at the turn of the millennium, and all the statistics indicate this: sales of new houses, sales of old houses, the prices of homes sold, employment figures in the real estate industry,

Sales of new single-family homes increased 50 per cent over the years 1999–2005, and then dropped off so dramatically that 2008 sales were one-half those of 1999 (see Table 3.1). Existing home sales grew 40 per cent before dropping off in 2005 (Table 3.2). During that same time, the number of real estate sales agents in the United States skyrocketed almost 70 per cent and reached 172,030 in 2007 (it took them a few

Table 3.1 Sales of new single-family homes in the United States, in thousands of units

Year	In thousands
1999	880
2000	877
2001	908
2002	973
2003	1086
2004	1203
2005	1283
2006	1051
2007	776
2008	485

Source: US Census Bureau accessed 25 March 2010 at http://www.census.gov/const/www/newressalesindex.html

Table 3.2 Number of existing homes resold in the United States

Year	2000	2001	2002	2003	2004	2005	2006	2007	2008
In thousands	5174	5335	5632	6175	6778	7076	6478	5652	4913

Source: US Census Bureau, accessed 25 March 2010 at http://www.census.gov/compendia/statab/2010/tables/10s0942.xls

months to realize their honeymoon with house sales was already over; see Table 3.3). The number of mortgage brokers increased from 7000 in 1987 (at which time they accounted for one origination in five) to 53,000 in 2006 (see Figure 3.1) and came to account for over two-thirds of originations (Barth, 2008). Normally all of these figures would stay more or less in the range of GDP growth, which would not even reach 34 per cent for the period in question, so there definitely was a bubble in US housing. During that period, prices for these new homes rose over 50 per cent and then dropped off (see Table 3.4). Family incomes did not increase much during that time. In fact, median household income actually decreased from 1999 to 2009 in constant dollars (although this may involve an increase in the number of single-person households). This increase led to an increase of the size of mortgages independent of any increase in income.

This growth in home sales and mortgage originations came in two waves. Over the years 2000–2003, the total volume of prime mortgage originations more than quadrupled, from under US$900 billion to nearly three and a half *trillion* US dollars! These were mortgages that conformed to the conventional criteria of Fannie Mae: a reasonable down payment by mortgagors with well-demonstrated capacity and willingness to meet mortgage payments that represented a modest portion of their monthly incomes. A second, smaller wave but which lasted longer began in 2000. This was the volume of subprime mortgages: loans for which the homebuyers had uncertain capacity to meet the payments. This figure also more than quadrupled, from around US$140 billion in 2000 to almost US$600 billion in 2006 (see Figures 3.2 and 3.3).

Although subprime and Alt-A mortgages are both smaller in volume than the prime mortgages, together they accounted for a similar volume as the volume of prime mortgages in 2005 and 2006, even though individual loans were smaller in size than prime loans. The number of loans is a factor which is omitted in most analyses because of the industry standard of measuring by dollar volume of loans. For example, Freddie Mac (2009) underlined that subprime mortgages account for half the foreclosures initiated in Pennsylvania between 2006 and 2008; a few slides later participants could note that subprime represented only 16.3 per cent of the volume (dollar value) of all mortgages at its peak in 2005 (see Figures 3.4 and 3.5). The 2009 presentation had a rhetorical objective (many subprime loans were problematic) rather than a scientific one, and there is no actual error in the data presented. The error, if there is one, would lie in conventional wisdom: that the seeds of the crisis lay primarily in subprime mortgage loans. DeGennaro (2009) has

Table 3.3 Employment in real estate services in the United States

	1999	2000	2001	2002	2003	2004	2005	2006	2007	2008
Property, real estate, and community association managers	143,040	145,340	156,180	156,290	156,120	159,980	154,230	156,880	159,660	159,700
Appraisers and assessors of real estate	52,520	53,560	59,630	57,160	61,070	62,270	63,800	66,420	66,210	66,260
Real estate brokers	26,760	31,120	38,530	40,810	40,590	40,050	41,760	46,950	49,270	51,390
Real estate sales agents	107,680	108,880	118,780	125,960	123,490	126,470	150,200	168,400	172,030	164,080

Source: Bureau of Labor Statistics. Annual data for 1999–2002.

78 *Genesis of the Financial Crisis*

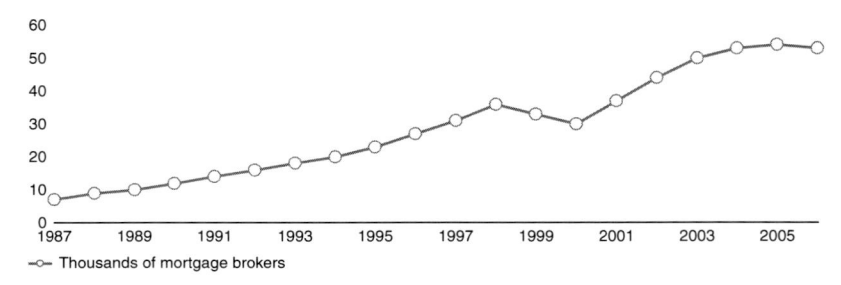

Figure 3.1 Number of mortgage brokers in the United States
Source: Barth et al., 2008.

Table 3.4 Prices for new single-family homes in the United States

Year	Median price	Average price
1999	$161,000	$195,600
2000	$169,000	$207,000
2001	$175,200	$213,200
2002	$187,600	$228,700
2003	$195,000	$246,300
2004	$221,000	$274,500
2005	$240,900	$297,000
2006	$246,500	$305,900
2007	$247,900	$313,600
2008	$232,100	$292,600

Source: US Census Bureau.

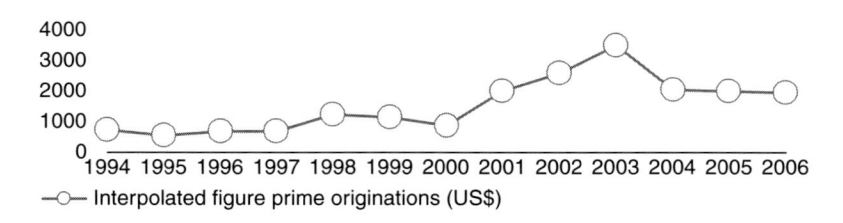

Figure 3.2 Evolution of the importance of prime mortgages
Source: Adapted from Barth et al., 2008.

emphasized how subprime mortgages were only part of the problem, however. There were other foreclosures, and their dollar volume was significant – and thus they had a significant impact on the cash flow of mortgage-based securities. Many people had purchased a home that was high-end relative to their income, either for pleasure or as a way to

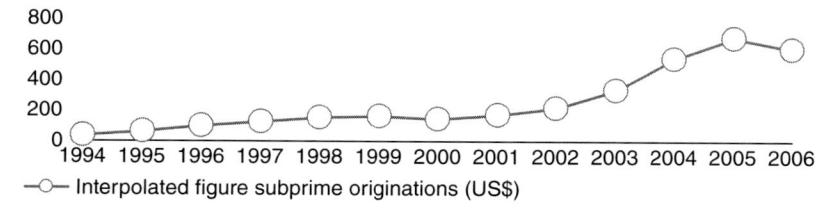

Figure 3.3 Evolution of the importance of subprime mortgages
Source: Adapted from Barth et al., 2008.

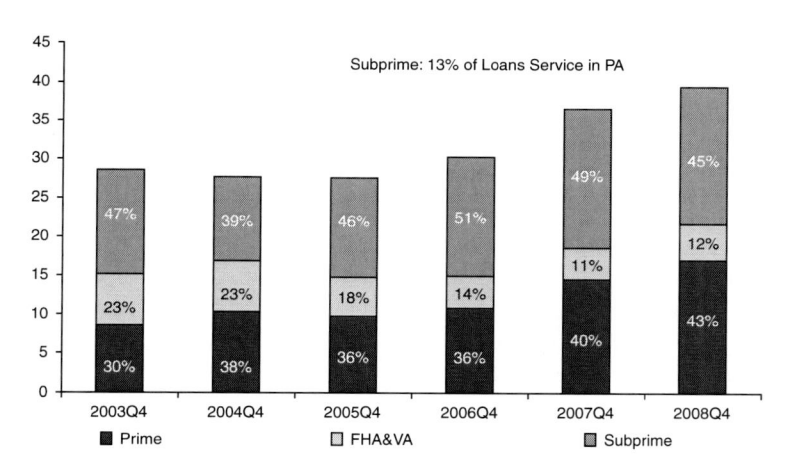

Figure 3.4 Number of foreclosures initiated in Pennsylvania, 2006 (annual rate in thousands)
Note: FHA – Federal Housing Administration; VA – Veterans Administration's loan program.
Source: Freddie Mac, 2009.

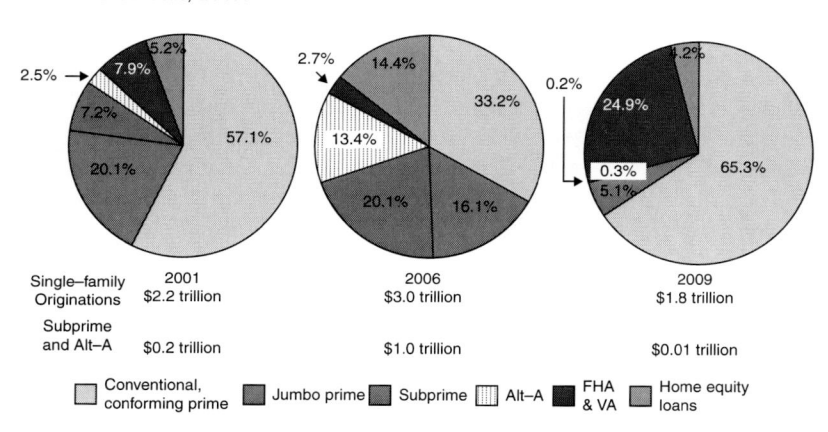

Figure 3.5 Categories of mortgages originated, 2001–2009
Source: Freddie Mac, 2009.

invest their money with the intent of flipping to an even more upscale home in the following years. Of these, many turned to strategic defaulting: walking away from their mortgages when the value of the home began to dip below the value of outstanding payments.

In a sense, the US government had achieved the goal of increasing homeownership: in 2004, 69.25 per cent of all US households owned their own homes, historically the highest ownership rate for that country. Not only that, the US Department of Housing and Urban Development was ambitious to do more! Arguing that it was the private sector that had taken the initiative in financing affordable housing, the HUD put pressure on Fannie Mae and Freddie Mac, as mentioned earlier. These purchased $434 billion in securities backed by subprime loans over the next couple of years.

But there were a few problems. First, although the ownership rate was at a historical high, the change was not revolutionary. Second, it was not affordable housing that was booming. Third, the boom was about to end – and the window would slam shut.

First, the change in US homeownership rate was not revolutionary. At the peak of the boom, almost 70 per cent of Americans owned the home they lived in. Although this is inferior to homeownership rates in Belgium (71 per cent), Spain (85 per cent) and Italy, one should be aware of a very different sociological reality in these countries: whereas in the United States children tend to move out of the house while still in their late teens or early twenties, in European countries children remain home, sometimes even after marriage, precisely because of the exorbitance of housing there. On the other hand, Norway and Ireland, both at 77 per cent in 2002, do represent a higher benchmark.

This 70 per cent ownership rate seemed to be the result of the previously described heroic efforts on the part of government to make affordable housing ownership accessible to lower-income households, rather than simply a consequence of generally increasing prosperity in the United States as a whole. There had been previous periods when the ownership rate decreased slightly while GDP increased. But were the results proportionate to the effort? And were the results real, given the foreclosure rates once the bubble burst?

The results were proportionate to the effort the government put out – and made the economy put out – if we simply take into account funds expended. Rather than an increase of government expenditures, most intervention took the form of diverting existing funds and motivating private industry to manage increased risks. Although the growth in the ownership rate may seem laughably small (2.5 per cent from 66.7 per cent in 1999 and only 3.7 per cent growth in 25 years from 65.5 per cent in 1980), the government was in fact trying to change the overall disposition of the economy, modifying the free allocation of wealth without increasing the total wealth available for allocation. It was trying to move a mountain.

These results were not proportionate, however, when we take into account the risks induced in private industry by government policies. This is something more obvious in hindsight than foresight, unless one is opposed to government intervention on principle. Austrian economists, who tend to oppose government intervention other than to facilitate the freedom of individuals to participate in the marketplace, were almost alone in predicting the bust, although many other economists joined them... as the crisis began. For a few percentage points improvement in homeownership rates in the United States, the government had put the entire world economy at risk. The disproportion is all the greater when we recall that homeownership versus rental is not the same as independence versus subjugation. Rental is only marginally inferior from the financial viewpoint within one generation, and many rich people opt to rent rather than own although homeownership does give a nice boost to the next generation.

The second problem with the boom was the dubiousness of the new ownership rate. Although the new owners did legally own their new homes, many did not have the capacity to make the mortgage payments they had contracted to make. Sometimes the terms of their mortgage were not appropriate. Sometimes they had purchased houses beyond their reach. Both of these cases led to defaults that exacerbated the end of the bubble: prices dropped even more quickly, and owners of second homes as investments were soon unable to flip these homes at a profit. The first case occurred both because homebuyers had over-represented their capacity to pay and because mortgage agents allowed themselves to be duped, while often counter-duping the homebuyers by offering them a mortgage at a higher rate than necessary –either classifying them as higher risk than necessary, or else hiding future increases in payments. This latter practice was possible because many people are intimidated when they enter into a transaction for a first time with someone who has made similar transactions several times a day for months or years; these clients also tend to be less zealous in ferreting out information when they think they are hiding information about themselves. In any case, not all the 2.5 per cent new owners would be able to retain their new home.

The third problem with the growth of the ownership rate is that it did not represent improvements for those with lower incomes. We need to examine the evolution of US house prices more closely to discover this. While the government had been attempting to make homeownership accessible to all, the real trend was towards more expensive housing. Table 3.5 shows this.

As we have already seen, the total number of houses sold in the United States grew by almost 50 per cent during the bubble. One would assume that government efforts to promote ownership of affordable housing targeted homes in the lower price categories. Surprisingly, there was actually a *decrease* in sales for the three lowest priced categories of homes grouped according to selling price. The most striking case was in the lowest priced category, which represented almost 12 per cent of all homes sold in 1999, but only 2.5 per cent in 2005. Perhaps the effect of inflation makes this data misrepresentative – if, for example, a $90,000 home increased to $110,000 over this period. However, we find that the next lowest priced category also decreased dramatically in the number of sales, shrinking from 126,000 to a little over 70,000. The housing bubble does not seem to have consisted in the poorest Americans buying their own homes, but simply in people buying more expensive homes. The three most expensive categories grew more quickly than the number of homes sold for all categories, with the most expensive homes more than quintupling – ten times the growth rate for all homes! In 2007, 21 per cent of homes purchased were purchased for investment, not as a primary residence. Another 12 per cent were purchased as a vacation residence. The boom does not seem to have benefitted the poorest Americans.

There is another possible interpretation. What if the price of housing inflated so much that the houses in the lowest category in 1999 would be priced in a higher category in 2005? The house price index of the Federal Housing Finance Agency is based on resales of houses and thus minimizes the effect of any trend to more expensive housing which otherwise would amplify any increase in house prices. The index was at 134.58 in December 1999 and reached 212.45 in December 2005, an appreciation of 58 per cent. (See Figure 3.6)

The results were thus doubly contrary to government intentions: not only did the boom seem to take place in the higher-priced categories, but real prices of houses in all categories (including the most affordable) were rising. Even if we minimize the trend towards purchasing more expensive houses, we still find that the price of housing was on the increase. How far does it go in explaining the decrease of the

Table 3.5 Number (in thousands) of houses sold in the United States, grouped by selling price

Year	Total	Under $100,000	$100,000 to $125,000	$124,999 to $150,000	$149,999 to $175,000	$174,999 to $200,000	$199,999 to $250,000	$249,999 to $300,000	$299,999 to $500,000	$499,999 and over
1999	880	102	126	155	119	89	110	65	89	25
2000	877	88	112	150	111	89	121	73	100	32
2001	908	75	105	143	130	91	135	86	110	32
2002	973	62	94	138	135	102	139	107	153	43
2003	1,086	54	96	146	150	114	148	112	197	68
2004	1,203	48	85	137	147	107	181	131	255	113
2005	1,283	33	71	122	127	119	200	152	315	144

Source: US Census Bureau.

84 Genesis of the Financial Crisis

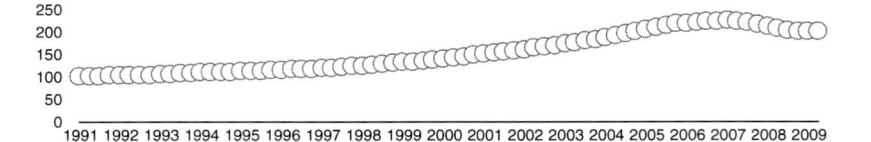

```
250
200
150
100
 50
  0
    1991 1992 1993 1994 1995 1996 1997 1998 1999 2000 2001 2002 2003 2004 2005 2006 2007 2008 2009
```

Figure 3.6 US house price index
Source: Data supplied by the Federal Housing Finance Agency (FHFA).

lowest-priced categories of housing? There is a rough and ready method to answer this question. Examining Table 3.5, we see that the increase basically moves homes up two categories. Thus, the lowest category still experiences a drop, while the next lowest categories experience slower growth than the more expensive homes.

The government had meant well, but the perversity of economics kept homeownership beyond the reach of those less well off. This is a lesson that governments never seem to learn, like King Canute trying to command ocean waves to stop coming to shore as a prelude to proclaiming vain all human kingship compared to the dominion of God.

To summarize then: there was a bubble in the US housing market from 1999 to 2005. This bubble consisted in the absolute number of houses sold, in the absolute number of existing houses resold, and in the absolute number of new single-family homes sold. More houses were sold, both old and new. The prices of houses increased. All these are characteristic of an economic bubble. Further, there was also a trend towards purchases and sales of more expensive homes: better located, larger, better finished. As a result, there was a dramatic surge in the total dollar sales in houses bought and sold and an increase in the number of real estate sales agents: people whose income is determined by the dollar volume of residential sales.

The ABCP (securitization) bubble that preceded the 2007 financial crisis

Securities

Figure 3.7 shows that securities issued in the United States reached two highs over the first decade of the new millennium: in 2003 and 2009. It is the former high which is relevant to the financial crisis. This growth in new issues found an echo in the New York Stock Exchange, where securities accounted for an ever-increasing portion of total trading. There had been ten years of steady growth for all kinds of asset-backed

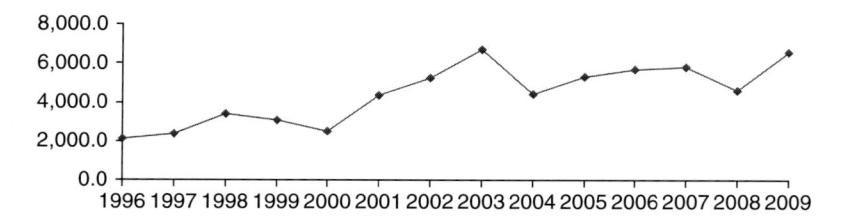

Figure 3.7 Volume of securities issued in the United States in billions of dollars, 1996–2009
Source: Based on data from Securities Industry and Financial Markets Association (SIFMA).

commercial paper since 1989, but the principal contributors to the peak were securities backed by one kind of asset: mortgage-related securities (see Figure 3.8).

There was also a slight upsurge of federal agency securities which follows the other upswings. The drop-off in 2004 reflects the privatization of 'Sallie Mae', which provides study loans to college students. However, 2004 also saw a sharp drop in mortgage-related securities and in securities in general. The reason was a sudden decrease in securities issued by the government-sponsored agencies Fannie Mae and Freddie Mac. This change was gradually and only partially supplanted by increasing 'private-label' issuance from 2000 to 2006 (see Figure 3.9). Private-label issuers were mostly banks, both the large Wall Street investment banks such as Lehman Brothers, often through subsidiaries, and banks specializing in mortgage lending such as New Century Financial.

Thus there would seem to be two waves of security issuances to consider: a push by the GSEs (privately owned corporations created by the US Congress, usually assumed to have an implicit guarantee since they are 'Government Sponsored Enterprises') that ended in 2004, year of criminal investigation of their non-compliance with new accounting principles for derivatives, and the longer wave of private wave issuance from 2000 to 2006. Another factor does not appear in these figures and charts, however. As already mentioned, in 2003, HUD began spurring the GSEs to increase their activity in terms of affordable housing by increasing the volume of subprime mortgages financed by their issuances. How did the portion of subprime mortgages in mortgage-backed security issues evolve over these years? The growth of private-label issuance is primarily in non-conventional mortgages (see OFHEO, 2007, p. 11). This is logical because these mortgages did not qualify for

86 Genesis of the Financial Crisis

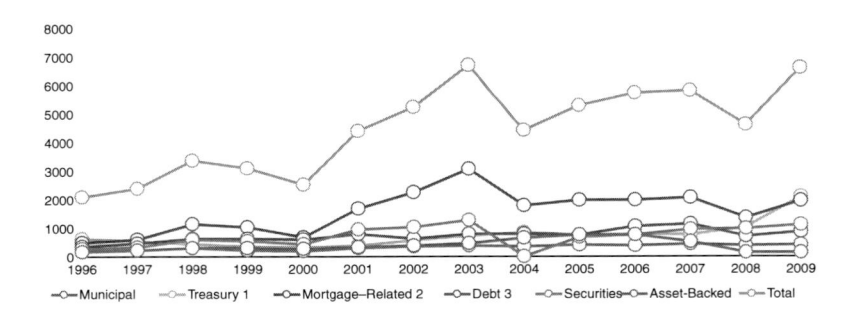

Figure 3.8 Issuance in the US bond markets in billions of dollars
Source: Based on data from Securities Industry and Financial Markets Association (SIFMA).

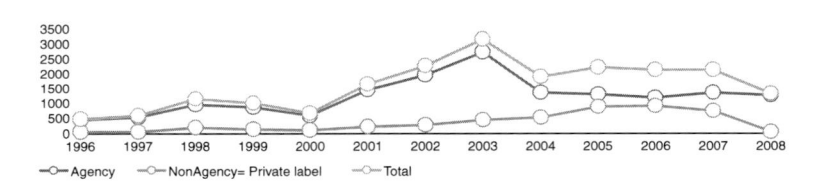

Figure 3.9 Agency and private-label mortgage-backed security issuance in billions of dollars
Source: Based on data from Securities Industry and Financial Markets Association (SIFMA).

securitization by the GSEs before 2004; only subprime and Alt-A mortgages qualified until 2008, at which time some jumbo mortgages also qualified temporarily (Fannie Mae, 6 March 2008). Fannie Mae bought and held a few hundred billion dollars' worth of these securities.

As the crisis began to unfold over 2006 and 2007, the holdings of two categories of mortgage-backed securities increased rapidly: foreign investors and that most mysterious category 'others'. The former was partly the result of the growing wealth of Asian economies and partly the result of European and other sources attracted to the past results of these investments, while unfortunately less familiar with the details of the US economy and requiring a learning period of familiarization with these instruments. This would help to internationalize the crisis. The category *others* 'includes hedge funds, nonprofits, and other groups for which detailed data are not available' (OFHEO, 2007). Hedge funds are believed to be the major demographic of this category.

They would provide one of the focal points for the developing crisis.

The ball of yarn unravels

The downward evolution of house prices, the upward evolution of the prime rate and the fruition of the logic of unattainable payment patterns contracted in many mortgages both for well-to-do mortgagors who had been intending to 'flip' a first or second residence and for lower-income mortgagors with subprime mortgages at adjustable rates all combined to increase the frequency of delinquent payments and eventually the rate of defaults in US single-family residential mortgages. How did the players on the ground react to these effects?

It was the issuers or 'arrangers' who first reacted to the problems with these mortgages, not the loan agents who, drumming up business for the lenders and dealing with the client, were the ones closest to mortgagees and the evidence that the payments would not be met. The loan agents knew the loans made no sense, but the money machine continued to work, so they did not slow in their efforts to find new business. The money lender suspected that the loans were weak, but was always able to sell them to an arranger – in fact arrangers had always been hungry for more blocks of mortgages. Thus, their money machine was also working, and they saw no need to slow down. The arrangers, however, began to see that the performance of the securities they were issuing was considerably lower than predicted by their models. This happened in October/November 2006, two years before the bankruptcy of Lehman Brothers brought the financial crisis to the attention of those not in the financial industry (This American Life, 2009).

More and more of these became more and more remiss to issue securities based on these mortgages (Barr, 2007). They could continue to sell their securities, but they were in danger of being caught with an unsellable issue. A further consideration was their reputation, which would suffer whether they were found to be knowingly selling trash or believed to be too incompetent to realize it. They liquidated their pending issuances and stopped buying blocks of mortgages (see Table 3.7).

Where did this leave the mortgage lenders? It left them with a block of mortgages that could not be sold. Ninety or ninety-five per cent of the capital tied up in those mortgages was owed to the warehouse lender. They were unable to pay back the loan to the warehouse lender. The mortgage lender declared bankruptcy. The warehouse lender would have to wait for the dispositions of the bankruptcy court to recover any assets it could from the mortgage lender. These assets were basically the mortgages. They would not prove to be a source of funding, although the warehouse lenders could ultimately, after some juridical delays, repossess the properties behind the mortgages. The values of those properties were soon to be in free fall.

Ownit Mortgage Solutions, a monoline mortgage lender, filed for bankruptcy on 28 December 2006.

Warehouse lenders began to react as well in the first few months of 2007 with margin calls: requiring more collateral for their loans since home values were decreasing. This led to the failure of dozens of monoline originators – mortgage lenders who had no other activities – in the first half of 2007.

The largest mortgage originators were also numbered among the largest arrangers (mortgage-backed security issuers) and, to a somewhat lesser extent, among the largest warehouse lenders (see Ashcraft and Schuermann, 2008). A given institution could be actively originating mortgages, lending or extending a warehouse line of credit to other originators, and issuing securities based on its own originations combined with those of other originators.[3]

As issues ceased and warehousing lending dwindled, many mortgage lenders had to close operations. Warehouse lenders soon followed the mortgage lenders into bankruptcy. There were around 15 warehouse lenders left in the United States as of January 2010, compared with 50 in 2003. There was a bloodbath among mortgage brokers and mortgage 'correspondents' (an intermediary between mortgagors and lenders, but with a one-to-one relationship with a lender, unlike brokers; many correspondents also serviced the mortgages once they had been originated). Mortgage originators culled their ranks as they sought to deal directly with the clients in an effort to assure the quality of the loans being made (OFHEO, 2007).

Meanwhile, issuers still had pools of mortgages in the process of issuance, many held securities as part of the underwriting process (having purchased some of the securities issued by themselves or by other originators on a temporary basis in order to give the market some time to absorb the issue) and many had even invested in some of these securities themselves. They now wanted to flog off all the securities they could. Within a couple of months, they began to find themselves as defendants in lawsuits brought by purchasers of mortgage-backed securities, as did the warehousers as co-defendants in suits by mortgagors for aiding and abetting mortgage originators in making predatory loans.

While some institutions covered various aspects of mortgage lending (retailing, warehouse lending, arranging securities) some of these and some of those strictly limited to mortgage originating, as well as some brokers, specialized in subprime mortgages. These were not the only

Table 3.6 Volume of the subprime mortgage originators

Rank	Lender	2006 Volume (billions US$)	Share (%)	2005 Volume (billions US$)	Change (%)
1	HSBC	52.8	8.8	58.6	8.83
2	New Century Financial	51.6	8.6	52.7	7.94
3	Countrywide	40.6	6.8	44.6	6.72
4	Citigroup	38.0	6.3	20.5	3.09
5	WMC Mortgage	33.2	5.5	31.8	4.79
6	Fremont	32.3	5.4	36.2	5.45
7	Ameriquest Mortgage	29.5	4.9	75.6	11.39
8	Option One	28.8	4.8	40.3	6.07
9	Wells Fargo	27.9	4.6	30.3	4.56
10	First Franklin	27.7	4.6	29.3	4.41
	All originators	600.0	100.0	664.0	100.0

Source: Cf. Ashcraft, 2008, p. 4.

Table 3.7 Top issuers of subprime mortgage-backed securities

Rank	Lender	2006 Volume (billions US$)	Share (%)	2005 Volume (billions US$)	Change (%)
1	Countrywide	38.5	8.6	38.1	7.50
2	New Century	33.9	7.6	32.4	6.38
3	Option One	31.3	7.0	27.2	5.35
4	Fremont	29.8	6.6	19.4	3.82
5	Washington Mutual	28.8	6.4	18.5	3.64
6	First Franklin	28.3	6.3	19.4	3.82
7	Residential Funding Corp	25.9	5.8	28.7	5.65
8	Lehman Brothers	24.4	5.4	35.3	6.95
9	WMC Mortgage	21.6	4.8	19.6	3.86
10	Ameriquest	21.4	4.8	54.2	10.67
	Total for all issuers	448.6	100.0	508.0	100.0

Source: Cf. Ashcraft, 2008, p. 4.

source of problems, since well-off mortgagors caught flipping a first or second residence were also fragile. Subprime loans were in the spotlight, however, and the subprime lenders Ownit Mortgage Solutions, Mortgage Lenders Network USA, ResMae Mortgage Corporation, People's Choice, New Century Financial and SouthStar Funding all declared bankruptcy between December 2006 and April 2007 (Frankel, 2009).

Some of these lenders were large, others small. Of the top ten lenders, New Century Financial went bankrupt and faced criminal investigation; Countrywide was acquired by Bank of America, which in turn had its troubles; GE Money closed the operations of WMC Mortgages; Fremont General Corporation (parent of Fremont) filed for bankruptcy; Ameriquest was acquired by Citigroup; Option One was acquired by American Home Servicing; and First Franklin halted loan originations on 5 March 2008. (Muolo, 2007). These firms accounted for 90 per cent of subprime originations. Those that remained were part of larger organizations that were deeply weakened by the fiasco, quite aside from the fact that they had also invested in the securities that were partially based on these subprime mortgages. Of those still standing, HSBC restructured its subprime operation (Muolo, 2007) with considerable losses (see next paragraph below), and Wells Fargo ceased offering (summer of 2007) subprime and Alt-A loans through brokers, reserving the decision to grant such loans to the judgement of its own employees, and in January 2009 was to more than double the number of its full-time default and home-retention employees in order to manage problem mortgages away from foreclosure.

Meanwhile, HSBC, the number one lender of subprime mortgages, announced a US$10.5 billion write-down in February 2007 and fired the head of its American mortgage-lending business. On 7 March, the FDIC issued a cease-and-desist order against subprime lender Fremont Investment & Loan, for 'operating without adequate subprime mortgage loan underwriting criteria'. In March, New Century Financial, the number two subprime lender, stopped lending and cut its workforce, and the New York Stock Exchange suspended trading on its shares; in April New Century Financial declared bankruptcy and cut its workforce in half again. In May, UBS closed its American subprime operations. Two Bear Stearns hedge funds exposed to the US housing market fizzled, and Bear Stearns spent US$3.2 billion to keep them from total collapse on 22 June 2007, but they ended up filing for bankruptcy protection on July 31. The day before, on July 30, HSBC announced that its charges for bad debts doubled because of exposure to US subprime loans.

American Home Mortgage, one of the top 25 subprime mortgage originators (See Table 3.6), filed for bankruptcy on 6 August. BNP Paribas (a French bank with operations worldwide and running several investment funds) stopped admitting withdrawals from three funds, stating that it was unable to calculate the value of participations in the funds because of instability in the markets. Thus the public could now recognize that toxic assets were international, although most people not working in finance were still unaware. Across the English Channel, the Bank of England provided emergency funding to Northern Rock Bank (the largest originator of low-quality mortgages in the UK) and this news led to a run on the bank on 13 September.

Behind the doors of investment banks and other financial firms, rumours and conjectures were seething. The month of October was marked with announcements of losses by several banks internationally: Citigroup (US$5.9 billion in subprime-related losses), Merrill Lynch (US$7.9 billion), Nomura (US$621 million), UBS (US$3.4 billion in losses), Wachovia, Countrywide (writing off US$1 billion in subprime mortgages) and even internally with Mitsubishi Financial Group writing off US$260 million in mortgage-related assets. This continued into November: Credit Suisse (US$1 billion), Citigroup (a US$8 billion and $11 billion decline in value for its $55 billion portfolio of subprime-related investments), BNP Paribas (about US$225 million), AIG (a US$2 billion write-down of mortgage investments), Wachovia (US$1.7 billion loss), Bank of America (US$3 billion subprime loss), HSBC (loss of US$3.4 billion), Barclays (US$2.7 billion loss), Swiss Re (this reinsurance company paid $1 billion on insurance to clients hit by subprime crises), Freddie Mac (US$2 billion loss). In December, Royal Bank of Scotland wrote off approximately US$2 billion of subprime-related assets, Morgan Stanley wrote off US$9.4 billion of mortgage-related assets, UBS wrote off US$10 billion of bad debts in housing, and Lloyds wrote off US$200 million.

Donald Tomnitz, the CEO of D. R. Horton, the largest American homebuilder, had told his investors, 'I don't want to be too sophisticated here, but '07 is going to suck, all 12 months of the calendar year'. His prophecy certainly held true for banks. The parade of announcements continued through January and February 2008.

Carlyle Capital and Peloton, two hedge funds, failed in early March. This was followed by general panic in financial circles (the equivalent of the music stopping in musical chairs), leaving Bear Stearns teetering on the edge of collapse. The Federal Reserve Bank offered a bridge loan and loss protection for the possibility of Bear Stearns toxic assets to incite JPMorgan Chase to take over it over on 16 March, at a price that saw Bear Stearns shareholders lose 90 per cent of their investment.

April, May and June saw another parade of bank losses being announced (UBS, Deutsche Bank, Lehman Brothers), and in July the share prices of Fannie Mae and Freddie Mac dropped 80 per cent. The FDIC then took Indy Mac into administrative receivership. Indy Mac (Independent National Mortgage Corporation) was a private thrift (savings and loan association) regulated by the state and not to be confused with Freddie Mac, which was a federally sponsored although privately owned firm. But the fate of this latter institution was similar, because on 5 September, the Federal Housing Finance Agency took Fannie Mae and Freddie Mac into conservatorship, lending them US$200 billion. The first conservators report, published in August 2010, revealed cumulative delinquency rates for the 2006 mortgages reaching almost six per cent by the second quarter of the second year for Freddie Mac and an astounding 11.58 per cent for Fannie Mae. Although the volume of subprime mortgages (for the industry, not just Freddie Mac and Fannie Mae) dropped from about US$600 billion to $200 billion in 2007, and Alt-A diminished a little, from around US$390 million to $265 million, the quality of these mortgages plummeted – perhaps because of the few candidates remaining in the US population – and the cumulative delinquency rates by the second quarter of the second year for the 2007 vintage were 22.29 per cent for Freddie Mac and 28.68 per cent for Fannie Mae. (FHFA, August 2010)

Up to that time there were five firms in the 'bulge bracket' (i.e., the biggest) of the US investment banks. Bear Stearns, the sixth largest, had been acquired in March. Ten days after the nationalization of Fannie Mae and Freddie Mac, two of the bulge bracket investment banks disappeared. Merrill Lynch approached Bank of America and was taken over by it. Lehman Brothers also sought a buyer, failed to close a deal, and filed for bankruptcy. This was the news item that brought the financial crisis to living rooms across the United States and to the attention of the world. It was followed by further takeovers, bankruptcies and announcements of losses (among the most spectacular: the country of Iceland, and AIG, the world's largest insurance company). It was also followed by more vigorous US federal government intervention than had been the case in the previous months, culminating in the greatest (in dollar terms) government intervention of all time, as over US$8 trillion in government loans and spending were announced and initiated: roughly the equivalent of a billion dollars per hour for a whole year!

Conclusion

An understanding of why certain assets are toxic and how various financial institutions came to acquire these assets is requisite to understanding the genesis of the financial crisis.

There are three kinds of toxic assets.

The first are the securities partially based on low-quality mortgages – or at least suspected low-quality mortgages – and their derivatives. Many pension funds, commercial banks, the investment banks themselves, mutual funds and hedge funds held these kinds of commercial paper in October 2008. They acquired them because they appeared to be a good value and came in variety of formats with respect to risk and timing of payments. Even the investment banks held them, not because they had not yet liquidated them in their underwriting function, but because they had been accumulating them as a good investment and were unable to liquidate them quickly enough once they realized that the game was up.

The second kind of toxic asset was also financial in nature and derived from the injudicious mortgages. These toxic assets included both the blocks of mortgages of varying quality and the warehouse loans with which the equity of the monoline lenders was leveraged. The mortgages had been acquired in the belief that once again they could be sold to larger financial institutions, and the warehouse loans had been made in the same belief. These assets were the first to lose their value.

The third kind of toxic asset was any contract to insure the first kind of toxic asset: in other words, companies like AIG and also specialized 'monoline' insurers sold credit default swaps (CDSs; see Chapter 1) in exchange for regular payments (a bit like insurance premiums) and thus the sales contract was an asset to these insurers which turned toxic when the vast majority of securities insured underwent a dramatic drop in value. Many of the companies selling the CDSs were unable to meet their obligation to compensate the holders of the CDSs and thus went bankrupt. The holders of a CDS had never really been insured because they were not the same people holding the assets being 'covered'. They were simply using the CDS as an investment in someone else's misfortune. They would have received a princely return had the counterparties not gone bankrupt.

Some have argued that the existence of these CDSs for the mortgage-backed securities prolonged the boom in these securities, and thus the supply of mortgages, and thereby the housing boom. The reasoning is that often firms buying the CDSs were also creating the mortgage-backed securities through the special purpose vehicles (holding the pools of mortgages and issuing the securities) and thus were betting against the securities they created and were motivated to create them with a high mortality rate. This has become almost conventional wisdom, but a lot of research (using hard-to-obtain data) is necessary to demonstrate this.

Part III
Remedies and Repartee

Part III covers opinion makers, particularly in the United States. My selection of opinion makers is perhaps peculiar. I exclude professional journalists as well as actors in the drama. Henry Paulson, Ben Bernanke and others have published books that are apologies explaining their past actions. I exclude these, although I do provide boxes with a summary of the statements of Ben Bernanke and Timothy Geithner below. I have also omitted the legal inquiries into the events surrounding the demise of Bear Stearns and Lehman Brothers.

The pundits and opinion makers whom I do examine fall into three groups. Chapter 4 covers vocal 'saltwater' economists, represented by two Nobel Prize winners considered to be somewhat left leaning in politics and social issues. Chapter 5 includes 'freshwater' economists, represented mostly by two authors somewhat present in the popular press, although less so than their saltwater counterparts, and considered to be more 'right wing', and 'Austrian' economists, who are excluded from the mainstream and are considered to be further to the right than freshwater economists.

The variety of viewpoints raises the issue as to whether there is a scientific basis on which to appraise, accept or reject these opinions or whether it is all a question of ideology. Chapter 6 examines this question and points to areas of convergence and lessons that researchers in each school can learn from others.

The crisis response of the main actors: Ben Bernanke and Timothy Geithner

Boxes 1 and 2 summarize the actions of the Federal Reserve System and the Treasury in responding to the financial and economic crisis, while respecting as much as possible the version of events as told by the head of each under the Obama administration.

> According to Ben Bernanke, the Federal reserve system responded to the financial crisis with four categories of action:
>
> 1. Interest rate cuts at the following times:
>   - August 2007
>   - September 2007 FOMC (Federal Open Market Committee) reduces the target rate by 50 points (1 point = one hundredth of one per cent)
>   - over the following months to spring 2008, reductions of another 325 points
>   - October 2008, a further 100 points (50 points co-ordinated with 6 central banks October 8)
>   - December: the 0–25 basis point range was targeted.
>
> In spite of the cheap access of funds for banks, there was no increase in lending, so the federal reserve moved to provide liquidity to the private sector. Besides the communication of policy communication, it used the following tools:
>
> 2. Using of federal Reserve assets to extend credit or purchase securities for bankers and primary securities dealers in the following ways:
>   - primary securities dealers (broker-dealers that trade in US government securities with the Federal Reserve Bank of New York) becoming eligible to borrow from the Fed
>   - credit facilities such as reduced spread between fed rate and discount rate, increased term to 90 days, etc
>   - bilateral currency swap agreements with 14 foreign central banks (impact on the dollar globally)
> 3. Using Federal Reserve assets to provide liquidity to borrowers and investors in critical nonbank credit markets:
>   - facilities to purchase commercial paper at three months term
>   - facilities for loans against AAA-rated asset-backed securities collateralized by student loans, auto loans, credit card loans, and loans guaranteed by the Small Business Administration
>   - a facility to finance bank purchases of high-quality asset-backed commercial paper from money market mutual funds
>   - a facility to buy high-quality (A1-P1) commercial paper at a term of three months
>   - a facility to provide three-year term loans to investors against AAA-rated securities backed by recently originated consumer and small-business loans
> 4. Purchasing long term securities for the Fed's portfolio
>
> Sources: Bernanke speeches 2008–2010

> The Narrative of Geithner and Treasury's Response to the Crisis:
>
> Geithner thought the best plan would align three cannons.
>
> a. Monetary policy: the Federal Reserve would lower borrowing costs to nearly nothing.
> b. Fiscal policy, through which massive government outlays – a stimulus – would help fill the gap in private spending.
> c. Recapitalization of the financial sector, which meant getting money into banks to help them absorb losses and continue lending
>
> Upping the degree of difficulty was the need to coordinate with other countries, since the crisis was already global. Geithner attacked the problem in two steps:
>
> a. "Stress tests" were designed to persuade panicked investors, amid what amounted to a run on every bank, to buy shares in any of them. This was an alternative to government buying shares, which would be seen as a step towards nationalization.
> b. Fix the system: by incremental and technical reform of regulation without dismantling the dominant institutions or restructuring the industry.
>
> Geithner said: "I think it's very important for banks to understand that they lost the basic confidence and trust of the American people. And they have a long way to go to earn that back. And every judgment they make now going forward – in terms of how they pay their employees, how they run their institutions, how they meet the needs of their customers, how much they support this very important effort of reform across the system – is going to be important to rebuilding that basic trust and confidence."
>
> (All things Considered, 2009)

4
Saltwater Economists

Saltwater economist number one: Paul Krugman

The Economist magazine criticized Professor Paul Krugman for being more politically partisan than scientifically rigorous in his writing for the general public. However, he does have impressive scientific credentials, Professor of Economics and International Affairs at Princeton University, he received the John Bates Medal in Economics in 1991 and the Nobel Memorial Prize in Economics in 2008 for his analysis of trade patterns and location of economic activity.

Three categories of comments compose his pronouncements on the crisis: observations on the bailouts of financial actors, his stance on fiscal remedies, and recommendations for reform of the finance industry.

He spoke out against bailouts in August 2007, a year before the general public became aware of the crisis. Hedge funds, not commercial or investment banks, were the candidates for bailouts at that time, although many large hedge funds belong to investment banking groups and were the origin of the demise of Bear Stearns. His reasoning then was that a bailout 'would be saving bad actors from the consequences of their misdeeds' (Workouts, Not Bailouts, 17 August 2007).

This reasoning was qualified a year later as it became clear that banks were going to need a bailout (Bailout questions answered, 29 September 2008). Because banks play a crucial role in the economy, there was no question in Krugman's mind that government money should be used to improve their capital position. One alternative would be to purchase bank assets, not shares. But this would provide needed capital only if the government paid a premium over the market price for those assets (Thinking the bailout through, 21 September 2008) because the problem was precisely that these assets had been overvalued. He felt this was unfair. He agreed with an alternative proposal that the government should receive shares in the banks in return for capital. The market capitalization of banks was greatly depressed in the fall of 2008, so a sufficient injection of capital by the government would have translated into majority ownership by the government. Krugman recognized that the administration wanted to avoid anything with the appearance of bank nationalizations, but he himself felt that such nationalization would be natural if politically difficult at that time (The good, the bad, and the ugly, 28 September 2008). Within a few months he repeated his observation that it was unjust to use taxpayers' money to bail out banks without getting ownership: 'Question: what happens if you lose vast amounts of other people's money? Answer: you get a big gift from the federal government – but the president says some very harsh things about you before forking over the cash' (Bailouts for Bunglers, 1 February 2009). As the US administration made an announcement of more funds for the banks, Krugman wrote in response: 'This is more than disappointing. In fact, it fills me with a sense of despair' (Financial Policy Despair, 22 March 2009).

Henry Paulson, secretary of the Treasury under the Bush administration, had wanted government to directly purchase toxic assets at their potential value – in other words, not at their current market value, but instead at their carrying values, which would have been much higher. Timothy Geithner, appointed by President Obama to succeed Paulson, lent government money to private investors to incite them to make the purchases. The programme was simple enough to describe in a couple of paragraphs, but complex and not intuitively evident for the uninitiated. The objective was to provide $1 trillion for the purchase of assets, without spending $1 trillion in government money. Part of the programme targeted loans, and another part targeted securities (mortgage-backed securities, but also credit card, student loans and other kinds of asset-backed securities as well):

- Loans: (A loan is an asset for the person lending money: it brings in revenue in the form of interest payments. If the borrower is insolvent or has no liquidity and cannot continue to make payments, however, the value of that asset drops. This happened with many loans on bank balance sheets.) Under Geithner's plan, a private buyer could purchase $10 million in loans with $2 million cash down – $1 million of its own cash, $1 million from TARP (see Chapter 1) – and then issue $8 million in bonds to come up with the rest of the cash, which is transferred to the seller of the loans. These bonds look like a bad investment because they are either based on the assets purchased (overvalued loans) or on the ability of the issuer to pay back those bonds – and that issuer has just spent money on overvalued loans. This perception changes when the FDIC guarantees these bonds: it guarantees that whoever buys the bonds will get their money back with interest. In this example (the proportion of government funds to private funds could vary somewhat depending on the assets being purchased) $1 million of government funds is used to engineer a $10 million transaction and to give the assets time to recover their value. If the value of these assets were suddenly to plunge to zero, then the government would lose $1 million, and then probably lose another $8 million as the bonds failed. However, this is not a realistic scenario – the assets perhaps could lose half their value or could eventually recover their full value. In other words, the government was involving its agencies in financial speculation to achieve an increased impact on the economy.

- Securities: (The FDIC insures deposits under $250,000 and acts a receiver if a bank fails. Thus, the FDIC, as the 'receiver' of the failed bank, assumes the task of selling/collecting the assets of the failed bank and settling its debts, including claims for deposits in excess of the insured limit (FDIC, n.d.)) Under the legacy securities programme, the FDIC was to create limited liability entities to which the failed bank would sell or transfer the toxic securities in exchange for ownership of the new entity and a note guaranteed by the FDIC. The bank would then turn around and sell a portion of its ownership stake to a private bidder.

There seems to be a world of difference between the programme that the media reported and Paul Krugman has criticized – the Treasury giving a trillion dollars to private banks to cover for their mistakes – and the intricate array of actions by which the Treasury in fact proposed to bail out financial institutions in this particular programme. Perhaps Krugman believed he had to 'dumb down' his message to make it strong and accessible to the American public. Perhaps Krugman dismissed the differences as irrelevant to the principle he was trying to communicate: public funds should not be exposed to risk if they are not also open to the benefit of a positive return. However, the details of the mechanisms employed by the Treasury do indeed provide the opportunity for a positive return. In the case of the legacy loans example, the million dollars from TARP was to be repaid with interest. In the case of the securities example, the transactions gave the FDIC a better chance of recovering the funds used to cover deposits under $250,000. In both the legacy loans and the legacy securities programme, there was a downside risk, with a particularly large potential dollar value compared to outlay in the case of the legacy loans. The expertise of Treasury economists worked to control the risk of each transaction, and the programme itself was an attempt to defuse the problems of systemic risk in the financial sector.

The effort seems to have been successful: although the economic crisis lingers, the financial crisis ended in the summer of 2010 and the Treasury was able to publish a favourable report in October 2010 in which it emphasized that the bailout efforts would cost one per cent of GDP compared to 2.4 per cent for the smaller savings and loan crisis of 1986 to 1995 and the 14 per cent average that the IMF had reported for over 40 banking crises since 1970. The Federal Reserve had heralded signs of victory a year earlier (Bernanke, 16 November 2009) – although it should be recalled that such optimistic announcements are part of its tool kit to stabilize the economy.

Fiscal stimulus was a second aspect of the US government's response to the crisis: spending taxpayers' dollars to create economic activity: jobs and demand. This is the topic on which Krugman was most vocal. A week before Christmas 2008 he reflected on the Bush administration's effort to jump-start the economy at the beginning of the year. That effort had very unspectacular results for two reasons, according to Krugman: (1) the numbers were too small – about 1.5 per cent of GDP, while Krugman militated for 4 per cent, and (2) only a fraction of that 1 per cent was true spending stimulus because more than half was a reduction in tax. In other words, the 2008 effort failed simply because it was far too small to have an impact (What to Do, 18 December 2008).

How much money should actually be spent to stimulate the economy? Krugman answered this question in two ways, of which one got him into trouble with his detractors (although not with his fans, who understood his point).

The answer that got him into trouble was that governments do not have the courage to spend at a sufficient volume to get the economy back into health and that an examination of history shows that wars have been the only motive which gets government to make sufficient expenditures. He observed: 'What ended up doing the trick in the 1930s (spending on the war effort) was actually destructive – a sort of cruel joke on the part of the gods of economics. It would have been better if the Depression had been ended through spending on useful things – on roads and railroads and schools and parks' (Economics: Not Nice, Not

Fair, Not Pretty, 25 November 2010). The reason there was no recession at the end of World War II was that businesses had been able to pay off their debts during the war years (Krugman and Wells, 2010).

Two years before making this dramatic point about the level of expenditure which was necessary (and it was hardly the first time Krugman's detractors had run into the argument that World War II had ended the Great Depression) Krugman had already explained the relation between economic dimensions and produced a ballpark figure for stimulus expenditure. Here are his words:

> GDP next year will be about $15 trillion, so 1% of GDP is $150 billion. The natural rate of unemployment is, say, 5% – maybe lower. Given Okun's law, every excess point of unemployment above 5 means a 2% output gap.
>
> Right now, we're at 6.5% unemployment and a 3% output gap – but those numbers are heading higher fast. Goldman predicts 8.5% unemployment, meaning a 7% output gap. That sounds reasonable to me.
>
> So we need a fiscal stimulus big enough to close a 7% output gap. Remember, if the stimulus is too big, it does much less harm than if it's too small. What's the multiplier? Better, we hope, than on the early-2008 package. But you'd be hard pressed to argue for an overall multiplier as high as 2.
>
> When I put all this together, I conclude that the stimulus package should be at least 4% of GDP, or $600 billion. (Stimulus math (wonkish), 10 November 2008; he reiterated the 4% figure in What to Do, 18 December 2008).

Although the Obama administration seemed to mobilize $600 billion of stimulus, Krugman argued that it really did not follow his advice: 'Of the roughly $600 billion cost of the Recovery Act in 2009 and 2010, more than 40 per cent came from tax cuts, while another large chunk consisted of aid to state and local governments. Only the remainder involved direct federal spending' (Debunking the myth of Obama's big spending, 12 October 2010). Krugman's message adopted a sharper tone a year later without providing precise figures: 'Obama's problem wasn't lack of focus; it was lack of audacity. At the start of his administration he settled for an economic plan that was far too weak. He compounded this original sin both by pretending that everything was on track and by adopting the rhetoric of his enemies…. he chose a seemingly safer course: a medium-size stimulus package that was clearly not up to the task. And that's not 20/20 hindsight. In early 2009, many economists, yours truly included, were more or less frantically warning that the administration's proposals were nowhere near bold enough. Worse, there was no Plan B. By late 2009, it was already obvious that the worriers had been right, that the program was much too small.... he and his officials continued to claim that their original plan was just right, damaging their credibility even further as the economy continued to fall short' (Obama's lack of audacity behind economy's woes, 5 November 2010).

Paul Krugman's consistent message has been purely Keynesian: the government must spend money. It must spend a lot of money (at least 4.5 per cent of GDP). It doesn't matter too much *how* it spends the money, because the important thing is not what is produced (roads and bridges or straw baskets and comedy shows) but rather to create work and get the machinery of the economy moving for all the population.

Although Krugman has been the most strident in advocating a more vigorous fiscal response to the crisis, he is not alone. Robert Shiller, Professor of Economics at Yale University, wrote in November 2010: 'It is strange that so many governments are now emphasizing fiscal consolidation, when they should be *increasing* their borrowing to take advantage of rock-bottom real interest rates. This would be an opportune time for governments to issue *more* inflation-indexed debt, to begin issuing it, or to issue nominal GDP-linked debt, which is analogous to it' (Shiller, 2010). In December 2010, Joseph Stiglitz, Professor of Economics at Columbia University, observed: 'What business wouldn't jump at investment opportunities yielding returns in excess of 10% if it could borrow capital – as the US government can – for less than 3% interest?' (Alternatives to Austerity, 6 December 2010).

Harvard economist Robert Barro examined the empirical data for World War II to see whether there is support for the idea that government spending can jump-start the economy. He examined World War II and the US economy for three reasons: there was spectacular variation up and down of government spending (such as a 26 per cent increase of the ratio of defense spending to GDP in 1942 and a 26 per cent drop in 1946), there was almost no destructive consequences on American soil to nullify the positive impact of spending, and finally the data allows an evaluation of the relation between the multiplier effect (the impact of a dollar of government money on GDP a factor of 1, meaning $1 spent increases GDP by $1) and the strength of the economy measured by the level of unemployment (which varied from 1 per cent in 1944 to 9 percent in 1949). Barro concluded that the multiplier was less than 1: 'For annual data that start in 1939 or earlier (and, thereby, include World War II), the defense-spending multiplier that applies at the average unemployment rate of 5.6% is in a range of 0.6–0.7' (Barro and Redlick, 2009). This multiplier increases with unemployment and would reach 1 when the unemployment level reached 12 per cent. It follows that the multiplier effect occurs only when at least one worker in eight cannot find a job.

The researchers concluded: 'The available empirical evidence does not support the idea that spending multipliers typically exceed one, and thus spending stimulus programs will likely raise GDP by less than the increase in government spending. Defense-spending multipliers exceeding one likely apply only at very high unemployment rates, and nondefense multipliers are probably smaller. However, there is empirical support for the proposition that tax rate reductions will increase real GDP.'

This was bad news for Krugman's arguments (Barro and Redlick, 2009). An opposing argument from Robert J. Gordon (Professor of Economics at Northwestern University) and Robert Krenn (equity analyst at Spot Trading LLC of Chicago and research assistant to Professor Gordon) was circulated in a September 2010 paper. (Gordon and Krenn, 2010). This paper came to the result of a multiplier greater than one and the observation that this multiplier was relevant to the 2009–2010 economy because of two factors: (1) the time period considered was shorter and earlier: 1939–1941 earlier; (2) capacity constraints (if factories are at 100 per cent, stimulus won't allow them to produce more) were taken into account by breaking the data into periods of constrained and unconstrained capacity. By examining the periods of unconstrained capacity, the authors argue, we can see the full effect of stimulus from deficit spending by government. They conclude that the government spending multiplier is 1.80 when the time period ends in 1941:Q2 and that 'while both fiscal and monetary policy contributed to the recovery from the Great Depression, fiscal policy innovations were the dominant force, especially after 1940:Q2 when government expenditures as a percentage of potential real GDP started to explode' (Gordon and Krenn, 2010).

Meanwhile, Krugman was chiding prominent actors and economists for lack of consistency in their conclusions. In his view, Larry Summers had made the case for fiscal stimulus and then recommended against it because of the danger that borrowing costs would rise. In his view, Roubini and Mihm also made the case for strong fiscal stimulus, and then backed down because of the potential for a rise in interest rates. (Krugman and Wells, 2010). Krugman may have felt that they were abandoning the 'liberal' cause, since 'conservative' economists, such as Niall Ferguson, had been warning of the dangers of the surge in US government debt: 'The risk is that at some point your fiscal policy loses credibility in the eyes of investors...Then, very quickly, you will find yourself in a debt spiral of rising rates, widening deficits, crumbling credibility and yet more rising rates' (Lim and Heath, 2010). Richard Koo alone earns Krugman's praise for recognizing that currently there is an abundance of savings, keeping interest rates down and allowing the government to borrow at three per cent.

While Krugman's point is undeniable, it does not seem to respond to the nature of Summers' and Roubini and Mihm's reservations. They were not arguing that interest rates were currently high or about to rise. They were arguing that worldwide opinion about the US economy was changing and that there was danger that increasing indebtedness could lead to a catastrophic reappraisal, which could induce a sudden and dramatic jump in interest rates. These reservations may be difficult or impossible to demonstrate or reject empirically, but that does not change the nature of these reservations nor allow us to reject them based on current rates.

Krugman also responded to the issue of debt in a more academic venue, via an as-yet unpublished paper circulated for comments (Eggertsson and Krugman, 2010; a cut and paste summary can be found in , Debt, deleveraging, and the liquidity trap, 18 November 2010). Arguing that the level of debt matters only if the distribution of that debt matters, Eggertsson and Krugman concluded that deficit-financed government spending can, at least in principle, allow the economy to avoid unemployment and deflation while highly indebted private-sector agents repair their balance sheets.[1]

At about the same time that this paper was circulated for comments, John Cochrane of the University of Chicago's Booth School of Business (Krugman's equivalent of a den of iniquity) wrote a piece for the general public in which he provided an overview of research on fiscal stimulus. He resumed the basic concept: '"Stimulus" supposes that if the government *borrows* $1 from A and gives it to B we get a fundamentally different result, and we all are $1.50 better off' (Fiscal Stimulus, RIP, 9 November 2010). Or $1.80 in the Gordon Krenn world. He then cites Robert Barro's 1974 'Ricardian Equivalence' theorem: given a series of assumptions, borrowing (to spend on stimulus) has the same effect as taxes (so borrowing for stimulus should have the same effect as taxing from stimulus – little or none). His point is not that the theorem is true in the real world, but that advocates of fiscal stimulus must address the suppositions of the theorem and show them to be unrealistic; in practice, according to Cochrane, they have not done so, but simply point to one or another supposition as being false, without empirical demonstration.

Finally, Cochrane points out that developments in macroeconomics in the 1970s have left Keynes behind due to major shortcomings in the logic of that approach. He summarizes, 'The whole business was simply discredited as being logically incoherent 30 years ago' (Fiscal Stimulus, RIP, 9 November 2010). Many economists nonetheless fall back into a Keynesian discourse when pressed by policymakers from the old school of thought, and many bandy such notions in the media.

Facts cannot resolve the differences of opinion as to the effectiveness of fiscal policy in specific cases, because one side or another can always cite specific circumstances that qualify the incidence. Similarly, empirical work is suspect in the absence of well-defined theory. Finally, Cochrane points out that all deficit spending is stimulus spending in the Keynesian vision. Thus the US government had made $1.5 trillion in stimulus spending, while labelling only $800 billion as 'stimulus'. Thus, there had already been 10 per cent of GDP of stimulus spending in the Keynesian sense, so it was rather hard on the Obama administration to say that it had not 'really' tried stimulus.

Reality is more complicated, of course. If government is routinely in deficit, what Professor Krugman wanted was a sizeable *increase* in spending. In addition, some of the increase had gone to bailing out banks via the Treasury. What portion of that money had seeped into the 'real economy'? Should it all be considered as part of the real economy? Although the 2009 budget had anticipated doubling Treasury outlays to over a trillion dollars, the 2011 budget decreased the 2009 figure to $701,775,000, so that the actual increase was half as large as foreseen. On the other hand, the budget figures do not include the expansion of the balance sheet of the Federal Reserve System – quantitative easing – and perhaps a portion of that had a stimulus effect.

Besides dealing with the crisis of 2007–2010, the US government should perhaps implement measures to avoid a recurrence of the crisis. What reforms does Krugman recommend? In a brief March 2010 article, Krugman writes, 'we have a choice: restore effective regulation or go back to the bad old days' (Jamie Dimon Was Right, 23 March 2010). His reasoning (citing Gary Gorton's Slapped by the Invisible Hand) is that there were no systemic banking crises during the period of strong regulation 1934–1999 up to the repeal of the Glass-Steagall Act under the Clinton administration.

He is not the only Nobel laureate to have said so. For example, Robert Lucas, of the University of Chicago, in a sense a competing school of thought, says: 'We macroeconomists have not been working on these problems. I had a seminar called 'Money and Banking' in which there was no article on the banking system for years. And why not? Because there had been no banking crisis in the United States since 1932; indeed, the biggest postwar problem was the inflation of the 1970s' (Deschamps 2010; translation by the current author). However, the blogosphere immediately produced a list of crises during that period (see Table 4.1). Although there may be room to debate whether each crisis was truly systemic, it is clear that each crisis brought on US government intervention in order to prevent more serious damage to the economy.

On the *Rachel Maddow Show*, 20 April 2010, Krugman provided a more systematic recommendation for reform, with four points: (1) the creation of a 'resolution authority' with clear legal power to seize the complex and large banks that were threatening the financial system in 2008; (2) regulation of derivatives, enforcing transparency and visibility; (3) consumer protection and (4) increasing the capital required of banks to diminish leveraging (Maddow 2010).

Regarding the first point, anyone who has examined the financial statements for Citibank, Goldman Sachs and other large financial entities has a sense of the complexity of ownership and managerial discretion involved in these institutions. If you are allergic to financial statements, take a look at Figure 2.5, the flow chart for the securitization of mortgage securities, and realize that an investment bank could have affiliates at almost every stage of the process. However, any student of management would be able to point out that a 'resolution authority' would most probably encounter the vicious circle of bureaucracy: new structures and rules breed evasive manoeuvres, which breed new rules and structures, which breed more evasion...Perhaps Krugman sensed the absence of any political will to undertake the labyrinth of legal challenges to multiple bank takeovers. That absence was based on not the unpopularity of takeovers among voters, but rather doubts about the advisability of temporary 'nationalization'. Seven months earlier, Joseph Stiglitz had pointed out that this issue could have been dealt with ad hoc (14 September 2009, For all Obama's talk of overhaul, the US has failed to wind in Wall Street; see also Financial Re-Regulation and Democracy, 4 June 2010).

Somewhat different comments hold for the regulation of derivatives enforcing transparency. Part of the innovation process in finance is analogous to the creation of many new industries: the first products/services are made-to-measure or at least small volume (even though the individual transaction may be large). This precludes standards and comparability, requirements for a public trading venue like the stock market. There are in fact disclosure rules already in place, but they require

Table 4.1 A list of financial and banking crises in the last 50 years

Year	Systemic	Nature
1971	D	Collapse of Bretton Woods
1970	D	Penn Central commercial paper crisis
1973–1974		Stock market crash following escalation of the price of oil in 1973
1973–1975		Secondary banking crisis in the UK
1975	D	New York City bankruptcy
1986–2003		Japanese asset price bubble and collapse
1980s	D	Latin American debt crisis – beginning in Mexico in 1982 with the Mexican Weekend
1983		Bank stock crisis in Israel
1987	D	Black Monday – the largest one-day percentage decline in stock market history (Daniels calls this 'Black Wednesday')
1985–1991	D; L	Savings and loan crisis in the US
1990s		Finnish banking crisis and Swedish banking crisis
1991	D	Commercial real estate crisis
1992–1993		Black Wednesday – speculative attacks on currencies in the European Exchange Rate Mechanism
1994		Venezuelan banking crisis
1994–1995	D	Economic crisis in Mexico – speculative attack and default on Mexican debt
1997–1998	D	Asian financial crisis
1998	D	Collapse of Long-Term Capital Management
1998	D	Russian financial crisis
1999–2002		Argentine economic crisis
1998–1999		Ecuador banking crisis
2000–2001		Turkish crisis
2001		Argentine crisis
2001	D	Bursting of dot-com bubble; collapse of telecommunications manufacturers
2002		Uruguay banking crisis
2002	D	Enron/Worldcom/Global Crossing crises

Notes: Those marked 'L' are included in Luc Laeven and Fabian Valencia's database of systemic banking crises (Laeven and Valencia, 2008). Those marked 'D' are included in Davies' list of systemic banking crises involving the US (Davies, 2010).

due diligence on the part of the buyer, and this due diligence requires expertise in the new products and services. In other words, we can solve the problem of derivatives today, but this guarantees nothing for the next new thing in finance.

What Krugman meant by the third point is unclear – perhaps he referred to the small purchaser of mortgage-backed securities either directly or through money-market funds. But most likely he referred to the problem of predatory lending, which Stiglitz explained as pointing to the need for better consumer protection. (Build strong rules for finance system, 12 April 2010)

The fourth point, increasing the capital required of banks, is a universal point of agreement among mainstream economists and was in process at the onset of the crisis. However, the 'vicious circle of bureaucracy' applies once again, and this concept may even explain the onset of off-balance-sheet assets. Clearly, there is a lot of work being done on accounting principles to remedy this situation. The problem seems less one of concept than one of application.

Obviously, any good prescription for reform will be based on a profound understanding of the roots of the crisis. Some of Krugman's critics simply feel that he does not understand the mechanisms that gave rise to the crisis (for example, Jackson 2008).

Saltwater economist number two: Joseph Stiglitz

Professor Joseph Stiglitz was awarded the Nobel Prize in 2001 along with George A. Akerlof and A. Michael Spence for their work on information effects in economics – what is often called the 'economics of information', which is partially about how information (and the lack of it, for some parties) influences market transactions and partially about the value of information in those circumstances. This background both influenced Stiglitz's understanding of the crisis and provided him with a language to communicate his understanding. This is perhaps best summarized by the *Economist*: 'As befits a man who won the Nobel Prize for his work on asymmetric information, Stiglitz dwells on the market imperfections and misaligned incentives that distorted decisions made by everyone from mortgage originators to credit-rating agencies. His depiction of finance's failures is not novel, but it is well done' (*Economist*, 18 March 2010).

The critique made by the *Economist* is that Stiglitz chastises government agencies for not doing their job, and then, by proposing more government intervention, proposes the remedy of greater involvement of those same agencies or others like them. This is inconsistent in the view of the *Economist* (although the word 'I' appears frequently in their blogs and sometimes in the printed magazine; the articles are rarely signed): 'After he has condemned today's policymakers so roundly as incompetent and beholden to special interests, that prescription, and the author's broader faith in government activism, sounds perverse.'

If government bungled the job in the past, how can you remedy it by proposing more bungling?

This critique is appealing at first glance, but it falls on deaf ears to anyone already convinced of government intervention and is really a caveat rather than a demonstration that government intervention is useless. If a father or mother forgets to pick up one of several children at a day centre, does that mean they should not do so as soon as they remember? Failure and error is part of the human condition, at least if one does not work for the *Economist*, and we continue to strive to do things better and overcome our weaknesses. The commentary of the *Economist* shows that this sort of situation should not be resolved at the level of ideological discourse, but at the level of technical detail.

Stiglitz's stance, be it ideological or verified, is that government intervention is necessary precisely to support the functioning of the market. (See, for example, 1 November 2010) This position is at least as old as Adam Smith (most business academics, and probably most economists, glibly refer to Smith but have never read even the first two books of *The Wealth of Nations*[2]). Virtually all economists also share this opinion. The difference of opinion is in the details: how the government can do this. Most accept the components of the notion of economic freedom: the importance of the rule of law, absence of corruption, stable monetary policy, and so on. A radical libertarian may argue that corruption defeats itself because no one wants to deal with a corrupt economic agent. (He or she should travel a bit: most poor countries are economic basket cases precisely because those in power are corrupt.)

For what level of intervention does Stiglitz call?

He rejects government involvement in mortgages and real estate, which he feels will only prolong the malaise and lead to a protracted economic stagnation like that experienced by Japan in the 1990s. Rather: 'What is needed is a quick write-down of the value of the mortgages. Banks will have to recognize the losses and, if necessary, find the additional capital to meet reserve requirements.' (A better way to fix the US housing crisis, 9 September 2010)

He rejects the manner in which the banks were bailed out by US government agencies, pointing out that even naked capitalism would find a way (bankruptcy, it is supposed) to maintain the function of the banks without rewarding shareholders and executives for bad decisions (as investors or as managers): 'Bailing out the US banks need not have meant bailing out the bankers, their shareholders, and bondholders. We could have kept the banks as ongoing institutions, even if we had played by the ordinary rules of capitalism which say that when a firm can't meet its obligations to creditors, the shareholders lose everything.' (For all Obama's talk of overhaul, the US has failed to wind in Wall Street, 14 September 2009). Like Krugman, Stiglitz criticized the Obama administration for under-reacting to the crisis, but at the same time he was worried that too much liquidity was getting into financial markets, driving down bond yields, and forcing investors to seek higher returns in emerging markets – and as a result driving up inflation and currency valuations in those countries (Vieira, 2010). Further, by giving money to these financial institutions (albeit temporarily to let them get back afloat), the administration was reinforcing old and failed business models precisely at a time when innovation was needed.

The money should have gone not to the banks, but rather directly to the holders of the mortgages which gave rise to the toxic assets: 'The problem is the government has been using its ability to lend to give money to the banks... If they had lent it on to households maybe with a little charge for transaction, 1 per cent or 2 per cent, that would bring down their payments and that would mean that the hundreds and hundreds of thousands of people losing their homes – and with that their life savings – all of that could have been stymied.' (Siegel, 2010)

Why didn't the US government give that money to millions of voters to help them save their mortgages? Why did it instead set up an almost inoperable mortgage revaluation system (inoperable because it is so difficult to see who holds the rights to the original mortgages)? According to Stiglitz, the answer lies in the prodigious lobbying power (read dollars) of the big investment banks and other financial behemoths.

The lobbying is a reality, but there may be a sound (if debatable) economic reason for parking funds with the banks. One could argue that the funds placed in the balance sheet of the banks never entered the economy or at least did so without affecting the price of goods and services in the economy. If the funds had gone to families, they would have affected the price of goods and services leading to inflation. Perhaps there would be a way to control that effect, but it is not evident. Even if all the money goes to mortgage payments, that will free up other monies for consuming.

Further, the problem is cast in high relief for Stiglitz because the banks that received money were not acting the same as the banks bailed out in the Great Depression had behaved: they were not lending money: 'The banks that survived 80 years ago continued to lend money. Today many banks aren't lending money anymore, above all the large investment banks. This will deepen the crisis.... We're just throwing money at them and they pay billions of it out in bonuses and dividends. We taxpayers are being robbed for all intents and purposes in order to reduce the losses that some wealthy people bear' (Spiegel, 1 April 2009).

This moral indignation is understandable: from Stiglitz's viewpoint, the banks should have been bailed out by an injection of capital via bankruptcy or nationalization. In other words: the institutions should have been kept, but the parties to the bad decisions (top management and shareholders) should have suffered the usual fate of bad deciders in management or investment: extinction. That public monies should serve private gain was scandalous.

Still, there is a logical error here that should be obvious if we put aside our moral sentiments for a moment.[3]

The Great Depression is often used as a template for financial crises. Financial crises and their resolution are often understood in comparison with the Great Depression. However, the one bit of Latin that economics students still learn (well, at least until recently) is *ceteris paribus* –other things being equal. The reason for this expression is that *cetera* are rarely all *paria*. There are so many factors in any economic situation that every situation ends up being unique. The point is that banks' not lending in the 2007–2010 crisis does not necessarily indicate bad will. It indicates that the situation of banks and the financial system in 2009 was not the same as in 1933. Although it was certainly desirable that banks start lending again with the injection of funds, perhaps that was not the only objective. Perhaps the first and most important goal was to provide them with technical solvability for long enough to return to normality on their own with minimal government involvement – be it by decision-making power or simply by the volume of funds provided. For this indeed is what has happened. (Citibank and Bank of America may need a few years of operations to convince everyone of their financial depth.) The government will perhaps make a small profit for its efforts (Fannie Mae and Freddie Mac remain great question marks at the time of writing), and the majority of banks are back to normal operations. The US economy is still in difficulty as of December 2010, and financial service reform has yet to be proven, but the financial community is unanimous in considering the *financial* crisis to have ended as of the summer of 2010, although some players may feel hard done by (see, for example, Greenberg, 2011).

What alternative can Stiglitz or Krugman propose? They can propose a similar plan where banks (and perhaps AIG) are put into bankruptcy or receivership with a US government agent as trustee or receiver. The bankruptcy resolution might take the 21 months that the historical process took to return things to normality in the financial world, and then government agents and government could retire to the role of watchman.

There is one shortcoming with such a proposition, if this is in fact what Stiglitz had in mind. The shortcoming is that such a process fixes things more than is absolutely necessary. To do so seems more 'fair' – both to the free marketers who argue the banks should be allowed to fail and the economy to heal 'naturally' and to left-leaning interventionists who argue that it is not ethical to take from the poor (and from the middle class) to reward the rich for their crass gambling. But we have to ask the question: can it be done? If we hesitate about the feasibility, then there is no point in pursuing principle blindly. To do so is the agnostic equivalent of clericalism: justifying an action on the basis of irrelevant authority.

There are two reasons for doubting the feasibility of this bankruptcy or receivership or temporary nationalization plan. The first is the sheer volume of the effort involved. The second is the problem of scarce expertise.

The volume of effort involved in a single bankruptcy case is enormous. A firm involves a whole community of partners both within the organization (the employees) and without (suppliers, customers, bankers, investors, etc.). This community, with its bundles of rights and obligations, hopes and expectations, has been built up over years, perhaps decades. A bankruptcy involves resolving this whole community and bundle of rights and obligations, first by manifold negotiations and then, if need be, via a *carefully considered* fiat by the trustee in accordance with law and jurisprudence. This is a complex process with a mid-sized firm. In the case of the large financial institutions –which are first and foremost relational in their nature, with hundreds if not thousands of distinct legal entities even within the purvey of the institution. To gain an idea of the volume of work involved, consider that the *report* on Lehman Brothers' bankruptcy is 2200 pages long and required a year-long investigation with a review of more than 10 million pages of documents and interviews with more than 100 witnesses (according to the *Wall Street Journal*), 34 million pages of documents and interviews with more than 250 people (according to the *Chicago Daily Law Bulletin*), or 10 million e-mails and 20 million documents (according to *Wealth Daily*). John Cochrane has observed: 'Our bankruptcy system is not well set up to handle complex financial institutions with lots of short-term debt and with complex derivative and swap transactions overhanging. Until that gets fixed, we have to muddle through' (The Monster Returns, 2 October 2008).

Given the choice between a complex process and (relatively) simple one, it appears to have been more practical to choose the simpler process, particularly because the health of the economy was in the balance.

The second consideration was the scarcity of competent managers for the financial institutions. Some may have stupidly put their firms at risk, others greedily and knowingly put the economy at risk – but they were and probably still are among the most qualified people for their jobs, and they were and are the only ones who are already up to speed in carrying out their work. Is it really a good idea to replace them precisely at the time of crisis?

If the driver of a car gets drunk, it is easy to replace him with another driver. If the top management of a business is impaired, there will be a dramatic drop in performance and the business may fail. In the case of the finance industry, eliminating the top management of all the major firms may not only lead to failure of these firms, but could also lead to catastrophic consequences for the firms and projects they would have financed, and thus to the economy as a whole.

Furthermore, who will throw the first stone? Simon Johnson, Professor at the MIT Sloan School of Management and former chief economist of the International Monetary Fund, pointed out the promiscuity between regulators and regulated as being a serious problem in the oversight of Wall Street by Pennsylvania Avenue. There simply is no independent pool of competent people, so we have to reply on the good faith of the people chosen. If this is a problem for regulation, then surely it would be a problem in selecting which executives to keep and which to fire based on competency and honesty.

Could these issues be dealt with and these problems be solved? Probably they could. Certainly the United Kingdom stands as an example of a successful resolution of the financial crisis via bankruptcy and government buyouts with systematic replacement of management. (P.W., 2010) Nevertheless, we can understand that decision-makers would hesitate to pursue this path, even if there were not the weight of a Wall Street lobby behind preserving the banks and the bankers' jobs.

Like Krugman, then, Stiglitz would have liked to see the bailout take the form of ousting the top management of the failing financial institutions, replacing them with a government agent temporarily, and giving the shareholders the natural market return (loss of most or all of their investment). He does so for somewhat different reasons. Both Krugman and Stiglitz believe in a market overseen by government, but Stiglitz is motivated by justice and has faith in the functioning of the market to provide appropriate information to all parties (if you risk everything, you

Table 4.2 Outside-the-box suggestions by Joseph Stiglitz on the use of bailout funds

1	Give the bailout money to mortgage holders rather than to the banks.
2	Give the bailout money to new banks rather than the failed banks: $700 billion would have created $7 trillion in loans.
3	Save only those parts of the banks that are systematically important, but not the "gambling" parts.

Sources: Siegel, 2010; Stiglitz, How to Fail to Recover, 6 March 2009; Stiglitz Says Government Misses Mark On Economy, 15 January 2010; Obama Has Confused Saving the Banks with Saving the Bankers, 25 February 2009.

are at risk), whereas Krugman is motivated by justice and has faith in government intervention. This is a caricature of their positions, of course.

Both are champions of a larger fiscal stimulus than that offered by the Obama administration; Stiglitz has the peculiarity of noting the possibility that the bailout could have been achieved specifically through a targeted stimulus, giving the bailout funds to beleaguered mortgage holders (See Table 4.2). Stiglitz explains the basic economic reasoning behind stimulus deficit spending: 'A household that owes more money than it can easily repay needs to cut back on spending. But when a government does that, output and incomes decline, unemployment increases, and the ability to repay may actually decrease' (Taming Finance in an Age of Austerity, 8 July 2010).

If we understand the mechanics of the economy, then, we may see that it makes sense for a country to spend, whereas a family should cut expenses. This does not mean that government expenditure should be unlimited and government debt unlimited; it means that such expenditure can have a beneficial effect on the debt in the mid-term, given certain conditions. Stiglitz felt that such conditions held during the crisis; other economists felt that the debt had become so great that those conditions were in danger of crashing down. Not only did Stiglitz feel those conditions held, but he asserted that they were propitious: 'What business wouldn't jump at investment opportunities yielding returns in excess of 10% if it could borrow capital – as the US government can – for less than 3% interest?' (Alternatives to Austerity, 6 December 2010).

Where does Stiglitz stand on the issue of reform? Better regulation alone is not enough:

> There are several important lessons to be learned from the crisis. One is that there is a need for better regulation. But reforms cannot be just cosmetic, and they have to go beyond the financial sector. Inadequate

enforcement of competition laws has allowed banks to grow to be too big to fail. Inadequate corporate governance resulted in incentive schemes that led to excessive risk taking and short sighted behavior, which did not even serve shareholders well. (Reform is needed. Reform is in the air. We can't afford to fail, 27 March 2009)

The public should not expect the old school of regulators to come up with a better solution: 'The usual approach – delegating responsibility to regulators to work out the details – will not suffice.'

So what precise reforms are necessary? Stiglitz offers two lists. One is conceptual and short; the other is substantive and long.

In the short list, reform is called for in which government agencies regulate financial 'institutions' size, their risk-taking, and their interconnectedness' (For all Obama's talk of overhaul, the US has failed to wind in Wall Street, 14 September 2009). Stiglitz believes that regulation can eliminate the argument of 'too big to fail' by keeping banks under the horizon of systemic importance; the implementation of such a regulation would have to be accompanied or preceded by a break-up of several of the largest banks in the United States. But breaking up legal entities alone would be insufficient, for two reasons. On the one hand, the interconnectedness of many such smaller institutions would lead to a similar systemic risk as from a single large institution. On the other hand, such small banks could continue to engage in relatively invisible connections with dubious partners, dubious either with respect to the level of risk or else with respect to the nature of their activities:

> We need to ring-fence the core financial system (commercial banks, pension funds, et cetera). We have seen the danger of allowing them to trade with risky unregulated parties. There will be ancillary benefits in restricting their dealing with offshore secretive banks, whose raison d'être is, for the most part, regulatory and tax evasion, facilitating terrorism, drugs and corruption. (A crisis of confidence, 22 October 2008)

Stiglitz provides the longer, substantive list in two dense paragraphs published on the *Guardian*'s website (A crisis of confidence, 22 October 2008):

1. More transparency (in particular, regarding compensation and incentives, and regarding conflicts of interest such as those leading to the creation of intentionally money-losing financial instruments).

2. Capital requirements for banks should be counter cyclical; in other words, they should increase as the state of the financial system becomes more precarious.
3. Predatory lending should be proscribed.
4. The erection of two agencies:
    a. financial products safety commission.
    b. financial systems stability commission.

Elsewhere, Stiglitz called for a worldwide financial oversight and stabilization agency. As chair of the Commission of Experts of the President of the UN General Assembly on Reforms of the International Monetary and Financial System, he 'called for the creation of a new global reserve system – away from the US dollar – that could be used not only to maintain financial stability but also finance development and the fight against climate change' (Professor Stiglitz addresses UNCTAD and ILO, 12 March 2009).

Predatory lending. Many laws in the United States attempt to proscribe predatory lending. But how can predatory lending as such be proscribed effectively? The problem is in the legal details. When is a loan predatory? It could be argued that most government programmes to promote homeownership among modest-income households in the 1960s, 1970s, 1980s and 1990s were precisely a mandate to engage in predatory lending. The FDIC (2006) describes predatory lending as the imposition of unfair or abusive terms on the borrower. Are terms abusive if the borrower cannot meet them? Then it would be predatory lending if the borrower lies about his income. Or are they abusive if the borrower pays a higher rate than another borrower? Then banks will have no incentive to lend to more risky borrowers. To be useful, this recommendation of Stiglitz needs to be more detailed; although in all fairness perhaps a lawyer rather than an economist would be best able to provide such detail.

He himself omitted this issue of predatory lending in a more mature overview of regulatory changes in an *Economist* debate in the spring of 2010. (Economist Debates, 20 March 2010). Here he mentions both regulatory reform and complementary changes beside those in the regulation of financial institutions:

1. Toughen regulations and regulatory structures to better align private rewards and social returns (and overcome the agency problem in banks).

2. Strengthen regulatory capacities to oversee new innovations to lessen the likelihood of abuse; for example, create a financial product safety commission.
3. Transparency regulation is necessary, but not sufficient.
4. If products like CDSs are sold as insurance products, then they should be subject to insurance regulation, ensuring that there is adequate capital to fulfil their promises; if they are gambling products, then they should be subject to gambling laws and regulated and taxed as such.

More changes are called for, beyond financial regulation reforms (Ibidem; Nasiripour, 2010):

1. Laws on corporate governance
2. Laws on bankruptcy
3. Taxation
4. Accounting principles and guidelines
5. Stronger competition and anti-trust laws, with better enforcement

Stiglitz made an unfortunate analogy regarding the creation of a financial product safety commission. To counter the idea that it would be difficult to staff such a commission, he wrote: 'The FDA (Food and Drug Administration) testing for the safety and efficacy of drugs has given the market confidence. Even if those working there are paid far less than those in the drug industry; the skills required for such testing is different from those required to create new products. A financial product safety commission, with commissioners drawn from those likely to be injured by 'defective' products rather than from those that would benefit, could similarly assess (if imperfectly) the safety and effectiveness of new financial innovations, including systemic effects that might arise if such products became widespread' (Nasiripour, 2010).

This analogy is unfortunate because perhaps the reverse is true. It is more difficult to guess the impact of a financial regulation because there are no standardized tests, as compared with food and drug safety tests. The unforeseen consequences of drugs usually follow familiar pathways verified by the tried and true routines developed over the years. Financial innovations are often an attempt to get outside the familiar pathways of the past. To the extent that we can develop simulations of the financial system and of the whole economy, we will then be able to develop products that both exploit and escape those simulations.

5
Freshwater Economists, Austrian Economists and Popular Opinion

Introduction

The previous chapter began an overview of opinions about the financial and economic crisis and its resolution, with particular attention to two 'saltwater' economists who have been media stars: Paul Krugman and Joseph Stiglitz. It should be noted that the younger generation of saltwater economists are less strident in their differences of opinion with 'freshwater' economists, who supposedly omit the 'synthesis' from what Samuelson called the 'neoclassical synthesis' that brought Keynes into the stream of neoclassical economic thought. In point of fact, the freshwater stream of thought operated a major progress in macroeconomic thinking in the 1970s, keeping much of Keynes' approach using mathematical models and examining aggregated behaviour, but correcting much of his method and conclusions. The younger generation of saltwater economists consults and incorporates the work done by freshwater economists to a greater extent than economists who studied before the research work of the 1970s reached the classrooms.

The current chapter summarizes the views of freshwater economists, with particular attention to Luigi Zingales and John Cochrane, respectively, and then the views of Austrian economists, with somewhat more attention paid to Peter Schiff, who, if not an academic, has been more visible in the media than most Austrian economists. The chapter ends with a consideration of popular opinion.

Freshwater economist number one: Luigi Zingales

Freshwater economists are far less visible in the media than Krugman and Stiglitz.

Luigi Zingales is a professor at the University of Chicago's Booth School of Business. With Paola Sapienza of Northwestern's Kellogg School of Management, he engineered a petition presented to Congress on 24 September 2008 regarding the Treasury plan as outlined on that date. The plan and the actions taken by Washington metamorphosed several times after that date, although the major thrust always remained to stabilize the financial system by injecting hundreds of billions of dollars into it. The petition presented three main objections: this was unfair, the plan was ambiguous, and the long-term effects could weaken the innovative financial markets of the United States. It asked Congress to proceed slowly and to ponder its decision well. With the benefit of hindsight, many economists now feel that Washington's rapid action, albeit imperfect and inconsistent, was more important to resolving the crisis than was choosing an optimal course of action. Further, it also seems clear now that Washington, through two administrations, was quick to learn and modify its plans while negotiating with the different partners. The last two objections are thus less crucial to understand the freshwater opinion and Zingales' position regarding the crisis and its remedy. The first is the most important: the plan was unfair because it took money from the victims of the crisis – the taxpayers on Main Street – and gave it to the perpetrators – the bankers on Wall Street.

The hundred signatories of the petition were economics professors of mostly but not exclusively American universities, so it is to be supposed that they understood the financial system had to be repaired for the good of Main Street. What they objected to was the mechanism proposed at that time (purchasing toxic assets), and most continued to object to future iterations of the mechanism in the coming months – such as loans and purchase of preferred stock with a hands-off approach to management. Like the saltwater economists Krugman and Stiglitz, they felt that the managers and shareholders who were party to bad decisions should bear the responsibility for their errors. Freshwater economists do so partly on moral grounds, but mostly on grounds of effectiveness.

Sapienza and Zingales noted that lobbying by financial institutions best explained the form that the bailout was taking and that the authorship of the plan was anything but transparent (Korn, 2008), noting a recent paper by three colleagues which found that 'controlling for ideology, the higher the amount of political contributions congresspeople receive from the financial industry, the more likely they are to vote for TARP'. (Zingales and Sapienza, 2009)

One of the dangers of the administration's plan would be to exacerbate one of the effects of the crisis: loss of trust in the finance industry and loss of trust in government. They offered an alternative plan – what they called 'Plan B':

> Saving banks will allow them to continue lending, which will sustain the economy.... This is certainly true, but restructuring mortgages and avoiding unnecessary and inefficient defaults will also help everybody. It will help the families who would otherwise lose their houses. It will help their neighbors who will not see the value of their homes depressed by a wave of foreclosures. It will help the economy, by supporting the consumption of all these families. It will also help banks, whose assets are directly and indirectly linked to the value of these mortgages. (Zingales and Sapienza, 2009)

Zingales thus rejects the bailout and suggests the funds could be used more appropriately helping troubled mortgage holders. This should not be confused with the notion of fiscal stimulus, although it is hard to distinguish the two: it would require deficit spending (which is what, strictly speaking, Keynesian fiscal stimulus is) and would inject billions of dollars into the economy.

However, Zingales explained that resolving the mortgage issues was really resolving the source of the crisis, which resided in a market failure: 'In this area the market failure is neither the falling of real estate prices nor the fact that people who cannot afford to live in their houses are forced out. Market prices adjust to direct the allocation of resources and foreclosure is a sad but necessary mechanism to address mistakes in resource allocation. The real inefficiency is that people who can afford living in their house at the current price are induced to default.... Thus, government intervention should not aim at supporting house prices, but at facilitating renegotiation in the most cost effective way' (2010 but undated, My Losing Battle Against the Leviathan, p. ii).

Such an intervention should avoid the extremes of making it too easy or too hard to obtain government help, so only those in need of help (those who hold little equity in a home that has lost more value than that equity) avail themselves of that aid. It would also need to keep the funds needed far below the US$1.3 trillion of subprime losses. Zingales proposes transferring a part of all appreciated value to the lender in the mortgage, as inspired by a plan that Stanford University had employed for housing its professors. (Zingales, 2008)

His main stand on reform of financial regulation, taken with Oliver Hart of Harvard, addresses the issue of systematic risk. He sees the Federal Reserve Bank defining criteria (Hart and Zingales, 2010) by which a financial institution is judged to be a systemic risk or not, with different regulations impinging on those institutions posing a systemic risk. The authors then proceed to explain how to use interest rate spreads as indicators of market perception of risk as a way to peg the level of risk posed by firms. This seems a really clever way to use the market to apply a rule ... until we consider how the market evaluated the risk of mortgage-backed securities through the intermediary of credit rating agencies.

Freshwater economist number two: John Cochrane

Also a professor at the University of Chicago's Booth School of Business, John Cochrane is the son-in-law of Eugene Fama, originator of the 'efficient market' hypothesis. Although he is more nuanced in his understanding of free markets than at least the caricature of the free-market hypothesis – the caricature being that the markets know everything already, so there is no point in having a business school – a recent interview in the French media contains a strong quote as to his confidence on the efficiency of markets: 'If the markets didn't see the crisis coming, it's because no one did' (Deschamps, 2010). (In fact, several Austrian economists did foresee the crisis, as did Nouriel Roubini of Columbia University – although the latter already had 'enjoyed' a reputation of predicting doom previous to this call on the crisis.)

As with the previous authors, Cochrane's comments cover his evaluation of the bailout, his view on stimulus spending, and insights into the nature of the crisis that can lead to reform of financial regulation. Distinct from previous authors, however, his position on the bailout is dependent on his understanding of the crisis in greater technical detail. Previous authors argued that it was a question of fairness that those who made the risky decisions that created the crisis bear the brunt of its fallout. Cochrane turns the bailout question on its head, pointing out that the anticipation of bailout was precisely the cause of the crisis. He arrives at that conclusion through his analysis of the Lehman Brothers failure. The Lehman Brothers failure was followed soon after by a panic that was the 'signature event' of the financial crisis. Without that panic, in Cochrane's view, there would have been only a mild recession similar to that of 2000.

The common belief was and is that Lehman Brothers' failure burst the dam of the crisis – there were other factors at play, but this failure brought them all to a head. Because Lehman Brothers failed, its partners were brought under duress, and the contagion spread throughout the financial system, putting it and the whole economy in jeopardy.

Cochrane points out that this was not the case: few of Lehman Brothers' creditors failed, most of Lehman Brothers' activities were taken over by others and were operating within a few days of the failure; Barclay's Bank and Nomura hired many former Lehman Brothers employees; there were only two easily remedied problems: some money market funds had to borrow from the Federal Reserve, and some assets were stalled in a bankruptcy court in Britain. He also pointed out what for him is a telling issue: 'Lehman's failure did not carry any news about asset values; it was obvious already that those assets were not worth much and illiquid anyway' (Cochrane, Winter 2009–2010, p. 34).

If the Lehman Brothers failure neither caused direct harm to the marketplace nor uncovered disrupting information about the state of that marketplace, why did it have such a catastrophic effect? Cochrane's answer is that the market had come 'to the conclusion that investment banks and bank holding companies were "too big to fail" and would be bailed out. But when the government did not bail out Lehman, and in fact said it lacked the legal authority to do so, everyone reassessed that expectation'. It now made sense to panic (Cochrane, Winter 2009–2010, p. 34).

What lesson does Cochrane conclude from his analysis? There is no problem of institutions too big in their systemic ramifications to be allowed to fail; there is rather a problem of systemic expectation of bailout, and the challenge is how to deal with this moral hazard. The only solution, in his view, is for government to give up the legal authority to bail out financial institutions. Clearly, he is more radical than both Krugman and Stiglitz in his condemnation of the bailout of financial institutions!

When Cochrane delves deeper into the history of the crisis, he seems to contradict this analysis. He asks why it was that so many financial institutions came so close to failure and does not respond, 'anticipation of bailout'. He answers rather 'fragile financial structures'. This is, however, completely in harmony with his previous argument: financial institutions may exploit 'fragile financial structures' precisely because of their anticipation of bailout in the case of failure.

Why were fragile financial structures a cause of the near demise of so many financial giants? Once again, the explanation can be confused with the systemic risk argument. According to Cochrane, these financial structures (from the special purpose vehicles discussed in Chapter 1 to highly leveraged long-term portfolios funded by overnight debt) have three effects: (1) converting assets with continuously corrected prices into assets with prices that are constant until unpredictable catastrophic failure; (2) turning a 'non-systemic' risk into a very 'systemic' one and (3) hiding risk and evading regulations (Cochrane, Winter 2009–2010, pp. 35–6).

The meaning of the second effect is unclear to anyone who does not share Cochrane's vantage point. He enlarges it by writing: 'For the fundamental investors to lose any money, we need to see a default or a bankruptcy, which is always expensive and chaotic. The losses can drag down brokerage, derivatives, market-making, and other "systemic" businesses having nothing to do with simply sitting on credit risk.' It is difficult to see how this affirmation can be true if 'there is nothing inherently "systemic" about the behavior of Lehman Brothers or other large banks' (Cochrane, Winter 2009–2010, p. 35). Perhaps the response is given when he explains his position on reform: 'In my view, there really aren't any genuinely systemic institutions, but there are systemically dangerous contracts.' He gives two examples of systematically dangerous contracts: bank deposits and derivatives (Cochrane, Winter 2009–2010, p. 37). He uses the former to illustrate his approach to financial reform:

> We all understand that markets can fail when there are externalities. If we need to allow bank deposits, we need a guarantee or priority in bankruptcy, which leads to moral hazard and puts taxpayer at risk. Some regulation and a forced separation of these 'systemic' contracts from arbitrary risk-taking are necessary. (Cochrane, Winter 2009–2010, p. 37)

The guarantee here is the deposit insurance provided by the FDIC, which would cover all deposits under $250,000 in the case of bank failure. This encourages clients to deposit their money even if they see the bank engaging in risky activities – all the more so if those risky activities allow the bank to offer a higher interest rate on savings accounts. Hence the need for regulation and/or separation from arbitrary risk-taking, so that the FDIC does not find itself inciting the banks to higher-risk activities.

Austrian economists

The Austrian school of economics is considered to be a heterodox school of economics – outside the mainstream. While there are a dozen or so well-known schools that are predominantly freshwater or saltwater, George Mason University is the only reasonably well-known post-secondary institution with an economics department that has a predominantly Austrian economics orientation. Although the rise of the economics school of the University of Chicago is associated with the Austrian school of economics –partly because that school was a formative influence on Milton Friedman and also because of the presence of Friedrich Hayek at the University of Chicago, there are several clear differences between the two perspectives:

1. The freshwater economists do tend to look into specific mechanisms more than the aggregates invoked by Krugman and Stiglitz; however, their approach is more 'scientific' than the Austrian school: they proceed empirically with models and testing of hypotheses. This divorces them somewhat from the realities that are the starting points of Austrian economics: subjective human intentions and judgements.
2. As such, freshwater economists have a model of the economy in their minds and try to understand its mechanics; Austrian economists are forever examining the myriads of interconnected elements of the real world (if you accept the capacity of the human mind to access reality at least imperfectly).
3. Austrian economists have more confidence in the wisdom of the mass of individual deciders in the market place than in the judgment – and disinterestedness – of powerful 'experts' in government bureaucracies and elsewhere.
4. Government agencies are part of the economic system in the freshwater vision; they are parasites external to the natural economy in the Austrian vision.
5. Government may help, hinder or supplement individual decision-making in the freshwater view, and economic science should teach government how to help and supplement individual decision-making. For Austrian economists, an important key to understanding the economy is the production of wealth via capital, which is structured into different degrees of proximity to ultimate consumption (and thus more or less lead time between investment and consumption). For example: manufacture of capital equipment, extraction or harvesting, distribution. Myriad individual decision-makers generate a good capital structure unless government-sponsored interference distorts individual decision-making.
6. Differences 3, 4 and 5 lead to an understanding of booms and busts which are particular to the Austrian school, as depicted in Table 5.1.

Table 5.1 Booms, busts and schools of economic theory

Theory/Phenomenon	Keynesian and variations	Freshwater, Chicago	Austrian	Others (Fisher, Minsky, post-Keynesians)
Root of economic crises	Fluctuations in aggregate demand mean equilibrium is temporarily short of full employment.	Real business cycle: something "outside" of the economy (war, technological change, politics) destabilizes the economy.	Excessive bank credit distorts investment decisions, leading to an inappropriate capital "structure" (proximity to serving consumption).	Credit cycle characterized by leveraged bidding during the expansion phase: accumulation of debt by private business is the root cause.
Government intervention	Fiscal policy: spend money to increase demand.	Monetary policy; regulate to mitigate bad effects.	Diminish or eliminate the discretion of central banks, particularly the fractional reserve system.	(Minsky) given the institutional set-up of modern capitalist economies, we need public control or ownership of large, capital-intensive production in order to pursue full employment. Economic growth will follow from this.
Predicted 2007–2010 crisis with a characteristic explanation?	No	No	Yes. All private contributions to the crisis were unintentionally incited by government interventions.	Yes: debt already there at the beginning, but increased with leveraged bidding during the various booms.

Austrian economists on the bailout

Almost all mainstream economists criticized the bailout plans announced by the Bush and the Obama administrations. Both criticized them as unfair; the freshwater economists added that they would be ineffective.[1] But neither rejected the concept of saving the banks and other financial institutions; their only concern was to avoid awarding shareholders and top management for putting the whole economy at risk. Their proposal was either shares for dollars (mostly the saltwater position), going as far as temporary de facto nationalization, or else due bankruptcy process or an expedited version thereof (mostly a freshwater position).

The Austrian position is almost identical to the latter proposition, but for subtly different reasons. Mark Thornton begins his 'Austrian recipe' for the economic crisis with 'Allow liquidation of bankrupt firms and debt (no bailouts)' (Thornton, 2009). In particular, he specified in an earlier blog posting:

1. Convert Fannie Mae and Freddie Mac's status from conservatorship into receivership.
2. Convert AIG's status from government owned to receivership.
3. Cancel the Primary Dealer Credit Facility (PDCF) and the Term Securities Lending Facility (TSLF) at the end of the announced programme (30 January 2009).
4. Announce that the federal funds rate will be allowed to 'float' at market rates starting 30 January 2009.

Each of these points contradicts or negates some point of the bailout plans as announced by Henry M. Paulson and then by his successor Timothy F. Geithner. They come down to two indications: (1) let the banks (and AIG and other large financial institutions) fail according to the rules of failure already in place; (2) don't confuse marketplace decision-makers with more tinkering. Not only does the precedent of bailout create a moral hazard that will encourage exaggerated (that is, irrational without a taxpayer-supplied safety net) risk-taking in the future, but the fact of bailout prevents the market from doing the best job it can at reorganizing the allocation of capital, which would be the most direct return route to prosperity.

This is the key to understanding the Austrian economist's vision as opposed to the Keynesian (or most mainstream economists when push comes to shove). The Keynesian method to reduce unemployment in times of recession or depression is to increase the GNP according to the simplified equation GNP = consumer spending + investment + government spending; in other words, increase government spending when investment and consumer spending are down. For the Austrian economist, capital distribution (across functions in the economy, not across potential owners of capital) is the key. If left to function on their own by governments that seek to support and enhance the efficiency of markets, economic agents in large numbers constantly correct this allocation of capital to near-optimal levels. When government intervenes, it can (and usually does) make dramatic mistakes, even if government decisions are a function of pure technical expertise rather than influenced either by political expediency or by special interests.

The Austrian viewpoint is the actual mechanism of the production of wealth. The Keynesian viewpoint would seem to be numbers on a sheet rather than the reality behind those numbers. Is the right-hand side or the left-hand side of the equation too low to support full employment? Not a problem: just have government increase spending to bring the numbers up. However, the Keynesian solution is not that fantastic. Rather, changing the figures on one side of the equation is a real adjustment in the mechanism of the economy as they understand it, so that the pump is primed, exchange is restored and the economy comes back into motion. The difference is not between psychotics and realists. The difference is between two different understandings of the workings of the economy.

Peter Schiff on stimulus

Perhaps the best-known contemporary Austrian economist is Peter Schiff, a professional money manager who has been reasonably popular in the American financial media, at least because of his strident differences from mainstream opinion and government policy and because of the accuracy of his predictions about the crisis when most economists were talking about growth. Most of his subsequent commentary over 2009–2010 was critical of specific government interventions, arguing they would have such and such an unintended effect weakening the economy. However, he has on occasion given an overview of his understanding of the crisis and his recommendations for government action.

Although Austrian economics conceives of government agencies as external to the economic and financial systems, they remain subject to the laws of economics. In the case of the United States in the winter of 2010–2011, for example, 'Given the short maturity of our national debt, a jump in short-term rates would either result in default or massive austerity. If we choose neither, and opt to print money instead, the runaway inflation that will ensue will produce an even greater austerity than the one our leaders lacked the courage to impose' (The Phantom Recovery, 8 June 2010). Elsewhere Schiff wrote: 'We don't have economic growth. GDP is going up, but that's not a sign of any economic growth. All we're measuring is what we're consuming. But we are paying for it by going into debt. As a nation, we're in worse shape because of the GDP growth. The real economy is shrinking' (Don't Bet on a Recovery, 2 March 2010). The point is that government can intervene to soften the immediate impact of a jump in interest rates, for example creating money to pay interest and simultaneously thereby reducing the value of that money and of future payments on the debt. However, this would *also* reduce the US wealth as measured in dollars and incomes of all Americans.

Part of the problem can be found in the dashboard of mainstream economists, at least those with a direct input to policy and perhaps academics as well. Economic growth is represented by GNP and GDP, so that growth seems to appear as soon as spending increases, even though all economists realize that the reality is more complex. The pressure or the ambition for results tends to measure those results by the gross product figures for the economy. Schiff reminds us, 'GDP largely measures spending, and spending is not growth' (The Phantom Recovery, 8 June 2010).

Besides the illusory nature of stimulus, however, there are substantive risks: growth in debt and braking of economic growth.

Regarding growth in debt, Schiff wrote eight months before the failure of Lehman Brothers:

> [The] Federal government is the biggest subprime borrower of all and it has committed the American taxpayer to the mother of all adjustable rate mortgages. With the majority of our near 10 trillion dollar national debt financed with short-term paper, what happens when interest rates rise? Will the government extend the maturities of one-year treasury bills, tuning them into 10-year treasury bonds, forcing holders of government debt to accept below market returns for extended time periods? These are real risks that will not go unnoticed by a world already saturated with depreciating U.S. dollar denominated debt. (The Mother of all Bad Ideas, 6 December 2007)

Schiff leaves us to guess that the rise in interest rates would lead to rapidly rising governmental interest charges at the federal, state and local levels, probably higher unemployment than we have today, a pullback in the worldwide stock exchanges, perhaps more tariffs as barriers go up to protect local providers, and so on, even though the United States has more than ample reserves to cover such increased interest payments.

Regarding braking of economic growth, he said the following in a 2010 interview:

> We have to stop stimulating. We have to shrink the government and cut government spending dramatically. The reason the economy is so screwed up is because government regulations and subsidies have created a slowing economy. They have prevented market forces from operating the way they need to be. They have prevented an efficient allocation of resources. (Schonberger, 2010)

Because 'stimulus' fiscal policy increases debt and the size of government (thus expending capital on less-productive or unproductive activities), Schiff argues, such policies act more as an economic sedative than a stimulant (Academic and Press Economic Forecasters Flying Blind, 28 August 2010).

He specifically takes issue with the argument that World War II spending brought about the end of the Great Depression, an argument that had been resurrected by Krugman and others. The massive spending of World War II is supposed to have finally provided sufficient fiscal stimulus to overcome the Great Depression, return the United States to full employment, and get the economy moving again. However, Krugman 'neglects to mention that during the five years from 1945 to 1949, federal spending dropped by 58 per cent and taxes fell by 12 per cent. Meanwhile, the budget deficit fell by 66 per cent in 1946 and was in surplus from 1947 to 1949' (Krugman Strikes Again, 9 April 2010). Further, there is a great financing difference between World War II expenditures and the fiscal spending of 2009–2010 (and counting): 'the US funded its World War II effort largely by raising taxes and tapping into Americans' personal savings.' As these savings are now at an all-time low, the closest recourse today would be to sell American 'non war' bonds to the Chinese...to the tune of US$10 trillion. The cost of borrowing would rapidly become exorbitant, confronting the government (or rather the Federal Reserve) with the dilemma of raising interest rates or buying bonds itself.

Finally, a telling point from the Austrian viewpoint is that wartime manufacturing installations could easily be mobilized for peacetime production: 'Also, after the war ended, American factories quickly retooled production from military hardware to consumer goods. The products not only created a domestic boom in living standards, but were also in high demand in war-ravaged Europe. The late 1940s and 1950s produced some of the largest U.S. trade surpluses (in relative terms) in our history' (Krugman Strikes Again, 9 April 2010).

Schiff underlines the severity of the US job situation in the fall of 2010 by reminding us that the situation is almost twice as severe as the most quoted figure would lead us to believe: 'The unemployment rate has now been above 9.5% for 14 consecutive months, the longest such streak since monthly records began in 1948. More importantly, the real unemployment rate, which factors in discouraged and under-employed workers, rose from 16.7% to 17.1%' (The Hail Mary, 8 October 2010). But,' he warns, stimulus spending is financed by debt 'that will further hinder the capital investment and business formation necessary to produce sustainable jobs' (More Stimulus Means Fewer Jobs, 3 December 2010).

Where Krugman had seen insufficient spending, Schiff saw a litmus test for stimulus (deficit) spending. If, he asks, 'printing money and dolling it out to the unemployed could create growth and jobs, why hasn't it already worked? After all, we have already extended benefits to 99 weeks. Where are all the jobs?' He continues, bordering on sarcasm: 'Also, if every dollar of unemployment benefits generates two dollars of growth, as our legislators claim, why not double or triple the benefits? In fact, why limit them to the unemployed? Just give the benefits to everyone – then we will really get this economy going.'

According to Schiff, Professor Krugman has misunderstood the problem if he believes that stimulating demand is a solution. In reality, stimulus spending diverts the benefits of current production from producers to consumers, and this has the effect of breaking the power and incentive of producers to invest in productive equipment and thus undermines economic growth. The problem lies not on the demand side, but on the supply side. '[U.S. Thanksgiving-weekend shopping news reports of] mobs of shoppers trampling over each other to fill their carts shows there is plenty of demand. What is truly lacking in our economy is supply. Those mobs are still filling their carts almost exclusively with imported products' (More Stimulus Means Fewer Jobs, 3 December 2010). Schiff concludes that demand is meaningless without the capacity to supply goods.

Popular opinion

The financial and economic crisis of 2007–2010 has been labelled as the 'worst recession since the Great Depression' or simply the 'Great Recession'. Nonetheless, the subject no longer preoccupies the average citizen, who has already formed a cursory opinion about this crisis and its resolution. That opinion may not be scientific, but it is worth consulting if only because common opinion has a way of imposing itself on history.

There are three elements to popular belief about the recent crisis. First, the crisis has reinforced the vague mistrust in the financial services industry present before the crisis. Second, people believe that government has dealt with the crisis and remedied it, although perhaps not in the best possible way. Third, there is a supposition that it could all happen once again because we have not learned sufficiently from our experience in this crisis. (All of this confused somewhat because of the onset and heightening of the euro crisis.)

The vague mistrust of the finance industry derives from the popular understanding or misunderstanding of the events of the financial crisis, from past impressions of the behaviour of the financial sector and from personal experience.

The popular understanding of the events of the financial crisis is that several high-profile players in the financial sector have paid their top employees large bonuses, turned healthy profits since the fall of 2008 and suffered little from the financial crisis. Many believe that precisely these high-profile players are responsible for the crisis, intentionally or unintentionally. They thus should have been forced to bear the brunt of the financial burden. Goldman Sachs, AIG and Morgan Stanley are some of the main actors considered to be guilty of profiting from a crisis they caused. This mistrust of a few players often extends to the entire industry. Little distinction is made between traders, top management of these institutions, and their shareholders.

This mistrust is founded on commentary in the media and also on the mistrust that preceded the whole financial crisis. Some economists are in part to blame, not because they accuse the financial industry but because of their explanation of economics. Their simplistic explanation is that the economy is based on selfishness. If indeed it were based on selfishness, it would be quite normal for the financial sector or players in the financial sector to pursue wealth at the expense of the rest of the economy. This would be particularly true if you believe that wealth is based on others' poverty. In reality, of course, the financial sector should profit only if the 'real' economy is profitable. For a few years, this did not happen, until the reality of leveraged risk turned around and bit the financial sector near the jugular vein.

The third contributing factor to the mistrust of the financial sector is personal experience. Almost everyone in North America and Europe has at least two contacts with the financial sector: the first with one or several banks for savings, a current account and perhaps mortgages; the second with a pension fund, usually a private account contracted by their employer. Many people have a further contact with the financial sector because they have invested some savings in bonds or in mutual funds. The diverse services provided to individual consumers are known as 'retail banking' in that industry. It is not a lucrative area, because transaction size is small while the number of transactions is elevated: a lot of work for minuscule sums. Bank employees have to be paid the same amount of money per hour independent of the size of the transaction they analyse. However, banks have found a way to make this retail banking profitable: service charges. In such countries as Canada, where there is a low level of competition among banks, consumers find themselves charged when they write a cheque, when they take cash out of their account and when they procure new cheques. In other words, it costs them money to bank their money. This was not the case 50 years ago. The notion that it would be cheaper for them to store money in their socks or under the mattress is irritating to them; this irritation is amplified because their understanding is that banks benefit by having their deposits, which they can then invest either in mortgages or in loans to businesses. They feel the banks should profit by using the money in this way rather than charging the consumer money to store their funds.

The other contact with banks is via mortgages. In the United States, consumers contracted mortgages either with banks or with specialized mortgage institutions. In the former case, the experience was very good. These banks retain their mortgages and make their profit through the performance of these mortgages. Those clients all were able to meet their payments and retain their houses. The performance of the specialized work institutions, however, was less consistent. We have seen this in the previous chapters of this book. Because these institutions did not retain mortgages, and because they made a profit independent of the forms of mortgages, many of them were less careful about the quality of mortgages. This meant that some consumers were able to buy a house even if they would have been rejected by the banks, but also meant that at least some portion of those consumers eventually could not make their payments or made their payments only under considerable economic duress. In these latter cases, once again there is mistrust of the industry both on the part of interested parties and on the part of their friends, their acquaintances and even those who read about their experience in the newspaper. Although perhaps only some employees in some institutions were truly irresponsible, the whole industry tends to be painted with the same brush.

The vast majority of people in North America and Europe also have a contact with the financial sector through their dealings with the pension fund chosen by their employer. Most of these choices are a good choice, and most pension funds are run according to high professional standards. They are constrained to a very narrow margin of risk. As a result, the profit level of investments is also often inferior to the profits seen elsewhere in the financial sector. The pension fund will never see the level of profits of hedge funds, simply because the hedge fund is unfettered in its choice of investments. When the entire economy flounders because of a crisis, the pension funds suffer also, because their investments by necessity are somewhere in the economy. Further, although they diversify their investments, this means that they will always have some investments in the poorly performing part of the economy. As a result, most people are usually a little unsatisfied with the performance of their pension fund. This vague dissatisfaction was compounded during the recent financial crisis. As we saw in previous chapters, the 'toxic assets' were presented and certified to be extremely low-risk investments with a reasonably good return. In other words, they were very good investments for pension funds. At least, this was the almost universal belief. As a result, many pension funds did invest heavily in toxic assets. Even in Canada, where the banking industry was almost unscathed by the financial crisis, many pension funds were badly burned. With hindsight, we can be very critical of the management of these pension funds. To expect exceptionally brilliant insight by the management of these funds is somewhat unrealistic. Yet, many people may be implicitly blaming their pension funds for not either foreseeing the financial crisis or at least being suspicious of the toxic assets.

A growing portion of the middle class in North America and Europe invests, at least buying Treasury bonds when the interest rate is higher or else putting some money into mutual funds. Currently the interest rate on Treasury bonds and interest rates on private bonds are at an all-time low. Mutual funds, on the other hand, are performing well and reflect the performance of both the stock market and commodities. Commodities have risen as the Third World economies grow and the US dollar has faltered. The stock market has risen as investors expect future benefits when the economy returns to normality after firms take some hits (declare losses) and reduce employment levels. It has also risen somewhat in response to quantitative easing. As a consequence, those who do not participate in these investment opportunities see the rich getting richer and the poor getting poorer. The members of the middle class who do invest are well aware that performance of their investments is not creating any new jobs.

Mistrust of government – or at least of politicians – is even more popular in North America and Europe than is mistrust of the financial sector. The latter is a vague apprehension born of ignorance of how the financial sector actually works and what it does, as well as the factors mentioned in the previous paragraphs. Mistrust of government is unfortunately reinforced by non-fulfilment of campaign promises and the improprieties of politicians who combine human weakness with opportunity and political power. We might expect a strong criticism of government interventions to remedy the crisis. There is no lack of theoretical sources of critique as well as vocal pundits, as we shall see. However, the financial and economic crisis is receding from people's minds – or at least is being replaced with the euro crisis – even as it disappears from headlines. Although the jobless rate remains high in the United States, this is not an issue for the 90 per cent of the workforce who have a job. Although part of the official motive for the quantitative easing being practised in the United States and Great Britain is the avoidance of deflation and economic stimulus needed to complete the remedy of the financial and economic crisis, most people are beginning to conceive it as either the first salvo in an undeclared currency war between the United States and China or else as a diplomatic path for those two countries to resolve their differences without government or politicians on either side losing face. In most people's minds, the crisis is over and their government has dealt with the crisis, albeit imperfectly. They may feel government could have been more vigorous in responding to the crisis, or that government could have had the same impact while spending less money, but they feel that once again their personal prospects are good because they are part of a prosperous economy with only a few hiccups on the radar: debt and the euro crisis. They do not fully understand what the government has done to intervene, but whatever it was seems to have dealt with the problems sufficiently well.

However, these same people do not think that government intervention to have been based on such a keen insight into the problem as to permit reform of the economy in general, and the financial sector in particular, in order to avoid a reoccurrence of the crisis. We are back to business as usual, and the creative talent of the financial sector will soon circumvent the changes that have been introduced. This vision is partly based upon the mistrust of that sector as actively seeking ways to exploit the rest of us in spite of the puny efforts of government to control it.

6
Conclusion

The views expressed by saltwater, freshwater and Austrian economists in the previous chapters do not easily lead us to a conclusion about the resolution of the financial and economic crisis of 2007–2010. The sole point of unanimity appears to be rejection of the bailout. Even this rallying point may be questionable, because authors in favour of the bailout remained almost invisible for that very reason. Rather than produce strong articles in support of the bailout, such authors would either write nothing or else discuss the details of fund allocation. It is in this use of funds that there was the greatest debate. Although we have stayed close to popular media and some trade publications, avoiding the exploding academic literature on the crisis,[1] clearly there are great differences of opinion regarding the actions of the US government and Federal Reserve. (I assumed the independence of the latter even as it bought hundreds of billions of dollars of Treasury bonds). Some of the criticisms of the Treasury's actions have proved dated, as the actual program carried out by the Treasury has evolved so that 2011 found some of the critics in awe of the reasonably cheap and perhaps even profitable resolution of the financial crisis, even if they considered it not 'fair' to keep management in their jobs and (sometimes) shareholders in the black. The intractable divergence of opinions remains remarkable, however.

The first section of this chapter summarizes the book and then looks for areas of agreement across expert opinion in the search for lessons to be gleaned from our experience of the first decade of the new millennium. The second section discusses our knowledge of economics and the state of economic theory. The final and third section observes some social and moral issues underlying the crisis but not dealt with previously in this book.

Overview of the book

The chapters reviewed

Chapter 1 covered the nature of the crisis. Individuals and enterprises had purchased assets that dropped dramatically in value. Financial institutions were among those enterprises. Financial institutions are entities that play a role in the circulation of wealth in the economy, so that economic systems were handicapped as a consequence. Part of the difficulty lay in uncertainty as to who would be able to meet their financial obligations. Therein lay the financial crisis. The prolonged period prior to the financial crisis was characterized by a remarkable abundance of capital. There was much less capital available throughout and after the crisis. This changed the constraints on business decision-making and led to a slowdown of the US and European economies, decreasing demand for the produce of developing countries as well as, by deferred purchases, for semi-durable and durable goods, such as cars. As a consequence, businesses dismissed some of their employees. The gross domestic product of the United States slowed from US$14,485,000,000 (annual rate) in the third quarter of 2008 to US$14,035,000,000 in the second quarter of 2009, then took another year to return to the level of 2008. The US unemployment rate doubled from five per cent in January 2008 to 10.1 per cent in October 2009; it was still at 9.2 per cent in June 2011. This was the economic crisis in the United States, and similar economic difficulties were experienced in most wealthy countries of the Occident and some Asian countries. Most countries worldwide experienced slowed growth because of diminished exports to rich countries.

Chapter 2 explained the historical context and the mechanisms through which the crisis had developed. The historical context included the rise of a new source of financing for house purchases. Financial securities provided a way to invest in mortgages, thereby multiplying the amount of capital available for home purchase. Changes in the financial world thus become relevant to the financing of home purchases. Two such changes led to riskier behaviour by financial institutions: (1) accounting tricks that allowed banks to keep risky assets off their balance sheets and (2) deregulation of the banking industry, in particular the bipartisan repeal of the Glass-Steagall Act, which heretofore had separated commercial and investment banking. Another change was the dramatic rise of 'merit' incentives in the financial sector that combined poorly with the mysterious (because poorly understood by upper management) workings of many new financial instruments, so that merit was attributed and rewarded prior to tangible returns for the employer. The dot-com boom and bust was an event in the financial sector that left capital searching for a haven from the contingencies of reality, and it found that haven in securities. Apparently.

Chapter 3 related the chronology of the crisis. A succession of Democratic and Republican US governments sought to increase homeownership among less wealthy Americans and among minority groups. Besides slightly increasing homeownership among these groups, the various interventions also stimulated the housing industry, ultimately leading to prices increasing at a rate that transformed real estate from a slow but safe long-term investment into a growth vehicle with the life cycle of a semi-durable good. This was exacerbated by efforts to resurrect the economy (read: investments) by aggressive monetary policy, and by the financial sector's unrestricted exploration of uncharted waters, particularly after the firms in that sector had gained experience with mortgage-backed securitization while working with the federally sponsored mortgage agencies (Fannie Mae, Freddie Mac and Ginnie Mae) and after several institutions experienced astronomic gains by following the quants (mathematicians who eschewed real math for money) and by converting the handcrafted products of lawyers (the carefully crafted contracts that were the first efforts at swapping risks) into mass-produced fungible goods. Already there was a plethora of capital as the first baby boomers began to retire, and the securitization of mortgages meant that this abundance became available to homebuyers. More strongly put: there was an oversupply of capital looking for an apparently safe investment, and mortgage-backed securities appeared to be that safe haven. The existence of one kind of security, the credit default swap (CDS), appeared to guarantee this safety, because it was often explained as an insurance policy for (among other things) mortgage-backed securities. This may have prolonged the market for such securities even once it was clear to all that the underlying mortgages often led to default. Unlike life insurance and other kinds of real insurance, anyone could buy this 'insurance', so that a total stranger could bet on the misfortune of a third party, and even the artisan of a security could bet against that security, creating a conflict with the interests of their clients, the purchasers of the securities. Marc Stern (2008 and 2009) provides a wonderful overview of many of the issues this book covers in Chapters 1, 2 and 3, as does the first dissenting statement of the final report of the FDIC (2010).

Chapters 4 and 5 provided a survey of the opinions of prominent American economists regarding the crisis and appropriate remedies and reform.

Chapter 4 focused on two 'saltwater' (more or less neo-Keynesian) economists: Paul Krugman and Joseph Stiglitz. Their positions cover three main topics: bailouts for banks, fiscal remedies and reform. Neither liked the notion of bailing out banks, seeing this as using other people's money to protect the banks from their own errors. However, Professor Krugman blinked in the face of the possibility that major banks might fail and proposed funding the banks in exchange for ownership, effectively nationalizing the banks on a temporary basis and supposedly exercising that majority ownership to rid the bank of the management that had brought them into crisis. Professor Stiglitz, on the other hand, felt that the standard mechanisms of the current capitalist system in the United States – namely, bankruptcy laws – were sufficient to keep the banks operating as institutions while revamping their management. The complexity of the large financial institutions would be arduous for the existent bankruptcy processes, however, and Krugman proposed (for the future) the creation of a 'resolution authority' with the powers to arbitrate the restructuring of such complex institutions. Stiglitz would have redirected the bailout funds to economic stimulus in the form of financial help for families unable to meet their mortgage payments. Krugman called for additional funding for fiscal stimulus, with most of his argumentation being about the real size of stimulus (at least US$800 billion cash up front) rather than on the way the funds would be used. Both Nobel laureates recommended reform via new agencies, more stringent regulation of banks' risk-taking and other new regulations. Krugman called for regulation of derivatives; Stiglitz, for transparency requirements regarding derivatives and other financial instruments as well as employee compensation. Krugman called for more stringent regulation of banks' risk-taking; Stiglitz specified that the rules should be counter-cyclical. He also pointed out the importance of controlling banks' interconnectedness. Both authors wanted greater consumer protection, with Stiglitz proposing a financial products safety commission. He also a proposed the creation of a financial systems stability commission within the United States and a worldwide financial oversight and stabilization agency. He also felt that banks' size should be limited. All of these suggestions appeared to have some merit, but most have come under criticism for undue complication, the introduction of new dangers, or the simple weakness of bureaucracies breeding byzantine evasive behaviour.

Chapter 5 illustrated the perspective of freshwater economists by giving overviews of comments by John Cochrane and by Luigi Zingales, and in addition provided the view of Austrian economists, with particular emphasis on the statements and writings of Peter Schiff. It ended with a discussion of popular opinion.

Professor Zingales and other freshwater economists agreed with saltwater economists that bailing out the investment banks was simply using taxpayers' money to save the banks from their own mistakes and in fact also rewarding key bank employees for sabotaging the banks for their own benefit. The banks' lobbying power explains this unjust and irrational behaviour on the part of Washington. Injustice was not the only problem with the bailout, however. The bailout's worst effect was to undermine trust in the finance industry and to undermine trust in government. Like Stiglitz, Zingales suggested the monies would better have been used to help beleaguered mortgage holders, but with a slightly different motivation and a slightly different mechanism. He saw the problem as one of market inefficiency in which mortgage holders had incentive to default – an economics problem rather than a social or moral problem, and one that should have been remedied by facilitating the renegotiation of the terms of each problematic mortgage. The funds used to do this were understood as having no fiscal stimulus effect, because freshwater economists believed that research in the 1970s had demonstrated fiscal stimulus to be a logical error on the part of Keynes. The principal reform Zingales proposed was to use interest rate spreads to classify financial institutions as occasioning systemic risk or not, with more stringent constraints regulating the former class.

Professor Cochrane's opinion regarding bank bailouts is far more radical than the opinions already considered: It was precisely the anticipation of a bailout that inspired banks to seek risky profits through the exploitation of fragile financial structures (such as long-term investments highly leveraged with short-term debt). In his view, the danger lies in contracts rather than in institutions. Reform should therefore regulate 'systemic' contracts and in particular separate them from arbitrary risk-taking. Cochrane's reforms appear to be the least unwieldy of reforms proposed, but he also wants to curb the power of government to bail out financial institutions in order to remove that moral hazard.

Chapter 5 also covered the Austrian economics view of the crisis. Austrian economists rejected the bailout as one more instance of government 'experts' trying to do a better job than the combined judgements of the marketplace in dealing with failed banks. Not only would they allow existent bankruptcy laws to resolve the failed banks, but they wanted AIG, Fannie Mae and Freddie Mac put into receivership as well. In a sense, they agreed with Cochrane that anticipation of bailout caused the crisis, but they further felt that the market would more judiciously correct the management errors made at the banks. Nor would Austrian economists use the bailout funds to help troubled mortgages, because the market would better resolve the problems than the judgement of any policymaker or arbitrator. Peter Schiff was the most vocal of the Austrian economists regarding fiscal stimulus. His point was that the widely used measure of economic size and growth, change in GDP, was in reality a measure of growth in consumption fuelled by increasing debt rather than growth in economic power. The result was a drop in the value of the US dollar and thereby in the wealth of Americans. He likened government debt in the United States to a gigantic subprime mortgage with variable interest rate. At some time the rest of the world would see US debt as risky and would dramatically increase the interest rate. Finally, Schiff argued that the problem in the US economy was not consumption but rather production: consumer goods were being imported. The best reform would be to reduce government presence in the economy to one of assuring maximal economic freedom through just business law, effectively sanctioned.

Chapter 5 finished with a brief overview of public opinion regarding the crisis: greater mistrust of government and of the financial sector.

Opinions reconciled... almost

The purview of opinions among economists is perplexing. While there is the usual almost ideological divide on the topics of stimulus and reform, there is an amazing unanimity in dislike for the bank bailouts. Nobody liked the idea of bailouts except bank employees with bonuses pending, bank shareholders, and the politicians and government agencies with the power to use tax monies in this way. In practice, however, the bailout of banks appears to have been a very successful series of measures. Less than one year after the nadir of the post–Lehman Brothers panic, when everyone pointed fingers at the government – for not bailing out Lehman Brothers, for guaranteeing the toxic assets of Bear Stearns to facilitate its merger with JPMorgan Chase, for spending too much money, for not spending enough money – it nevertheless was recognized that the financial crisis had been resolved and that Wall Street once again was functioning at a level comparable to pre-crisis activity. Even more surprisingly, Washington made a tidy profit on the bailout if we exclude the conservatorship of the government-sponsored agencies.

Other financial centres around the world also seem to have recovered, at least to the extent that we can ignore other problems such as Europe's Greek sovereign debt crisis and the 2011 catastrophes in Japan.

On the other hand, the US economy cannot be said to have recovered because GDP has returned to pre-crisis levels but unemployment has not. US government intervention has not healed the economic woes of the United States. Perhaps more months are needed. At the time of this writing, however, a year has passed since the recovery of the financial sector without signs of improved employment. It may also be due to deeper, more structural problems with the US economy, primarily the level of debt. If structure were truly a problem, however, then surely the demographic burden – the proportion of employable people to retired or unemployable ones – would have an opposing effect and decrease unemployment.

The great question, then, is whether the measures that saved the financial sector have been beneficial for the economy and the country or whether they simply benefitted the employees and shareholders of financial institutions whose destiny is slowly detaching itself from the performance of the economy as a whole. The justification for bailing out the banks and temporarily taking over AIG is the role these play in the economy. If the effort to govern risk severs the linkage between financial institutions and all other firms, then saving those financial institutions does not automatically save the economy.

There remain two alternatives: intervene directly in the economy (as Stiglitz and Zingales proposed) or simply recognize that the harm has been done, recognize that we have the power to harm others as well as ourselves, and refrain from any intervention. If predatory lending is a way for the rich to steal from the poor, then the poor suffer. If receiving a bonus for burdening your employer with toxic assets is a way to steal from your employer, then the shareholders suffer. While most judicial systems punish crime, they do not restitute damages; at best, they provide a costly recourse for obliging the guilty party to offer restitution. Why should taxpayers' money be used to restitute damages within the financial sector if this restitution does not heal the economy?

Who are the guilty parties behind the financial crisis of 2007–2010? Bank employees each taking home tens of millions of dollars of bonus for the Christmas of 2008 are an attractive target of blame. Sleazy touts flogging mortgages with balloon payments to uneducated immigrants who have purchased a middle-class or better home are also attractive targets of blame. Rating agencies who rated junk as triple A securities appear guilty. But what about middle-class Americans who purchased one or more homes beyond their means as a short-term investment, with the intent of flipping the home already purchased and moving upscale to a bigger investment? They took a risk and lost. The risk they took diminished their own wealth, but we have since learned that it also weakened the whole economy. Can we accuse them of greed that has harmed us all? Or of stupidity that has dragged us all down? And the poor, uneducated and naïve immigrant workers from Mexico, Jamaica and the Philippines who invested their earnings in upscale homes near Los Angeles or townhouses in New York City: did they not enjoy luxury beyond their means for a couple of years and then walk away with only their credit rating damaged for a few years?

There are many guilty parties, not all easily distinguishable from innocent victims. King Solomon would have to sunder the child in many parts, and even if the real mother wished to preserve the child intact, her voice would be lost in the cacophony of interested parties clamouring for their pound of flesh. A confusing array of agencies and pundits jostle on the seat of King Solomon, and the US system replaces the imperfect integrity of the individual to a supposedly visible and above-board lobbying system. However, as Johnson, Krugman, Stiglitz, Zingales and Cochrane have argued, and the Austrian economists would ratify, the influence of Wall Street is far too great for anyone to imagine that the lobby system permits a disinterested (or 'balancedly' interested) governance of Wall Street.

No government is likely to adopt the Austrian recommendation of zero intervention by government. Only a dictator would have the real discretionary power to do that, and dictators are unlikely to give up their power to tinker with the economy. Further, the only advanced economy in the world that is directed with anything near autonomy of public opinion is Singapore's. All other rich economies are political regimes characterized by stability of system and instability of people.

The realistic alternative, then, lies in the responsiveness of the governance system to public opinion. Unfortunately, there are two major barriers to the effectiveness of any responsiveness there might be. First, the complexity of the problem and the multiplicity of opposing voices are daunting for an expert, let alone the common citizen. Second, the common citizen is profoundly ignorant of the workings of the economy, let alone the more arcane financial motor of that economy. Just as the citizens of many Latin American countries are vulnerable to the demagogy of unscrupulous politicians who bandy such words as 'liberalism' and 'communism' while enriching themselves and their families, so too the citizens of the world's most powerful economy are incapable of critiquing the verbiage of their representatives and senators in regard to economic and financial affairs. Without educated and understanding citizens, the most enlightened approaches to policy, such as Richard Thaler's 'nudging' of decision-making (Thaler, 2011) lead to disguised manipulation by Big Brother.

In spite of the strong disagreement about the utility – and even about the reality – of fiscal stimulus, there would appear to be room for discussion about a pragmatic exception to the 'no government interference' principle of the Austrian economist. Perverse incentives have led financial institutions to misappropriate capital in the US economy. Government could compound this error by allocating still more capital to the financial institutions, albeit temporarily to allow them to recover the health of their balance sheets. Alternatively, government could put those same funds into the hands of myriad decision-makers in the marketplace to re-sanitize decisions made under those same perverse incentives. If – and this is a big 'if' – those funds are kept within the mortgage payment system, the funds would also disappear, absorbed as toxic assets became good assets once again and the banks became solvent. The problem, Austrian economists would object, is that this would lead to false prices in the housing market even if general inflation would be avoided.

The third area, reform, holds little promise for agreement. While the mainstream seeks to fine-tune anterior regulation, the Austrian economists wish to eliminate it wholesale. However, even if this latter proposal is the best economic answer, it does not seem politically viable at the present time. The former solution poses real difficulties. Regulation is clearly an insufficient answer: the same authors proposing new regulation typically undermine their own proposals by demonstrating the past ineffectiveness of regulators in sanctioning relevant regulation.

Power and information pose two obstacles to regulation.

The reality is that Wall Street is powerful and the homologues of Wall Street around the world are powerful: the intimacy of political power and economic wealth is a reality. Wall Street can and has influenced legislation, regulations, and application of sanctions. Individuals in investment banks have bullied and resisted regulators by personal prestige, evasiveness in complying, mind games and harassment. Michael Lewis and other writers have underlined the disdain of the financial sector for the professional calibre of regulatory employees and perhaps unintentionally communicate this disdain to their readers. This disdain supposes that everyone is motivated by money and independence. It also ignores an important element of the relation between regulators and financial services: initiative is with the industry, not with the regulators. Anyone who has experienced competition or combat knows that this places regulators at a disadvantage. An example of such initiative is the ability of individuals in financial services to recognize and exploit weaknesses and simplistic assumptions in the mathematical models of finance.

This disadvantage can be removed, although potentially at tremendous cost, by treating financial activity as a privilege rather than as a right. This would return initiative to the agents of government, but shackle the innovative capacity of the financial sector and perhaps lead to a migration of financial heavyweights to the global equivalent of Delaware corporate law – any land providing sufficient stability and infrastructure and minimal legal constraints.

Part of Wall Street's advantage resides in its opacity (reinforced by the complexity of the firms and by the audacity and sense of supremacy of its employees). Not only have regulators insufficient information to regulate, but Wall Street employees also can selectively invoke information to contradict any inconvenient assertions by regulators. This opacity could possibly be neutralized, or at least could soon be neutralized, by an integration of the business intelligence systems of financial firms with those of government agents. Again, the potential cost is tremendous, at least for anyone distrustful of Big Brother. Further, mere access to information is futile without the will and available manpower to analyse and comprehend it. In addition, a basic tenet of business intelligence and of all information systems is 'garbage in, garbage out'. The input comes from employees of the financial services, and access to information is problematic even within these services. Inaccurate accounting is a problem not only for regulators, but also for the management of these firms.

There is one solution that might be able to recruit support from all sides of the ideological turf wars, but mentioned by no author, although Cochrane provided a criteria for application of this restriction. Should the market indicate that a firm represents systematic risk, a real-person ownership structure should be required: either majority ownership by an individual (a physical person) or else a partnership of real persons. Deprived of legal limits to their liability, the ultimate commanders of the firm will have an incentive to understand and govern the risks being taken by employees both for the firm and for their clients. The current public ownership permits a few reckless gamblers to lead their firms to a short-term dominant position in the competitive landscape, encouraging their homologues in rival firms to lose confidence in reasonable, prudential management, to act irresponsibly and adopt a magical approach to oversight (they don't know how the employees make those profits, but it seems to work).

Regulation is an instance of control, and a basic characteristic of a good control system is that it should be adequate rather than perfect. The problems of the financial crisis lie not in dishonesty and errors, but in the fact that dishonesty and errors were allowed to accumulate to the extent that they did.

One issue that was not raised by any of the experts covered in Chapters 4 and 5 is fungibility. Nothing can be traded easily in an anonymous market unless it is a perfect substitute for other goods of the same class. The perfection of that substitution is often conventional, but that convention must have a solid foundation in reality. If we were able to interview pigs, we would quickly find that each pork belly is unique, yet they are identical enough to be valued identically, and futures can be derived from the market for pork bellies. The toxic assets of the financial crisis of 2007–2010 are contracts – and sometimes contracts about contracts – between various parties about varied goods, particularly residential housing of varied construction in different locations and of different ages. Part of the genius of securitization is to transform this variety into fungible bits of risk and return. It does so by routinizing the legal work (when individually crafted contracts suppose due diligence), using mathematical models to standardize the risk (these models suppose continuity but model discontinuous reality), and supposes good faith in the composition of the goods underlying the contracts (when credit default swaps can create an incentive to select those goods in a such a way as to increase the likelihood that the original security becomes toxic), with standards controlled by rating agencies with insufficient data and who are compensated by the vendors of the security. It is hard to see how such assets can be considered fungible if some people are honest and others are not. On the other hand, such fungibility is most desirable, so there is room for valuable economic research on this topic.

Reflections on economics as a science

Economic models

There are two positions on the validity of economic and financial models: keep them or trash them.

John Kay provides a simple but lucid insight into the status of economic models:

> It is a mistake to believe the efficient-market theory is false. The insight that information is essentially incorporated in prices is important. It is an equally big mistake to believe that the EMH [the efficient market hypothesis] is true. Market prices do not necessarily represent a considered, weighted assessment of available information. ... The second model that is neither true nor false is the prevailing approach to risk and uncertainty. It is essential to know that theory if you are dealing with financial markets. It is a mistake to think it false, and may prove to be an expensive mistake. But it is also a mistake to believe the theory is true. Both the EMH and the theory of subjective expected utility are theories that are illuminating, useful, but not true. That is the nature of knowledge in economics. Good theories are theories that are useful – no more, no less. (Kay, 2010)

This is not an apology for scepticism but rather an observation that models are tools that help us apprehend (in the sense of 'perceive') reality. They are more like reading glasses than like the abstract ideas of Aristotelian epistemology by which the knower is united with the known. This bears on the current reception of Smith's 'invisible hand'. While Smith observed an effect present in market economies, some free-market economists exalt it into a natural law that would have a beneficial effect if only government would stop getting in the way. Smith, on the contrary, warned that capitalists and top management (he used the word 'masters' and dealt mostly with owner-managers) would often collude against their counterparties in other markets (labour, land and supplies) if government did not intervene to keep them honest. Smith did not have a 'model' of the invisible hand, although he demonstrated it with a non-mathematical argument involving four markets (product/service, labour, financing, and real estate). He did not confuse his observation of the 'invisible hand' effect with the determinism of an immutable natural law, although his century is considered to be the century of natural law, and Google points us to several web pages on Adam Smith's three 'natural laws of economics'. In fact, the eighteenth-century notion of natural law was a decadent and simplistic derivative of a more profound notion of natural law characteristic of medieval thought and inspired by classic Greek philosophy. It was functional enough for the development of the scientific method in modern thought (from

Descartes through Kant to Newton) but not worthy of Adam Smith, who was not studying a mechanism.

What changes would enhance the accuracy of the models we now possess? After the fiasco of models as a contributing cause of the crisis, the move is to incorporate the financial sector into models of the economy and thus, supposedly, to provide more realistic input back into the financial models. 'Buttonwood' – the blog alias of one *Economist* journalist – tells us, 'In my view, economists have failed to take enough account of the impact of financial markets, perhaps because, until the 1980s, these markets seemed relatively unimportant' (Buttonwood, 9 August 2010). Another, unsigned, article from the *Economist* also testifies to the need for incorporating financial markets, with their imperfections, into economic models, but warns that it is the basic models that end up influencing policy rather than the nuances of the more complicated models. (*Economist*, 16 July 2009, The other-worldly philosophers)

One of the proponents of trashing models is George Soros. After observing that economics has had a tendency to model itself on theoretical physics – recall that at least two of the articles cited in this volume are from the journal *Physica* – with an intellectual structure of axioms and hypotheses derived from these axioms, asks whether the axioms resemble reality. He notes that Euclidean axioms resemble reality and produce a viable geometry. The axioms of economics do not resemble reality according to Soros, and he cites precisely the two theories cited by John Kay:

> Rational expectations theory and the efficient market hypothesis are products of this approach. Unfortunately they proved to be unsound.... rational expectations theory does not [resemble reality]. It postulates that there is a correct view of the future to which the views of all the participants tend to converge. But the correct view is correct only if it is universally adopted by all the participants –an unlikely prospect. Indeed, if it is unrealistic to expect all participants to subscribe to the theory of rational expectations, it is irrational for any participant to adopt it. Anyhow, rational expectations theory was pretty conclusively falsified by the crash of 2008 which caught most participants and most regulators unawares. The crash of 2008 also falsified the Efficient Market Hypothesis because it was generated by internal developments within the financial markets, not by external shocks, as the hypothesis postulates. (Soros, 2010)

Soros expects a good model to tell us about the future; Professor Kay, Professor Makiw and a myriad of other economists tell us that economists and their models are not for predicting.[2] What is the purpose of these models if they do not serve for predicting? They illuminate, responds Kay. But they can clearly mislead us, as they did prior to the 2001 crisis. Where was the illumination then?

Soros suggests a return to the human decision-maker to found a more realistic economics.[3] This is precisely the approach of the Austrian economists from whom he has such great distance both politically and in terms of conclusions. Roger E. Backhouse, Professor of Economics at the University of Birmingham, United Kingdom, not an Austrian economist, writes, 'It is my view that the distinctive feature of mainstream economics, distinguishing it from Austrian economics, is model-building and the important point about models is that they are not the real thing'. This does not mean that there is nothing for mainstream economists to learn from Austrian economics, nor vice versa. It means, on the contrary, that there is an opportunity for much cross-pollination. Among the many recommendations that Backhouse offers both mainstream economists and Austrian economists, two are relevant here. First, mainstream economists would do well to adopt more awareness of their models: perfect competition, equilibrium, stable preferences, given technology and Pareto efficiency as a welfare criterion. This will help remind them that those models are not reality. Second, Austrian economists in turn need to rediscover that, with all its shortcomings, mathematics can help us gain insight alongside natural language explanations.

The twentieth-century understanding of the scientific method was to refine scientific models by falsification. Perhaps this is more useful in the natural sciences than in economics. In economics, the push towards more 'realistic' models has taken the form of behavioural economics, in which additions to the rational model are made either piecemeal, based on oversimplified experimentation, or else using whole-cloth theories of human behaviour which are alternative, but no more accurate than the basic rational model.

The science of economics does not seek to model human economic behaviour. Perhaps that would be the goal of economic anthropology. The object of economic science is the economic dimension of human life, and that dimension is an abstraction from human life. If we seek to predict human behaviour in things economic, then we must await conclusive research from economic anthropology and economic sociology.

Economists often think that this is their job and thus wander from their field of competence and impose dogma on other human sciences.

Difference of opinion, or different scientific conclusions?
Edward L. Glaeser, an economics professor at Harvard, noted that we all have learned a lesson on the fragility of the economy. In order to fix things, however, we face problems that require two sets of tools: problems that require 'microeconomic analysis, where we have some hope of consensus, and those that require the tools of macroeconomics, where intellectual wars still rage' (Glaeser, 2010). These same wars are evident in the media.

If economists are so strongly divided, we may well entertain doubts as to the nature of our knowledge about economics. Is economics indeed a science, in which only incidental issues and new frontiers give rise to differences of opinion? Or is much of economics really just ideology, with competing systems of ideas justifying the worldview of different economists? Alan Lewis writes, 'it is difficult to see how these competing claims can be resolved by any kind of empirical test as these belief systems are resistant to change, comprising, in a Kuhnian sense, incommensurate paradigms' (Lewis, 2010).

An unintended rebuttal comes from Guy Sorman (2009). He demonstrates that economics *does* follow an empirical method and has used it to arrive at a series of conclusions about the roads that do *not* lead to prosperity. Although his conclusions are quite moderate and probably acceptable to both saltwater and freshwater and all mainstream economists, the spirit of freshwater economists (even if tenured at Columbia, Stanford and Princeton) predominates in his evidence. So, whether or not it is valid, the rebuttal does not work; it ends up being one more missile in the intellectual war.

Peter Foster (2008) of the *National Post* in Canada wrote: 'The very fact that Messrs. Stiglitz and Buchanan are Nobel economics laureates with diametrically opposed views was one of the reasons Alfred Nobel never set up a prize for economics in the first place (it was added later by Swedish bankers). Economics is not a science in which there is a broad body of knowledge on which all economists agree. Rather – when it is not mathematically abstruse and irrelevant – it is a field of ideological conflict which many economists enter intent on "improving" markets without understanding them in the first place.'

While this assertion may be partly correct, perhaps there is room to learn a little from each of the positions we have seen, in terms of both what knowledge economics does afford and what it tells us about the financial crisis.

Because the 2007–2010 financial crisis is fading into the background – at least for now, as reforms are newly minted and the euro crisis begins to blur with the 2007–2010 crisis in popular consciousness – a good place to begin is a comparison of views relevant to the economic crisis, such as those on the question of full employment. The following quote from a saltwater economist presents two views on employment: 'One can view mass unemployment as a phenomenon of "imperfect labor markets" (the neoclassical framework) requiring real wage reductions as the principal solution. Or, one can view mass unemployment as mainly a phenomenon of inadequate effective demand (the Keynesian theoretical position), requiring mechanisms to support the incomes of those who are not adequately paid in private markets' (Galbraith 2001).

Both perspectives understand the problem as one of mechanisms. They differ as to the precise mechanism, the means to address the problem, and also in the human issue behind the problem. Unemployment or low-wage labour is not a good thing for human beings, although generous unemployment benefits can both mitigate and complicate the problem. The Keynesian approach addresses this issue by seeking employment for all at high wages; the neoclassical approach addresses it by supply and demand for labour – lowering the price of labour until there is demand for it.

Of the two approaches, the neoclassical as stated by John Kenneth Galbraith is clearly further abstracted from the reality of the economy. It recovers from this position with another abstraction. The following paragraphs explain this.

The neoclassical solution for unemployment is lower wages, but these lower wages do not always help in the search for a job. Someone living in Calgary, Canada (the city with the highest GDP per capita in North America) soon learns that transport and lodging issues impose a lower limit on salary. In other words, there are other supply and demand curves for economists to draw. Economics teaching is a little bit guilty here: the supply and demand curves, already an abstract from the real marketplace, are a good way of depicting how economists conceive of price equilibrium. They certainly do not depict how Adam Smith conceived price is determination and the distribution of goods and services across all of society, because Adam Smith, aside from not drawing any curves, used four different markets simultaneously to explain the effect.

Also, if you cannot eat and sleep, you cannot work. If you have no education, you cannot work well. Beyond eating and shelter, there are a series of basic human needs and rights that are constrained by economic reality: founding a family and educating children, for example. It is not the job of the economy or economists to provide for those rights, but 'temporary' changes in the economy can have dramatic impacts on those rights once they have been exercised.

The neoclassical response is not to increase wages – which would eliminate their solution to full employment – but rather to observe that there are too many workers at the low end of the wage scale. They argue that this is not a wage problem, but rather a structural problem. There are not enough skilled workers, perhaps. This may be a problem of general education (blame the government?) or of changes in technology that require new skills and replace others (blame employers for not 'retooling' their employees or government for not foreseeing this change?), or of migration of low-skill jobs out of the country (blame McDonald's for not opening enough franchises?)

Thus the neoclassical approach to full employment has at least two components: workers have to negotiate their wage on the marketplace, and they have to have relevant skills to negotiate a higher wage. Government interference in the first component can discourage adequate action on the second. By providing timely information (perhaps an impossible task), the government can encourage people to acquire the right skills. This clearly enters difficult social territory. If a boy grows up in a ghetto with his single mum where his only role models are transient drugs dealers, star athletes and rap singers, then drug dealing and gang membership may seem like his only choice if he lacks rapping or athletic talent. There are difficult social issues impacted by economics, but they should not be solved by economists, or at least not at the moment of arriving at a general understanding of the economy.

The Keynesian approach is to inject money into the economy in order to create jobs; this should have the added effect of raising the demand curve (for jobs) and thus the 'equilibrium price' for jobs: higher wages. This again is an abstraction: what kind of jobs will be created – high end or low end? Keynes said it didn't matter how the money was spent, so low-end jobs would do just fine – digging holes and then refilling them. His point was that while the purpose of the economy was to create wealth as well as distribute it, the distribution of wealth is crucial for the operation of the economic mechanism. Wealth distribution would thus be an effectiveness issue as well as a social justice issue. In a sense, this is a somewhat more sophisticated version of Marx's theory of crises and the ultimate failure of the capitalist system.[4] Keynes was interested not in furthering the failure of capitalism, but in overcoming the crises that it might encounter. He seems to have found a solution in terms of his model of the economy, although perhaps he did not sufficiently consider all the possible consequences of his spending solution. He probably would agree today that money would be better spent improving strategic transportation and education (both technically useful and culturally enriching) than on digging holes and then refilling them, provided those monies arrived to people who needed greater purchasing power. Thus it would be more faithful to Keynes, if not to his writings, to fund poor parents who want to send their children to (better-quality) private schools, rather than increase teachers' salaries or purchase computers for use in public schools.

Although Keynes saw that spending power could prime the pump, he could not foresee that the executors of his intellectual inheritance would spend the money without putting it into the hands of those with no purchasing power.

Austrian economists are justly proud of emphasizing the 'intertemporal' effects on capital structure. They also understand that education for skills, although it is not capital, is an important factor in the creation of wealth and obtaining employment. They rephrase this as a 'structural problem'. Why can they not recover the insight of Keynes described in the previous paragraphs, if not as a general principle, at least as a compromise solution in the real-world economy as we find it? The starting point of Austrian economics is the individual human actor, with his intentions and his limitations. Is not the reality of government part of the limitations of the individual? Cannot the government – albeit heavy-handedly – aid the individual to get better education by increasing his purchasing power to do so without imposing this or that educational institution? What is wrong with the classic solution of redistributing wealth for education in the form of vouchers with which parents can select the school of their choice?

This cursory examination of the models of the Keynesians and the neoclassical economists has revealed a few points for potential agreement among those academics across the intellectual divide who are willing to compromise their political agendas. But perhaps this way out of the intellectual war is a false path if their models themselves are fictions.

At a more theoretical level, examination of the three schools leads to the conclusion that the economy does not exist; there are only human beings acting in human communities. The mechanisms to which the mainstream economists allude are in fact the constraints under which individual human actors – and the moral persons they create – make decisions. These constraints of decision-making are interrelated, and this mesh of interconnectedness is the abstraction we call the 'economy'. This connectedness is affected by the decisions of the actors, by actors in 'other' economies, by government agency, by natural events, by technology and by other human activities. In response to these influences, and in pursuit of their personal goals, individual actors negotiate solutions/transactions that impinge on other transactions via this connectedness, in a gradual process culminating in constant reallocation of capital resources. This may or may not lead to full employment for all. This is called the 'working of the market'. Government can also respond to these influences in an attempt to guide the market back to full employment for all. Two questions must be asked of this possibility: (1) Which does a better job (in terms of employment, prosperity, distribution): market or government? (2) Which is faster: government or market?

The social and moral underpinnings of the crisis

Pensions and the pill

The financial crisis arose from a concurrence of multiple factors in the financial and juridical systems of the United States as well as the public administration of that country. One of the factors was the tremendous availability of capital in search of investment opportunities. In their dissenting statement, Hennessey, Holtz-Eagan and Thomas, commissioners of the US National Commission on the Causes of the Financial and Economic Crisis in the United States, present this availability of capital as the combined effect of the rise of China and the accumulated sovereign funds of oil-rich nations. However, it is also the product of a more profound underlying problem in Western society that contemporary society has avoided addressing in any systematic way, perhaps because it is too obvious to be noticed, perhaps because the topic is taboo.

We could say that the crisis is a side effect of the birth control pill.

An increasingly unbalanced population pyramid characterizes Western societies because of the birth control pill, or at least because of the use we have made of it, and an ever-larger burden of a retired or disabled population rests on the shoulders of an ever-smaller working population. Although an obvious corollary to what some demographers have called the 'demographic dividend', this negative effect of decreased fertility is kept in the silo of 'ageing societies' (usually pointing to Japan) separate from the silo of the demographic dividend. Nonetheless, the reality behind the shift in the population pyramid first gave great impulse to pension funds as money replaced children as the key to retirement, and then subsequently, as baby boomers reached retirement, has put great pressure on these pension funds, which have been seeking creative ways to obtain a higher return on investments while respecting the prudential constraints on the risk they may incur. Mortgage-backed securities seemed a solution made in heaven: great returns, almost no risk. Indeed, how could any decision-maker/portfolio manager of a pension fund keep his job if he had not invested in such securities?

We may perhaps deal with the fallacies that led to the mortgage-backed securities blow-up: poor models, superficial rating, incompetent (or overly routine) due diligence, and so on. In this way, mortgage-backed securities may no longer tempt pension funds again. But something else will, unless we accept the consequences of underfunding or else adopt policies of massive immigration of youth.

Of course, even if there were no tremendous pressure for performance on these funds, individual investors for these funds would still have the ambition to excel in their personal performance.

Individual citizens

Many explain the crisis with one word: greed. If pressed, they might give a second word: avarice. For similar reasons, others blame the free market because it is based – they say – on greed. The greedy people wear navy blue suits and work on Wall Street. We have to stop lying to ourselves. By the time a tot reaches three years old, he has mastered a phrase that he will often repeat to his parents: 'not me'. Who stole the biscuits? Who broke the lamp? Not me. Assuming responsibility and recognizing our faults is part of growing into maturity. Perhaps we never completely do that. Certainly there has been a lot of finger pointing during and following the crisis. But most of the victims of the crisis have been willing victims. Some of them work on Wall Street; others work (or worked) on Main Street.

A second issue is the human tendency to reduce our work to a game.

Blogger and best-selling author Tim Ferris claims he won the 1999 USAWKF Sanshou championship. By exploiting the loopholes in the rulebook, he was able to combat opponents from a lower weight category and win by pushing his opponent out of the ring. His tactics were effective for the 'game', but would be completely ineffective in the real-world application of the martial art. This does not mean that he cheated. In a sense, creating an unfair advantage is a fundamental principle of the martial arts. Rather, it means that his tactics would be useless on the street (where of course he would use other tactics because he is intelligent and has martial skills). In an analogous way, we do the same when we work for extrinsic incentives rather than the desire to do a great job. The beauty of the sophisticated crafts of the financial industry have been completely lost in the competition to bring home the most goodies and to boast about hoodwinking a naïve client – or naïve employer. We are far removed from the Zen of Motorcycle Maintenance, never mind the lessons of the story of Cain and Abel. This is a problem in any profession, but it is exacerbated in the case of the finance industry.

Even the notion of success can divert us from the pursuit of high-quality work. Success is socially defined and socially contrived as well. In most of South-east Asia, success depends far more on contacts and influence than it does on performance. In most advanced economies, success is far more performance based. But that performance is still judged, measured and defined by other people.

Many trace the origins of Western civilization to the encounter of the Judaeo-Christian tradition, which valued work, with the acme of classic Greek civilization, which valued leisure for the pursuit of truth and beauty, and with the rational and effective juridical system of the Roman empire. It is striking to contemplate the artistic and intellectual achievements of the golden age of Greece and to realize they were made possible not by enterprise but by piracy and barbaric warfare which were as much about raids and economic advantage as they were about power. Although we owe some of the first notions of economics to the Greeks – Aristotle wrote a treatise on the topic, and Xenophon provides a description of crop futures – they had disdain for productive work and the 'sleazy' activities of business. To this day, many Romance languages use a negative term for business: *neg-ocio*, or the absence of leisure. One of the highest values of the Greeks was fame or glory – not the mysterious divine glory of Christian theology, but simple crass public opinion. Can it surprise us if so many of us eschew quality and detail in our work to pursue success and to quiet our neurosis about what others think?

Notes

1 The Nature and Effects of the 2007–2010 Crisis and Ways to Resolve It

1. http://en.wikipedia.org/wiki/Lehman_Brothers_bankruptcy, accessed 17 February 2012.
2. http://en.wikipedia.org/wiki/Austrian_economics, accessed 17 February 2012.

2 The Roots of the Crisis

1. The agenda item for the 'open meeting' (anyone could attend; few did) reads as follows: Alternative Net Capital Requirements for Broker-Dealers that are Part of Consolidated Supervised Facilities and Supervised Investment Bank Holding Companies. See http://www.sec.gov/news/openmeetings/agenda042804.htm, accessed 25 January 2010. The rule change had been proposed in writing several months before the meeting. Comments on the proposal are to be found at http://www.sec.gov/rules/proposed/s72103.shtml, accessed 25 January 2010. The risk and software consultant Leonard D. Bole was the sole opponent to the change among those who commented the proposal; Commissioner Goldschmid expressed reserves at the meeting but received no support.
2. Some of the investors in these mortgage-backed securities again sought to maximize the return on their capital, and again used other people's money to do that. They bought a portion of the entire issue of securities and combined it with other kinds of debt that they purchased – such as long-term leases, credit card debt – and create another legal entity, to which they sold this debt and which in turn issued securities which gave a right to a participation in the payments on these debts.

    Mortgage-backed securities are part of a more general category called asset-backed securities. These assets may be of many kinds – such as debts, for example. (Debts in the sense that the holder of the debt has a contractual right to a series of payments against the debt.) Thus, within asset-backed securities there is a class of securities that are all backed by debt. The nomenclature for this is not 'debt-backed securities' but rather 'credit debt obligations', with the more often used acronym 'CDO'. When different securities that are all various kinds of CDOs are incorporated into a new issue of securities, as we saw in the previous paragraph, the result is called a 'CDO squared'. (Note that the homeowner with a mortgage would have great difficulty in finding where his mortgage payments go, and so would have an almost impossible task if he wanted to renegotiate different terms with the recipients of his payments.) Including other CDOs in a new CDO issue had the effect of creating demand for the first CDO, somewhat analogous to illegal practices in promoting Ponzi-scheme investments. The SEC has been investigating several ex-investment banks for securities fraud in this regard. Unfortunately, the cases are usually settled with a payment before completion of the process, so that detailed judgements are not rendered and the data will not be accessible to the public. For interesting analyses and graphics illustrating the ownership of CDOs, see http://projects.propublica.org/tables/circular_cdos and also http://www.propublica.org/special/a-banks-best-customer-its-own-cdos. On the cross-ownership of CDOs, see http://orgnet.com/cdo.html.

3 Three Chronologies and the Genesis of the 2007–2010 Crisis

1. Both commercial banks and thrifts ('savings and loans') are depository financial institutions in the United States. In other words, people deposit money in accounts with them. Thrifts are intended to encourage saving capital and homebuying, whereas banks exploit a variety of assets (lending activities).
2. While an individual participates in the economy as a real person, groups of people may act in concert by constituting a moral person, for example a registered business. This registered business has little juridical status, and 'employees', for example, are treated as independent agents before the law with limited legal obligation or right to loyalty to and from the 'employer'. This situation is remedied by obtaining juridical status for the moral person, constituting a new legal entity. Different laws may apply to this new legal entity depending on the goals for which it is created and also depending on the juridical authority that proclaimed and sanctions the law under which it was constituted. In the present case, corporations created to provide financial services may be constituted according to federal law (Washington) or the law of a specific US state, and the constraint is mentioned for those created with a federal charter.
3. The concrete reality of business does not assemble itself in straightforward conceptual ranks, at least in the United States of America. Business law there does not inhibit initiative, at least not to the extent of making facts easier to gather for the researcher! As opportunities arise, businesses exploit them, and thus history is as important as logic in explaining the particular configuration a business organization may have. Some opportunities are... opportune to exploit, others are not. In the case of the warehouse business, warehouse lending can be a way to participate in the business drummed up by competitors. Some warehouse lenders were also originators, some were not. This empirical complexity of business in free markets gives rise to many questions that can only be answered by hard work – either by years of experience in the field or by painstakingly detailed research. For example, how did the multifaceted organizations deal with the unraveling of the securities and securities boom? Were those warehouse lenders that also issued securities the first to stop warehousing lending? Did they have the courage to act more rapidly because they had other sources of income than mortgages? Or did warehouse lenders who were not active in issuing securities react as quickly?

4 Saltwater Economists

References will be given in title, date format for Professors Krugman and Stiglitz, due to the abundance of sources for 2008, 2009 and 2010.

1. Their argument was based upon the behaviour of a mathematical model: a series of equations that represent all of their hypotheses. Because the human mind can handle more than four or five variables only with great difficulty, economists resort to this method to 'verify' the import of a series of hypotheses. Fortunately or unfortunately, such mathematical models require a simplification of reality; for example, one improvement of the Eggertsson and Krugman model was to explicitly take into account... the distinction between debtors and creditors!
2. Although Stiglitz does not actually say that Adam Smith was against government intervention, he comes close: 'Interestingly, there has been no intellectual challenge to the refutation of Adam Smith's invisible hand: individuals and firms, in the pursuit of their self-interest, are not necessarily, or in general, led as if by an invisible hand, to economic efficiency.' Beppe Grillo's Blog (From an interview with Joseph E. Stiglitz entitled *The pact with the devil*, available at http://www.beppegrillo.it/eng/2007/01/stiglitz.html, accessed 10 December 2010.)

    Stiglitz does *not* say that Adam Smith is against any government intervention, but most readers assume this. Smith uses the expression 'invisible hand' once only, in order to explain an effect present in economic transactions. Elsewhere he recognizes that businesses often attempt to avoid this effect. Stiglitz knows this: 'Even Adam Smith recognised that unregulated markets will try to restrict competition' (A crisis of confidence, 22 October 2008).
3. I do not mean that morality is only sentiment, as do some philosophers – simply that some people are emotional rather than rational in their moral judgements and that most of us react emotionally to bad moral behaviour (particularly if we are victims, or the weak are victims).

5 Freshwater Economists, Austrian Economists and Popular Opinion

References will be given in title, date format for Professors Zingales and Cochrane and Schiff due to the abundance of sources for 2007, 2008, 2009 and 2010.

1. In practice the bailouts appear to have been very effective and perhaps a fair deal for taxpayers because the majority of the firms helped (particularly if we look at the size of the firms helped) are back to normal operations, and most have also returned the money received with interest or with a profit. Although this latter fact does not necessarily make the bailout fair, it certainly would reduce the gravity of the injustice if it had been unfair to help the banks and not the average citizen.

6 Conclusion

1. In October 2010 I still entertained the possibility of covering the academic literature and narrowed down the field to 30 articles available on the Social

Science Network website. A week before Christmas 2010, a cursory search for papers on the financial crisis submitted over the previous month returned 178 papers. In March 2011, there were over 4500 papers available on the same database. At the start of November 2011, nearly 8000 documents. While many of these are too specific (to less relevant topics, such as changes in consumer behaviour during the financial crisis), this indicates that it is still too soon to do a literature review.
2. This then raises the inconvenient question of what service economists provide to governments. Perhaps the Austrians are right in wanting governments out of the economy. Austrian economists do recognize a role for government in supporting the market with adequate laws and their sanction. The followers of Ayn Rand – perhaps more radical than Rand herself – go further. See Epstein, 2010.
3. Soros provides an alternative, but with a caveat that he did not permit the models he wishes to replace: 'Some timelessly valid generalizations can serve to explain events but not to predict them.' His alternative, reflexivity, is actually a very interesting insight for the professional investor with a few hundred million to spare, as it provides a rule of thumb for recognizing opportunities for 'arbitrage' between fanciful investors (victims of what he calls 'positive feedback reflexivity') and a more sober appreciation of the market.
4. Marx built his theory on David Ricardo's theory of value, leading necessarily to an unjust (of course in Marx there should be no moral values) distribution of wealth, and on the extension to the whole economy of the tendency of some kinds of manufacture towards scale and concentration. As a result, the end state of the economy was supply in the hands of a few rich families, with the vast mass of population without work and impoverished: thus there would be no demand to supply goods to. There are three problems with Marx's theory. First, even if we accept the incorrect hypotheses about value and concentration, the supply-demand problem would be corrected long before the ultimate crash he alludes to. Second, not all manufacture tends towards concentration, and certainly not all services. Third, Marx is right in concluding that wages are necessarily unjust if we accept Ricardo's incorrect theory of value. This theory is that the value of a good or service is the amount of work 'contained' in it. This is very appealing because it would mean – in theory, not in practice – that we could account for the value of any good or service given the time and the money to get all the information. We would simply have to account for all the work involved from the moment shovel hit the ground (well, we may have a vicious circle here, since you need to dig to get the iron ore for the shovel – but that is just going into too much detail, and we guess the contribution of that vicious circle). It is also very illusory, because no one values anything simply because there is a lot of work put into it (an exception being middle-level art, such as the small series silk embroideries of Vietnam, for which prices vary according to the complexity of the image rather than the size of the embroidery). This illusion leads to subsistence wages. How much work is 'contained' in a worker? There is the work used to produce food, shelter and sufficient education to do his job, count his money and communicate with workers: the work that produces a subsistence level of goods and services.

Bibliography

Statistical sources such as agencies dependent on the federal government of the United States of America, readily localized on the Internet, are not listed in this bibliography.

Ashcraft, Adam B. and Schuermann, Til (July 2008), 'Understanding the Securitization of Subprime Mortgage Credit', *Federal Reserve Bank of New York*, available at http://www.newyorkfed.org/research/staff_reports/sr318.pdf; later published as 'Understanding the Securitization of Subprime Mortgage Credit', *Foundations and Trends in Finance* 2, No. 3, 191–309.

Backhouse, Roger E. (Summer 2000), 'Austrian Economics and the Mainstream: View from the Boundary', *The Quarterly Journal of Austrian Economics*, Vol. 3, No. 2, 31–43.

Baily, Martin Neil, Litan, Robert E. and Johnson, Matthew S. (2008), 'The Origins of the Financial Crisis', *The Initiative on Business and Public Policy Fixing Finance Series* – Paper 3, 32.

Baker, Dean (2007), 'Housing bubble update: 10 economic indicator to watch', available at http://www.cepr.net/documents/publications/housing_indicators_2007_02.pdf, accessed 5 January 2011.

Balzli, Beat and Schiessi, Michaela (8 July 2009), 'The Man Nobody Wanted to Hear. Global Banking Economist Warned of Coming Crisis', *Spiegel Online International*, available at http://www.spiegel.de/international/business/0,1518,635051,00.html, accessed 18 December 2010.

Barr, Alistair (2 August 2007), 'Parts of secondary mortgage market freeze up', *MarketWatch*, http://www.marketwatch.com/story/parts-of-secondary-mortgage-market-freeze-up-for-lenders?siteid=rss, accessed 3 February 2010.

Barro, Robert J. and Redlick, Charles J. (1 October 2009), 'Stimulus Spending Doesn't Work', *Wall Street Journal*, available at http://online.wsj.com/article/SB10001424052748704471504574440723298786310.html, accessed 8 December 2010.

Barth, James R., Tong Li, Triphon Phumiwasana and Glenn Yago (January–March 2008), 'A Short History of the Sub-Prime Mortgage Market Meltdown', *GH Bank Housing Journal*, Vol. 2, No. 2, available at http://www.ghbhomecenter.com/journal/GHBEng-sub.php?ids=19, accessed 20 November 2011.

Bernanke, Ben S. (2008), 'Federal Reserve Policies in the Financial Crisis', available at http://www.federalreserve.gov/newsevents/speech/bernanke20081201a.htm, accessed 8 December 2010.

Bernanke, Ben S. (15 October 2008), 'Stabilizing the Financial Markets and the Economy', speech given at the Economic Club of New York, New York, available at http://www.federalreserve.gov/newsevents/speech/bernanke20081015a.htm accessed 10 November 2011.

Bernanke, Ben S. (16 November 2009), 'On the Outlook for the Economy and Policy', speech at the Economic Club of New York, available at http://www.

Bibliography 163

federalreserve.gov/newsevents/speech/bernanke20091116a.htm, accessed 12 December 2010.

Brooks, Rick and Simon, Ruth (3 December 2007), 'Subprime debacle traps even very credit-worthy', http://online.wsj.com/article/SB119662974358911035.html, accessed 5 January 2010.

Brunnermeier, Markus K. (December 2008), 'Deciphering the Liquidity and Credit Crunch', *Working Paper*. Later published in the *Journal of Economic Perspectives*, American Economic Association, Vol. 23, No. 1, 77–100 (Winter 2009).

Buffet, Warren (2003), Letter to shareholders, *2002 Annual Report - Berkshire Hathaway Inc*, 3–23 (the section on derivatives begins on page13), available at http://www.berkshirehathaway.com/2002ar/2002ar.pdf.

Burry, Michael (7 November 2006), *A Primer on Scion Capital's Subprime Mortgage Short*, letter to clients of Scion Capital, available at http://www.scioncapital.com/PDFs/Scion%202006%204Q%20RMBS%20CDS%20Primer%20and%20FAQ.pdf, accessed 2 August 2011.

Buttonwood (9 August 2010), 'Day of the (brain) dead', Buttonwood's notebook, *The Economist Online*, available at http://www.economist.com/blogs/buttonwood/2010/08/fiscal_monetary_policy_and_state_economics, accessed 4 January 2011.

Carrick, Alex (3 December 2009), 'U.S. and Canada Moved away from Deflation in October', *Daily Commercial News and Construction Record*, available at http://dcnonl.com/article/id36595, accessed 19 March 2010.

Chandra, Shobhana (4 August 2009), 'U.S. Incomes Fall 1.3%, Biggest Drop in Four Years (Update3)', *Bloomberg*, available at http://www.bloomberg.com/apps/news?pid=newsarchive&sid=aT8rdIv7186Q Accessed 20 December 2010.

Cochrane, John H. (n.d.), *'Fiscal Stimulus, RIP'*, available at http://faculty.chicagobooth.edu/john.cochrane/research/papers/stimulus_rip.html, accessed 3 January 2011.

Cochrane, John H. (2 October 2008), 'The Monster Returns', *The New York Times*, available at http://freakonomics.blogs.nytimes.com/2008/10/02/john-cochrane-on-why-the-bailout-plan-would-be-a-disaster, accessed 15 December 2010.

Cochrane, John H. (Winter 2009–2010) 'Lessons from the Financial Crisis', *Regulation*, 34.

Cochrane, John P. (Fall 2010), 'Capital in Disequilibrium: Understanding the "Great Recession" and the Potential for Recovery', *Quarterly Journal of Austrian Economics*, Vol. 13, No. 3, 42–63, specifically on pages 42 and 52.

Davies, Daniel (23 March 2010), 'Crisis is the normal state', available at http://crookedtimber.org/?s=krugman+banking+crises, accessed 8 December 2010.

de Nooy, Wouter, Andrej Mrvar and Vladimir Batagelj (2005), *Exploratory Social Network Analysis with Pajek*, Cambridge University Press, Cambridge.

DeGennaro, Ramon P. (Fall 2009), 'It's Not Just Subprime!', *The Journal of Private Enterprise*, Vol. 25, No. 1, 23–30.

Deschamps, Pascale-Marie (8 December 2010, updated 13 December 2010), 'Les cerveaux de Chicago à l'épreuve de la crise', *Les Echos*, available at http://www.lesechos.fr/management/actu/020989490016-les-cerveaux-de-chicago-a-l-epreuve-de-la-crise.htm, accessed 15 December 2010.

Bibliography

Dodd, Randall (December 2007), 'Tentacles of a Crisis Finance and Development', *Finanace & Development*, Vol. 44, No. 4, 2.

Economist Debates (20 March 2010), available at http://www.economist.com/debate/days/view/473, accessed 21 March 2012.

Eggertsson, Gauti B, and Krugman, Paul (16 November 2010) 'Debt, deleveraging, and the liquidity trap: A Fisher-Minsky-Koo approach', available at http://www.princeton.edu/~pkrugman/debt_deleveraging_ge_pk.pdf, accessed 3 January 2010.

Eggertsson, Gauti B. and Krugman, Paul (November 2010), 'Debt, Deleveraging, and the Liquidity Trap: A Fisher-Minsky-Koo approach'. A cut and paste summary can be found in Paul Krugman, 18 November 2010, Debt, Deleveraging, and the Liquidity Trap, at http://www.voxeu.org/index.php?q=node/5823 accessed 8 December 2010.

Epstein, Alex (n.d.), *A Call for the Separation of State and Economics*, available at www.aynrand.org/site/DocServer/separation_of_econ_and_state_long.pdf The authorship is stated at http://blog.aynrandcenter.org/separation-of-state-and-economics-a-new-ideal-for-america/ both pages were accessed 1 August 2011.

FCIC (The National Commission on the Causes of the Financial and Economic Crisis in the United States) (2011), *Financial Commission Inquiry Report*, US Independent Agencies and Commissions. Also available at http://www.fcic.gov/report

FDIC (2006), Report No. 06-011, Challenges and FDIC Efforts Related to Predatory Lending, available at www.fdicig.gov/2006reports.asp accessed 11 November 2011.

FDIC (n.d.), *When a Bank Fails – Facts for Depositors, Creditors, and Borrowers*, available at http://www.fdic.gov/consumers/banking/facts/index.html Accessed 10 November 2011.

FHFA (2010), http://www.fhfa.gov/webfiles/16591/ConservatorsRpt82610.pdf accessed 16 December 2010.

Fannie Mae (FNMA) (6 March 2008), *Announcement 08-0, Amends these Guides: Selling Temporary Increase to Our Conventional Loan Limits*.

Federal Reserve Bank (updated regularly), *Flow of Funds accounts* at http://www.federalreserve.gov/releases/z1/Current/z1r-2.pdf, accessed 16 March 2010.

Federal Reserve Bank of Boston (1993), *A Guide To Equal Opportunity Lending*, available at http://www.bos.frb.org/commdev/commaff/closingt.pdf

Frankel, Allen B. (2009), 'The risk of relying on reputational capital: a case study of the 2007 failure of New Century Financial', *BIS Working Papers* No. 294.

Freddie Mac or Federal Home Mortgage Corporation (6 May 2009), 'Housing and Mortgage Market Update', *Philadelphia Council for Business Economics*, Philadelphia, PA (presented by Frank Nothaft, chief economist for Freddie Mac).

Foster, Peter (2008), 'Nobel savages', *The National Post*, available at http://www.canada.com/nationalpost/columnists/story.html?id=b5e83ae5-2eb6-4448-94d8-e4abe7349959&k=92292, accessed 1 August 2011.

Galbraith, James K. (January 2001), 'A contribution on the state of economics in France and the world', *Post-autistic Economics Newsletter*, No. 4, available at http://www.paecon.net/PAEtexts/Galbraith1.htm, accessed 21 December 2010.

Bibliography 165

Geithner, Timothy F. (9 June 2008), 'Reducing systemic risk in a dynamic financial system', *The Economic Club of New York*, New York City, available at http://www.newyorkfed.org/newsevents/speeches/2008/tfg080609.html, accessed on 18 January 2010.

Ginnie Mae (n.d.), *Who we are. What we do. Why it makes a difference*, available at http://www.ginniemae.gov/about/about.asp?Section=About, accessed 3 February 2010.

Glaeser, Edward L. (1 June 2010), 'What we don't know, and perhaps can't', *New York Times*, available at http://economix.blogs.nytimes.com/2010/06/01/what-we-dont-know-and-perhaps-cant, accessed 20 December 2010.

Goldman Sachs (2008), Annual Report 2008.

Gordon, Robert J. and Krenn, Robert (2010), 'The end of the great depression, 1939–41: policy contributions and fiscal multipliers', *NBER Working Paper*, No. 16380.

Greenberg, Hank (5 January 2011), 'Why did we nationalize AIG?', *Wall Street Journal*, available online at http://online.wsj.com/article/SB10001424052748704723104576062083357423022.html, accessed 10 November 2011.

Grillo, Beppe (2007), from an interview with Joseph E. Stiglitz entitled 'The pact with the devil', available at http://www.beppegrillo.it/eng/2007/01/stiglitz.html, accessed 10 December 2010.

Hart, Oliver and Luigi Zingales (23 November 2010), 'How to improve the financial-reform law a brief proposal to protect the system – without stifling innovation', *City Journal*, reproduced in Luigi Zingales (2010) but undated, *My Losing Battle Against the Leviathan* (Public interventions of a desperate free-market economist), p.95, The University of Chicago Booth School of Business, available at http://faculty.chicagobooth.edu/luigi.zingales/papers/2010ZingalesPamphlet.pdf, accessed 15 December 2010.

Jackson, Gerard (27 October 2008), 'Paul Krugman's explanation of the financial crisis is pure baloney', *Brookes.com* available at http://www.brookesnews.com/082710krugman.html, accessed 11 November 2011.

Johnson, Simon (May 2009), 'The quiet coup', *The Atlantic Monthly*, available at http://www.theatlantic.com/magazine/archive/2009/05/the-quiet-coup/7364, accessed 23 March 2010.

Kay, John (2010), 'Knowledge in economics', in *The Economic Crisis and the State of Economics*, edited by Robert Skidelsky and Christian Westerlind Wigström, Palgrave Macmillan, 91–92 .

Korn, Marjorie (1 October 2008) 'Bailout bill's stealthy authorship potentially problematic', *Medill Reports*, available at http://news.medill.northwestern.edu/washington/news.aspx?id=99511, accessed 15 December 2010.

Krugman, Paul (2007), 'Workouts, not bailouts', available at http://www.nytimes.com/2007/08/17/opinion/17krugman.html, accessed 10 November 2011. A version of this op-ed appeared in print on 17 August 2007, on page A23 of the New York edition of the New York Times.

Krugman, Paul (21 September 2008), 'Thinking the bailout through', available at http://krugman.blogs.nytimes.com/2008/09/21/thinking-the-bailout-through/ accessed 10 November 2011.

Krugman, Paul (28 September 2008), 'The good, the bad, and the ugly', available at http://krugman.blogs.nytimes.com/2008/09/28/the-good-the-bad-and-the-ugly/ accessed 10 November 2011.

166 Bibliography

Krugman, Paul (29 September 2008), 'Bailout questions answered', available at http://krugman.blogs.nytimes.com/2008/09/29/bailout-questions-answered/, accessed 10 November 2011.

Krugman, Paul (10 November 2008), 'Stimulus math (wonkish)', available at http://krugman.blogs.nytimes.com/2008/11/10/stimulus-math-wonkish/, accessed 10 November 2011.

Krugman, Paul (18 December 2008), 'What to do', available at http://www.nybooks.com/articles/archives/2008/dec/18/what-to-do/, accessed 10 November 2011. This appeared in print in the18 December 2008 issue of *The New York Review of Books*.

Krugman, Paul (1 February 2009), 'Bailouts for bunglers', available at http://www.nytimes.com/2009/02/02/opinion/02krugman.html, accessed 10 November 2011. A version of this article appeared in print on 2 February 2009, on page A21 of the New York edition of *The New York Times*.

Krugman, Paul (22 March 2009), 'Financial policy despair', available at http://www.nytimes.com/2009/03/23/opinion/23krugman.html, accessed 10 November 2011.

Krugman, Paul (23 March 2010), 'Jamie Dimon was right', available at http://krugman.blogs.nytimes.com/2010/03/23/jamie-dimon-was-right, accessed 8 December 2010.

Krugman, Paul (12 October 2010), 'Debunking the myth of Obama's big spending', available at http://www.pressdemocrat.com/article/20101012/opinion/101019940, accessed 7 December 2010.

Krugman, Paul (5 November 2010), 'Obama's lack of audacity behind economy's woes', *The New York Times*. No longer available on the Internet.

Krugman, Paul (18 November 2010), 'Debt, Deleveraging, and the Liquidity Trap', available at http://www.voxeu.org/index.php?q=node/5823, accessed 8 December 2010.

Krugman & Co. (25 November 2010), 'Economics: not nice, not fair, not pretty', *The New York Times*, available at http://archive.truthout.org/economics-not-nice-not-fair-not-pretty65362, accessed 10 November 2011.

Krugman, Paul and Wells, Robin (14 October 2010), 'The Way out of the slump', *The New York Review of Books*, available at http://www.nybooks.com/articles/archives/2010/oct/14/way-out-slump/?pagination=false, accessed 10 November 2011.

Lacroix, Kevin M. (13 January 2008), '"CDO squared securities" lawsuit hits MBIA', available at http://www.dandodiary.com/2008/01/articles/subprime-litigation/cdo-squared-securities-lawsuit-hits-mbia, accessed September 2009.

Laeven, Luc and Valencia, Fabian (2008), 'Systemic Banking Crises: A New Database', *IMF Working Paper* 08/224.

Leonnig ,Carol D. (10 June 2008), 'How HUD mortgage policy fed the crisis', *Washington Post*.

Lewis, Alan (2010), 'The Credit Crunch: Ideological, Psychological and Epistemological Perspectives', *The Journal of Socio-Economics*, Vol. 39, 127–131.

Liebowitz, Stan (5 February 2008), 'How feds invited the mortgage mess', *New York Post*, available at http://www.nypost.com/p/news/opinion/opedcolumnists/item_Qjl08vDbysbe6LWDxcq03J, accessed 11 January 2010.

Bibliography 167

Lim, Bomi and Heath, Michael (13 October 2010), 'Krugman, Ferguson Argue over U.S. Fiscal Stimulus', *Bloomberg News*, available at http://www.bloomberg.com/news/2010-10-13/krugman-clashes-with-niall-ferguson-over-u-s-fiscal-stimulus-second-round.html, accessed 8 December 2010.

Maddow, Rachel (20 April 2010), Interview with Paul Krugman, *The Rachel Maddow Show*: transcript available at http://www.pkarchive.org/economy/RMS042010.html, accessed 11 November 2011.

Meredith Whitney Advisory Group LLC (2010), 'Tragedy of the commons: launching ratings on the top 15 States', reported at http://finance.fortune.cnn.com/2010/09/28/meredith-whitneys-new-target-the-states/ and reiterated here http://www.bloomberg.com/news/2011-05-04/whitney-defends-her-prediction-of-hundreds-of-billions-in-muni-defaults.html, both accessed 1 June 2011.

Mirowski, Philip (Summer 2010), 'The Great Mortification: Economists' Responses to the Crisis of 2007-(and counting)', *The Hedgehog Review* 12.3, available at http://www.iasc-culture.org/publications_article_2010_Summer_mirowski.php#, accessed 20 December 2010.

Muolo, Paul (July 2007), 'Of Top-25 subprime funders, four in '06 went bust', *US Banker*. available at http://findarticles.com/p/articles/mi_km2929/is_200707/ai_n19396632/?tag=content;col1, accessed 18 January 2011.

Nasiripour, Shahien (2010), Stiglitz, Nobel Prize-Winning Economist, Says Federal Reserve System 'Corrupt', *Huffington Post*, available at http://www.huffingtonpost.com/2010/03/03/stiglitz-nobel-prize-winn_n_484943.html, accessed 29 August 2011.

Office of the Comptroller of the Currency, Board of Governors of the Federal Reserve System, Federal Deposit Insurance Corporation, and Office of Thrift Supervision (2001), Interagency Expanded Guidance for Subprime Lending Programs, available at http://www.occ.treas.gov/news-issuances/bulletins/2001/bulletin-2001-6a.pdf.

Office of Federal Housing Enterprise Oversight (OFHEO) (2007), Mortgage Markets and the Enterprises in 2007, original publication July 2008, revised February 2009, OFHEO research paper.

P.W. (17 December 2010), 'Shafts of light between the storm clouds', *The Economist*, available at http://www.economist.com/blogs/blighty/2010/12/bank_englands_financial_stability_report, accessed 19 December 2010.

Philippon, Thomas (2008), '*The Evolution of the US Financial Industry from 1860 to 2007: Theory and Evidence*', NYU working paper available at http://economics.stanford.edu/files/Philippon5_20.pdf

Rajan, Raghuram (2005), *The Greenspan Era: Lessons for the Future*, speech transcript available at http://www.imf.org/external/np/speeches/2005/082705.htm The published article is Raghuram Rajan (2006), 'Has Financial Development Made the World Riskier?', *European Financial Management*, Vol. 12, No. 4, 499–533, available at http://onlinelibrary.wiley.com/doi/10.1111/j.1468-036X.2006.00330.x/full Donald L Kohn's commentary on the paper is a tribute to the Greenspan 'doctrine' and makes the unfortunate implication that systematic risk had NOT increased -although in remarkably unquotable wording. See http://kcfed.org/publicat/sympos/2005/pdf/Kohn2005.pdf, p.373. In contrast, Hun Song Shin's commentary provided and a simple

168 Bibliography

metaphor to understand the potential for systematic risk. This metaphor provides a complement to Keynes metaphor of musical chairs. The Hun Song Shin commentary is available at http://www.kc.frb.org/publicat/sympos/2005/pdf/Shin2005.pdf. All documents accessed 1 June 2011.

Rockwell, Llewellyn H. (10 September 2008), *Don't Bail Them Out*, available at http://mises.org/story/3104, accessed 12 August 2009.

Rothbard, Murray N. (1969), *Economic Depressions: Their Cause and Cure*, available at http://mises.org/tradcycl/econdepr.asp, accessed 11 February 2010.

Schiff, Peter (6 December 2007), 'The mother of all bad ideas', http://www.europac.net/commentaries/mother_all_bad_ideas, accessed 11 November 2011.

Schiff, Peter (2 March 2010), 'Don't bet on a recovery', LewRockwell.com, available at http://www.lewrockwell.com/schiff/schiff75.1.html, accessed 11 November 2011.

Schiff, Peter (9 April 2010), 'Krugman strikes again', available at http://www.europac.net/commentaries/krugman_strikes_again, accessed 20 December 2010.

Schiff, Peter, (8 June 2010), 'The phantom recovery', available at http://www.lewrockwell.com/schiff/schiff92.1.html, accessed 5 November 2011.

Schiff, Peter (19 July 2010), 'Why not another world war?', available at http://www.europac.net/commentaries/why_not_another_world_war, accessed 13 December 2010.

Schiff, Peter (28 August 2010) 'Academic and press economic forecasters flying blind', available at http://www.marketoracle.co.uk/article22253.html, accessed 12 December 2010.

Schiff, Peter (8 October 2010), 'The hail Mary', available at http://www.europac.net/commentaries/hail_mary, accessed 13 December 2010.

Schiff, Peter (3 December 2010), 'More stimulus means fewer jobs', available at http://www.europac.net/commentaries/more_stimulus_means_fewer_jobs, accessed 13 December 2010.

Schonberger, Jennifer (9 August 2010), Peter Schiff: 'We're in the early stages of a depression', *The Motley Fool*, available at http://www.fool.com/investing/general/2010/08/09/peter-schiff-were-in-the-early-stagesof-a-depress.aspx, accessed 11 November 2011.

Shiller, Robert J. (18 November 2010), 'Shorting fiscal consolidation', available at http://www.project-syndicate.org/commentary/shiller74/English, accessed 8 December 2010.

Shostak, Frank (29 September 2008) 'The Rescue Package Will Delay Recovery', *Ludwig von Mises Institute*, available at http://mises.org/daily/3131/The-Rescue-Package-Will-Delay-Recovery, accessed 9 November 2011.

Siegel, Robert (15 January 2010), 'Stiglitz says government misses mark on economy', Joseph Stiglitz interviewed by Robert Siegel on All Things Considered, NPR, Audio and transcript of quote available at http://www.npr.org/templates/story/story.php?storyId=122620894, accessed 8 December 2010.

Smith, Yves (2010), *How Unenlightened Self Interest Undermined Democracy and Corrupted Capitalism*, Palgrave Macmillan, New York.

Soramäki, Kimmo, Morten L. Bech, Jeffrey Arnold, Robert J. Glass, Walter E. Beyeler (2007), 'The topology of interbank payment flows', *Physica* A 379, 317–333.

Sorman, Guy (2009), *Economics Does Not Lie: A Defense of the Free Market in a Time of Crisis*, Encounter Books, New York.
Sorman, Guy (2010), 'The Free-Marketeers Strike Back', *City Journal*, Vol. 20, No. 3, available at http://www.city-journal.org/2010/20_3_free-marketeers.html, accessed 20 December 2010.
Soros, George (2010), 'Anatomy of crisis – the living history of the last 30 years: economic theory, politics and policy', presented at the INET Conference at King's College, 8–11 April 2010, available at http://www.youtube.com/watch?v=XVC9mwQqWIY, accessed 4 January 2011.
Spiegel (1 April 2009), 'Government stimulus plans are "not enough"', available at http://www.spiegel.de/international/world/0,1518,druck-616743,00.html, accessed 8 December 2010.
Spruiell, Stephen (14 July 2009), 'Lies, damned lies, and economics', article is available at http://www.nationalreview.com/articles/227879/lies-damned-lies-and-economics/stephen-spruiell, accessed 20 December 2010.
Stein, Gabrielle (16 July 2007), 'RMBS downgrades feed subprime market frenzy', Asset Securitization Report, available at http://www.securitization.net/news/article.asp?id=284&aid=7471, accessed 1 June 2011.
Stern, Marc (October 2008), *The Washington and Wall Street (Financial) Orgy*, available at http://www.pwlcapital.com/pwl/files/42/4293f650-396d-4e41-9064-b5a188a6a339.pdf, accessed 1 August 2011.
Stern, Marc (November 2008), *The (Sur) Realistic World of Credit Default Swaps (CDS)*, available at https://www.pwlcapital.com/pwl/files/f7/f79b61b9-c89c-4082-ae0c-201a411fd747.pdf, accessed 1 August 2011.
Stern, Marc (12 February 2009), *The Epiphany of a Declining Economic Empire*, available at http://www.pwlcapital.com/pwl/files/21/21cdc28e-350c-4b34-9-dd5-6340e001ae5a.pdf, accessed 1 August 2011.
Stern, Marc (8 March 2009), *Is This the Last Arrow in the Treasury's Quiver or Simply the Continuation of the Wall Street Handout and Bailout Programs?* available at http://www.pwlcapital.com/pwl/files/5d/5d832750-e1a4-4551-83d4-e0111d709fef.pdf, accessed 1 August 2011.
Stiglitz, Joseph E. (22 October 2008), 'A crisis of confidence', *The Guardian*, available at http://www.guardian.co.uk/commentisfree/cifamerica/2008/oct/22/economy-financial-crisis-regulation, accessed 12 December 2010.
Stiglitz, Joseph E. (25 February 2009), *Obama Has Confused Saving the Banks with Saving the Bankers*, available at http://www.democracynow.org/2009/2/25/stieglitz, accessed 12 December 2010.
Stiglitz, Joseph E. (6 March 2009), 'How to Fail to Recover', available at http://www.project-syndicate.org/commentary/stiglitz110/English, accessed 12 December 2010.
Stiglitz, Joseph E (12 March 2009), Professor Stiglitz addresses UNCTAD and ILO, summarized at http://www.un-ngls.org/spip.php?page=article_s&id_article=794, accessed 11 November 2011. An audio clip of the full lecture is available at http://www.ilo.org/global/about-the-ilo/press-and-media-centre/videos/events-coverage/WCMS_103603/lang--en/index.htm
Stiglitz, Joseph E. (27 March 2009), 'Reform is needed. Reform is in the air. We can't afford to fail', *The Guardian*, available at http://www.guardian.co.uk/commentisfree/2009/mar/27/global-recession-reform, accessed 10 December 2010.

Stiglitz, Joseph E. (14 September 2009), 'For all Obama's talk of overhaul, the US has failed to wind in Wall Street', *The Guardian*, available at http://www.guardian.co.uk/commentisfree/2009/sep/14/lehmans-one-year-after1, accessed 10 November 2011.

Stiglitz, Joseph E. (12 April 2010), 'Build strong rules for finance system', available at http://www.politico.com/news/stories/0410/35636.html, accessed 12 December 2010.

Stiglitz, Joseph E. (4 June 2010), 'Financial Re-Regulation and Democracy', available at http://www.project-syndicate.org/commentary/stiglitz126/English, accessed 12 December 2010.

Stiglitz, Joseph E. (8 July 2010), 'Taming Finance in an Age of Austerity', available at http://www.project-syndicate.org/commentary/stiglitz127/English, accessed 12 December 2010.

Stiglitz, Joseph E. (9 September 2010), 'A better way to fix the US housing crisis', available at http://www.guardian.co.uk/commentisfree/cifamerica/2010/sep/09/us-housing-crisis-policies, accessed 8 December 2010.

Stiglitz, Joseph E. (1 November 2010), 'One of the Main Lessons from the Financial Crisis is that the State Must Play a Key Role in Sustaining Economic Development', *African Development Bank Group*, available at http://afdb.org/en/news-events/article/joseph-stiglitz-one-of-the-main-lessons-from-the-financial-crisis-is-that-the-state-must-play-a-key-role-in-sustaining-economic-development-5524, accessed 15 December 2010.

Stiglitz, Joseph E. (6 December 2010), *Alternatives to Austerity*, available at http://www.project-syndicate.org/commentary/stiglitz133/English, accessed 10 December 2010.

Thaler, Richard (June 2011) interviewed in Nudging the world toward smarter public policy: An interview with Richard Thaler, *McKinsey Quarterly*, available at https://www.mckinseyquarterly.com/Nudging_the_world_toward_smarter_public_policy_An_interview_with_Richard_Thaler_2817, accessed 15 November 2011.

The Economist (12 February 2009), 'Out of Keynes's shadow', available at http://www.economist.com/businessfinance/displaystory.cfm?story_id=13104022, accessed 30 December 2010.

The Economist (16 July 2009), 'The other-worldly philosophers', available at http://www.economist.com/node/14030288, accessed 4 January 2010.

The Economist (18 March 2010), 'Blame game. Two influential economists take a potshot at financial policymakers. Why don't their criticisms add up?', available at http://www.economist.com/node/15716841, accessed 8 December 2010.

This American Life (2009), Episode Transcript Program #355, 'The Giant Pool of Money', p.9, available at http://www.thisamericanlife.org/sites/default/files/355_transcript.pdf

Thornton, Mark (21 May 2009), 'Austrian recipe vs. Keynesian Fantasy', *Ludwig von Mises Institute*, available at http://mises.org/daily/3465, accessed 18 December 2010.

U.S. Securities and Exchange Commission (n.d.), *Comments on Proposed Rule: Alternative Net Capital Requirements for Broker-Dealers That Are Part of Consolidated Supervised Entities*, available at http://www.sec.gov/rules/proposed/s72103.shtml, last accessed 25 January 2010.

Valukas, Anton R. (13 March 2010), *Lehman Brothers Holdings Inc. Chapter 11 Proceedings Examiner's Report*, available at http://lehmanreport.jenner.com/

Vieira, Paul (5 October 2010), 'Flood of liquidity risks market "chaos"', *Financial Post*, available at http://www.nationalpost.com/news/canada/politics/Flood+li quidity+risks+market+chaos/3628324/story.html, accessed 8 December 2010.

von Nordenflycht, Andrew (2008), 'The Demise of the Professional Partnership? The Emergence and Diffusion of Publicly-traded Professional Service Firms', *Working Paper*, Faculty of Business, Simon Fraser University.

Willis, Bob and Courtney Schlisserman (2008), 'U.S. Economy: Consumer Prices, Housing Starts Slide (Update 1)', *Bloomberg*, available at http://www.bloomberg.com/apps/news?pid=20601205&sid=a73N6LrkY5zo, retrieved 5 August 2009.

Woellert, Lorraine and Christine Harper (28 October 2008), 'Citigroup, Goldman Asked by Waxman to Justify Bonuses (Update2)', *Bloomberg*.

Zingales, Luigi (2008), 'Plan B', *The Economist's Voice*, Vol. 5, No. 6, Article 4.

Zingales, Luigi (2010 but undated), *My Losing Battle against the Leviathan (Public interventions of a desperate free-market economist)*, The University of Chicago Booth School of Business, available at http://faculty.chicagobooth.edu/luigi.zingales/papers/2010_Zingales_Losing_Battle_Leviathan.pdf, accessed 15 November 2011.

Zingales, Luigi and Sapienza, Paola (13 February 2009), 'How Big Finance Bought the Bailout Plan', *Foreign Policy*, available at http://www.foreignpolicy.com/articles/2009/02/12/how_big_finance_bought_the_bailout_plan, accessed 15 December 2010.

Index

adjustable-rate mortgages, 41, 63
adverse selection, 65
affordable housing, 72–4, 80, 82
aging population, 155–6
agriculture, 44
Akerlof, George A., 109
Alt-A mortgages, 38, 58, 66, 76, 86
American Dream Down Payment Act, 74
American Home Mortgage, 91
American Home Servicing, 90
American International Group (AIG), 3, 12, 24, 91, 92, 93, 132
Ameriquest, 90
assets
   see also toxic assets
   distress selling of, 17–18
Austrian economics, 30–3, 81, 124–31, 141–2, 145, 150, 154
automobile industry, 44

Backhouse, Roger E., 150
bailouts, 2–3, 6
   alternative view of, 30–3
   Austrian economists on, 127–8
   critics of, 98–9, 110–13, 120–3, 127
   mainstream view of, 21–30
Bank of America, 90, 91, 92, 112
Bank of England, 91
Bank of Japan, 20
bankruptcy, 25–6, 29, 112–14
banks
   see also financial sector
   bailout of, 2–3, 6, 21–33, 98–9, 110–13, 120–3
   bankruptcy for, 112–14
   Canadian, 13–14, 133
   capitalization of, 5
   central, 19–20
   commercial, 4, 6, 49, 93
   competitive markets and, 31
   deregulation of, 43–4
   failures, 4–5, 25–8

investment, 6, 43–4, 47–52, 91, 93, 111–12
   loans by, 4, 5, 43
   regulation of, 4, 42–3, 106–9
   risk to, 42–3
   service charges, 133
   "too big to fail," 2–3, 116–17
   types of, 4, 6
Barclays, 91
Barro, Robert, 103–4
Basel I, 6
Basel II, 4, 5, 6
Bear Stearns, 2, 24, 90, 91, 92, 98
Berkshire Hathaway, 50–1
Bernanke, Ben S., 20, 95–6
BNP Paribas, 91
bonds, 28–9
   insuring, 11
   issuance of, 86
   municipal, 10, 11, 48
   Treasury, 134–5
bonuses, 45–6
booms, 125–6
bubbles
   dot-com, 46–7, 73, 139
   housing, 74–6, 81–2, 84
   securitization, 84–6
Buffet, Warren, 50–2
Burry, Michael, 2
Bush, George W., 74, 127
busts, 125–6

Canadian banks, 13–14, 133
capital, 6–7, 109
   availability of, 13
capital gains tax, 72–3
capital requirements, 44, 107, 117
capital reserves, 43
capital-to-assets ratio, 5–6
Carrick, Alex, 21
central banks, 19–20
China, 135, 155
Citibank, 112

174 *Index*

Citigroup, 3, 5–6, 24, 26–9, 90, 91
Clinton, Bill (William), 72
Cochrane, John, 105–6, 113, 122–4, 141, 146
collaterized debt obligations (CDOs), 11, 59
collaterized mortgage obligations (CMOs), 59
commercial banks, 4, 6, 49, 93
commodities, 134–5
Community Reinvestment Act, 72, 73
construction, 53, 74
consumer protection, 107, 109
Countrywide, 90, 91
credit crunch, 13–16, 36
credit default swaps (CDSs), 11, 93–4, 139, 147
credit rating agencies, 65–7, 122, 143, 147
credit risk, 51–2
Credit Suisse, 91
criminal investigations, 90

debt
  deflation and, 17–18
  funding, 54
  government, 104–5, 115, 129
  long-term, 28–9
  in US economy, 19
defaults, 5, 10–11, 39, 56, 59, 66–8, 80, 87, 121
deflation, 16–21
de-linking, 57
demographics, 155–6
Department of Housing and Urban Development, 72, 73, 74, 80
deposits, 124
  insurance on, 4–5, 26–8
deregulation, of banking industry, 43–4
derivatives, 50–1, 85, 107, 108, 124
discrimination, 71, 72
dot-com bubble, 46–7, 73, 139

economic crisis, as result of financial crisis, 11–12
economic growth, 8–9, 129, 130
economic models, 147–51
economic policy, 31–3
economic transactions, 13–14

economists
  Austrian, 30–3, 81, 124–31, 141–2, 145, 150, 154
  differences of opinion among, 151–5
  freshwater, 119–24, 125, 126, 141
  opinions of, 142–7
  saltwater, 98–118, 140
economy
  government intervention in, 31–3
  Japanese, 20
  real, 22, 28, 46–7, 129, 133, 153
  stabilization of, 19
  US, 11–12, 19, 44–5, 138, 143
education, 154
efficient market hypothesis, 122, 149
employment
  in real estate sector, 77
  views on, 152–4
Equal Credit Opportunity Act, 71
equilibrium price, 153
escrow funds, 67

Fama, Eugene, 122
Fannie Mae (FNMA or Federal National Mortgage Association), 58, 70–4, 80, 85–6, 92, 112
Federal Deposit Insurance Corporation (FDIC), 4–5, 6, 26–8, 42–3
federal funds rate, 127
Federal Home Loan Mortgage Corporation (FHMC), *see* Freddie Mac
Federal Housing Finance Agency, 92
Federal National Mortgage Association (FNMA), *see* Fannie Mae
Federal Reserve, 31
  quantitative easing by, 106
  reaction to crisis by, 2, 20, 95–7
Ferguson, Niall, 104–5
fiduciary duties, 8
financial crisis (2007)
  alternative view of, 30–3
  awareness of, 2–3
  effects of, 13–21
  end of, 112, 142–3
  extent of, 11–13
  genesis of, 35–6

financial crisis (2007) – *continued*
  historical context, 41–7, 138–9
  market imperfections and, 59–68
  mechanics of, 47–55
  nature of, 3–13, 138
  opinions on, 140–7
  overview of, 139
  popular opinion on, 132–6
  reforms following, 106–9, 115–18
  response to, 95–7, 99–106, 120–1
  responsibility for, ix, 143–4
  roots of, 37–68
  social and moral underpinnings of, 155–7
financial guarantors, 10–12
financial institutions, 4–11
  see also banks
  acquisition of, 24
  bailouts of, 3, 21–33
  bankruptcy by, 25–6, 29
  lobbying by, 111, 120, 144
  managers of, 114
  role of, 12–13
  types of, 3
financial product safety commission, 118
financial sector
  deregulation of, 43–4
  government intervention in, 92, 99–100, 109–18
  increase in, 44–5
  mistrust of, 132–4, 136
  overview of, 4–11
  profits in, 47
  recapitalization of, 97
  regulation of, 106–9, 145–7
  salaries in, 45–6
financing, 6–7, 22–3
  shrinking of sources of, 14–16
  structured, 58
First Franklin, 90
fiscal policy, 32, 97, 106, 128–31
fiscal stimulus, 101–6, 115–16, 128–31, 145
Fitch, 65
fixed-rate mortgages, 41
foreclosures, 35, 58, 66–8, 78–80
foreign investors, 86
Foster, Peter, 151

Freddie Mac (FHLMC or Federal Home Loan Mortgage Corporation), 58, 71–3, 76, 80, 85, 91, 92, 112
free markets, 122
Fremont General Corporation, 90
freshwater economists, 119–24, 125, 126, 141
Friedman, Milton, 125
full employment, 152–4
fund managers, 47–52
fungibility, 147

Galbraith, John Kenneth, 152
Garn-St Germaine Depository Institutions Act, 71
Geithner, Timothy, 97, 99, 127
GE Money, 90
George Mason University, 125
German Historical school, 30
Ginnie Mae, 58, 70–1
Glaeser, Edward L., 151
Glass-Steagall Deposit Insurance Act, 4–5, 43, 106, 138
global reserve system, 117
Goldman Sachs, 3, 6, 49, 50, 132
Gordon, Robert J., 104
government
  bank bailout by, 21–33
  mistrust of, 135
government debt, 104–5, 115, 129
government intervention, 31–3, 143
  Austrian economists on, 127–8
  economic theory and, 126
  in financial sector, 92, 99–100, 109–18, 120–1
  in housing market, 69–74, 80–1
  stimulus spending, 101–6, 115–16, 128–31, 145
Government National Mortgage Association (GNMA), 58, 70–1
Great Depression, 111–13, 130
greed, 156
Greek civilization, 157
Greenspan, Alan, 32–3, 73

Hart, Oliver, 122
Hayek, Friedrich, 31, 125
hedge funds, 9, 12, 49, 86, 91, 93, 98, 134

historical context, 41–7, 138–9
Home Mortgage Disclosure Act, 72
homeownership, 37–41, 53, 69, 74, 80–2, 84, 139
home sales, 74–6, 83
house flipping, 63–4, 66, 80, 87, 144
household incomes, 76
Housing and Community Development Act, 72
housing bubble, 74–6, 81, 82, 84
housing discrimination, 71, 72
housing market, 33, 35, 37–41, 66, 139
  government intervention in, 69–74, 80–1
  overview of, 69–70
  spasms in, 74–84
  unraveling of, 86–92
housing prices, 39–40, 67–8, 72, 74, 76, 81–4, 87–8
HSBC, 90, 91

Iceland, 92
imperfections, *see* market imperfections
incentive system, 45–6
Independent National Mortgage Corporation (Indy Mac), 92
individual responsibility, 156–7
inflation, 16, 32
information
  economics of, 109
  inaccurate, 67
  lack of, 146
insurance companies, 12, 49
insurers, 10–11
interest rates, 19–20
  cuts in, 73
  increase in, 130
  low, 33
  mortgage, 41, 53–4, 61, 63, 71–3
  on municipal bonds, 10
  zero per cent, 19–20
interest-rate swaps, 57
interest spread, 4
investment, 7, 8–9
  loss of, 28–30
  short-term, 47
investment banks, 6, 43–4, 47–52, 91, 93, 111
investment managers, 7–8, 47–52

Japan, lost decade, 20, 110
Johnson, Simon, 114
JPMorgan Chase, 24, 92
jumbo asset mortgages, 38, 58, 85
junior tranche, 58, 59

Kay, John, 148, 149–50
Keynesian economics, 106, 119, 126, 127–8, 153–4
Krenn, Robert, 104
Krugman, Paul, 98–109, 114–15, 130–1, 140

legacy loans, 99–101
legacy securities, 100–1
Lehman Brothers, 2, 3, 24, 29, 85, 87, 92, 113, 122–3
Lewis, Alan, 151
liquidity, 49–52
Lloyds, 91
loans, 4, 5, 43, 48–50, 61, 99–100
  see also mortgages
lobbying, 111, 120, 144
long-term debt, 28–9
low-income households, 72, 80, 82, 84
Lucas, Robert, 106–7

making markets, 48
manufacturing sector, 44
market failure, 121
market imperfections, 59–68, 109
McAdoo, William Gibbs, 3
Menger, Carl, 30
Merrill Lynch, 92
minorities, 69, 71, 74
monetary policy, 32, 97
money supply, 19
Moody's, 65
moral hazard, 123
moral underpinnings, 155–7
Morgan Stanley, 91, 132
mortgage-backed securities, 52–9, 66–7, 85–6, 89, 93–4, 139
mortgage brokers, 55, 60–4, 76, 78, 88
mortgage fraud, 65
mortgage lenders, 87–8, 90
mortgage originators, 54–5, 59, 62–5, 88, 89

mortgages, 37–41, 42, 52–5, 133–4
  adjustable-rate, 41, 63
  Alt-A, 38, 58, 66, 76, 86
  defaults, 87
  fixed-rate, 41
  foreclosures, 58, 66–8, 78–80
  government-backed, 70–1, 73
  increase in, 76
  interest rates, 41, 53–4, 61, 63, 71–3
  jumbo, 38, 58, 85
  prime, 76, 78
  subprime, 38–40, 58, 66, 76, 78–9, 86, 88–91
  underwriting, 64–5
mortgage securitization, *see* securitization
mortgage trust, 55–6
multiplier effect, 42
municipal bonds, 10, 11, 48
mutual funds, 93, 134–5

nationalization, 127
neoclassical economics, 152, 153
New Century Financial, 85, 90
New York Stock Exchange (NYSE), 44, 84–5
Nomura, 91
Nortel, 46
Northern Rock Bank, 91

Obama administration, 101, 102, 107, 111, 127
off-balance-sheet activity, 43, 109
Office of Federal Housing Enterprise Oversight, 72
opacity, 146
opinion makers, 95
Option One, 90
origination fees, 54
overcollateralization, 58
Ownit Mortgage Solutions, 88

Paulson, Henry, 95, 99, 127
pension funds, 6, 8–9, 12, 49, 93, 134
perfect substitutes, 147
popular opinion, 132–6
power, of Wall Street, 145–6
predatory lending, 63–5, 72, 88, 109, 117–18, 143
price bubbles, 32

prices
  declining, 16–21
  determination of, 152
  housing, 39–40, 67–8, 72, 74, 76, 81–4, 87–8
Primary Dealer Credit Facility (PDCF), 127
prime mortgages, 76, 78
private-label issuers, 85, 86
public opinion, 132–6, 144–5

quantitative easing, 20, 106, 135

Rajan, Raghuram, 2
rating agencies, 65–7, 122, 143, 147
rational expectations theory, 149
real economy, 22, 28, 46–7, 129, 133
real estate, 9
  see also housing market
real estate agents, 75–6, 77
reforms, 106–9, 115–18, 122, 145
regulation, 106–9, 147
  of banking industry, 4, 42–3
  of derivatives, 107, 108
  obstacles to, 145–6
  reforms, 117–18, 122
regulators, 114–16
Reinhart, Vincent R., 20
rentals, 41, 81
reserve requirements, 43, 44, 107, 116
resolution authority, 107
retail banking, 133
risk, 5–9, 61
  to banks, 42–3
  concentration of, 52
  credit, 51–2
  guarantors of, 10
  investment, 29
  management of, 48, 56–8
  mortgage, 39, 57
  spreading, 7, 11
  systemic, 122, 124, 146
Roubini, Nouriel, 2
Royal Bank of Scotland, 91

Sack, Brian P., 20
salaries, 45–6
Sallie Mae (SLM Corporation, originally the Student Loan Marketing Association), 85

saltwater economists, 98–118, 140
Sapienza, Paola, 120
Schiff, Peter, 2, 128–31, 142
science of economics, 147–51
scientific method, 150
Scotiabank, 14
second homes, 73, 81, 82
securities, 47, 100
  legacy, 100–1
  mortgage-backed, 52–9, 66–7, 85–6, 93–4, 139
  tranched, 58, 59
  volume of, 84–6
Securities Exchange Commission (SEC), 44
securitization, 35, 47, 52, 55–59, 71, 84–6, 139
  market imperfections in, 59–68
selfishness, 132–3
service charges, 133
services sector, 44–5
Shiller, Robert, 103
Smith, Adam, 110, 148–9, 152
social underpinnings, 155–7
Sorman, Guy, 151
Soros, George, 149–50
sovereign funds, 9, 155
special purpose vehicles, 55–7, 93–4
Spence, A. Michael, 109
Standard and Poor, 65
Stiglitz, Joseph, 103, 109–18, 140
stimulus spending, 101–6, 115–16, 128–31, 145
stock market, 134–5
stress tests, 97
structured finance, 58
student loans, Student Loan Marketing Association, 85
subprime mortgages, 38–40, 58, 66, 76, 78–9, 86, 88–91
success, 157
Summers, Larry, 104, 105
Swiss RE, 91
systemic risk, 122, 124, 146

Taxpayer Relief Act, 72–3
telecommunications, 46–7
Term Securities Lending Facility (TSLF), 127

Thornton, Mark, 127
Tomnitz, Donald, 91
"too big to fail," 3, 116–17
toxic assets, 3–4, 9–12, 134, 147
  bankruptcy law and, 25–6
  effects of, 13–21
  government purchase of, 24, 99
  types of, 93
  tranches, 58, 59
  transparency, 116
Treasury bonds, 134–5
Treasury Department
  criticisms of, 137
  reaction to crisis by, 97, 99–101
Troubled Asset Relief Program (TARP), 24

UBS, 90, 91, 92
underwriting, 48, 64–5, 88
unemployment, 130, 131, 138, 152, 153
United Kingdom, 114
University of Chicago, 125
US economy, 138, 143
  debt in, 19
  evolution of, 44–5
  international opinion on, 105
  shrinking, 11–12
US housing market, 69–93, 139
  government intervention in, 69–74, 80–1
  overview of, 69–70
  spasms in, 74–84
  unraveling of, 86–92

Wachovia, 91
wages, 45–6, 152, 153
Wall Street
  see also financial sector
  lobbying by, 111, 120, 144
  power of, 145–6
warehouse lenders, 55, 87–8
Wells Fargo, 90
Western civilization, 157
Whitney, Meredith, 10
WMC Mortgages, 90
World War II as fiscal stimulus, 102–4, 130–1

Zingales, Luigi, 119–22, 141